WARRIOR GENTLEMEN

....

"Gurkhas" in the Western Imagination

To the Memory of

Lieutenant Chitahang Thegim
Subedar Man Prasad Thegim
Havildar Juwar Singh Nogu
Rifleman Karna Bir Jabegu

of the 'Indreni' settlements, Ilam, Nepal

WARRIOR GENTLEMAN

•••••••••••

"Gurkhas" in the Western Imagination

by
Lionel Caplan

Berghahn Books
Providence • Oxford

First published in 1995 by

Berghahn Books
Editorial offices:
165 Taber Avenue, Providence, RI 02906, USA
Bush House, Merewood Avenue, Oxford, OX3 8EF, UK

Library of Congress Cataloging-in-Publication Data
Caplan, Lionel.
  Warrior gentlemen. 'Gurkhas' in the Western imagination / by
Lionel Caplan.
      p.   cm.
  Includes bibliographical references and index.
  ISBN 1-57181-852-9
  1. Gurkha soldiers. 2. Great Britain. Army. Brigade of Gurkhas--
History. 3. Nepal--Social life and customs. 4. Great Britain
Army--Officers--Attitudes. I. Title. II. Title: 'Gurkhas' in the
Western imagination.
UA853.N35C36   1994   94-37858
356'.189'095496--dc20   CIP

British Library Cataloguing in Publication Data
A catalogue record for this book is available from
the British Library.

Printed in the United States.

Cover photograph courtesy of the Director, National Army Museum, London.

CONTENTS

PREFACE   vii

ABBREVIATIONS   ix

CHAPTER 1
INTRODUCTION *Discovering Gurkhas*   1

Introduction: Texts and their Worldly Contexts—The Gurkha
Literature—Who are the Gurkhas?—Encountering the
Gurkhas—The Anglo-Nepal War—Recruiting Gurkhas—
Gurkhas in the Twentieth Century

CHAPTER 2
GURKHAS AT HOME *The ecology of military service*   28

Introduction—Populations of the Middle Hills—Becoming
Gurkhas—The Economics of Gurkha Service—The Social
Implications of Gurkha Service—The Political Implications of
Gurkha Service—Ex-Gurkhas in Town—Conclusion

CHAPTER 3
OFFICERING GURKHAS *The culture of command*   55

Introduction—Royal and Indian Officers—British Officers
and the Public Schools—Sporting Officers—The Gurkha
Regiments as an Elite Corps—British Officer-Gurkha Officer—
Regimental Cultures—The Regimental Officer—The Career
Officer—Conclusion

CHAPTER 4

REPRESENTING GURKHAS *The rhetoric of martiality*   87

Introduction—Martiality—Martial Nepalis—The Place
of Martiality—The Persistence of Martial Thinking—
Masculinity—Masculine Nepal—Loyalty—The Bond of Trust—
Defiant Gurkhas—Conclusion

CHAPTER 5

COURAGEOUS GURKHAS *The making of warrior gentlemen*   126

Introduction—The Concept of Courage—Military perspectives
on courage—Warrior Gurkhas—Gurkha Perspectives on
Courage—Gentlemen Gurkhas—Conclusion

CHAPTER 6

CONCLUSION *Gurkha fictions and political realities*   152

REFERENCES   159

INDEX   174

PREFACE

The legendary Gurkhas have inspired a considerable literature about their character, quality and exploits under British command, much of it written by the very officers who have selected, trained and led them in war and peace. Thirty years ago, when I returned from east Nepal after a stay of thirteen months in an area inhabited by Limbus, many of whom had served in Gurkha regiments, I began to read some of the military literature for background purposes, to enable me to complete a research project on 'Hindu-tribal' relations. It struck me then that the Gurkhas I was being presented with in this literature bore little resemblance to the former soldiers I had come to know in the settlements of Ilam.

Why this should be so was a question which intrigued me, and therefore my return to these texts after many years—during which time incidentally, many more have appeared—to make them the centre-piece of the present study, stems from a long-standing curiosity about these representations of the Gurkhas. In the intervening period, too, anthropologists (along with the practitioners of other disciplines) have focused increasing attention on the manner in which Westerners (Euro-American anthropologists included) depict their (mainly non-Western) subjects. This essay constitutes an attempt to relate the rhetorical devices employed to depict Gurkhas to the wider historical, political and military contexts affecting these soldiers and, in particular, their European officer-chroniclers. It thus relies on a variety of literary, historical and ethnographic sources, published and unpublished, as well as on supplementary interviews with British officers who served and continue to serve with Gurkhas.

Thanks are due to numerous individuals and institutions whose assistance helped to make this work possible. I express my appreciation to the staff at the Oriental and India Office Collections of the British Library, the Imperial War Museum, the National Army Museum and the Gurkha Museum. At the latter I am much beholden to the archivist Claire Mason and her many volunteer helpers, in particular Colonel Michael Broadway, who was especially assiduous in tracking down elusive material. A number of officers and former officers gave generously of their time to answer my many questions, or to provide assistance of other kinds, and I record my thanks in particular to General Sir John Chapple, Brigadier E.D. 'Birdie' Smith, Colonel C.E. Jarvis, Colonel D.R. Wood, Lieutenant-Colonel W.J. Dawson, Lieutenant-Colonel R.C. Couldrey, Lieutenant-Colonel C.N. Fraser, Lieutenant-Colonel J.S. Roberts, Lieutant-Colonel H.C.S. Gregory, Major R.L. Willis, Major J.J. Burlison, Major J.B. Oliphant, Major J.E.G. Lamond, Captain A.P.M. Griffith and Captain A.P. Coleman. Needless to say, they are not responsible for the views expressed here.

An award from the Nuffield Foundation enabled me to spend four months in east Nepal in 1988, and provided the opportunity to discuss various issues regarding their military service with former Gurkha soldiers in the 'Indreni' settlements in Ilam, east Nepal. The School of Oriental and African Studies gave me a small grant to cover the costs of travel in Britain in connection with the project, and to make a brief visit to Nepal in early 1992 while I was engaged on other research in India. I gratefully acknowledge the generosity of both institutions.

I am also beholden to academic colleagues at SOAS, Bergen and Oxford who provided helpful criticisms in seminars which outlined some of the arguments presented here, and to Dr Michael Hutt for his comments on the manuscript. Finally, this project would almost certainly not have come to fruition without the abiding interest, constant encouragement and discerning judgements of Pat Caplan. To her, as always, I am most indebted.

L.C.

July 1994

ABBREVIATIONS

CO	Commanding Officer
DSM	Distinguished Service Medal
GR	Gurkha Rifles
ICO	Indian Commissioned Officer
ICS	Indian Civil Service
MC	Military Cross
MM	Military Medal
NCO	Non-Commissioned Officer
OTC	Officers' Training Corps
QGO	Queen's Gurkha Officer
VC	Victoria Cross
VCO	Viceroy's Commissioned Officer

CHAPTER 1

....

INTRODUCTION

Discovering Gurkhas

It was ... an eye-opener to our army in India to find
another race which ... could meet them and beat them
on equal terms.

Brigadier-General C.G. Bruce *The Gurkhas*, 1928.

Introduction: Texts and their Worldly Contexts

While publications of all kinds on military subjects have a wide readership
in the English-speaking world, the army of pre-Independence India continues to exert a strong fascination among that section of the reading public
partial to military exotica and adventure. According to one historian, no
other formation of the old Indian army (nor, he might have added, of the
British army since the Second World War), has 'received more printer's ink'
than the Gurkhas (Haycock 1988:464).[1]

These military writings, which are authored principally by British officers
who have served with Gurkhas, may be said to constitute a particular mode
of 'orientalist' discourse, in as much as they pass as an authoritative and
superior body of knowledge about 'others' which these others can or do not
possess about themselves, and also in the sense that they essentialise these
others through generalisation about their inherent natures (see Said 1978;
Clifford 1980). The production of the discourse, moreover, cannot be separated from the issue of power, both in the narrow sense that those in an

unambiguously superordinate position (the European officers) produce peremptory knowledge about their military subordinates, and in the wider sense of the unequal economic, political and social structures within which the depictions occur. This marks it out as a species of colonial or neo-colonial discourse, which refers to 'knowledges developed in the course of domination, and "rhetorical strategies" employed to describe colonial peoples ...' (Mani 1986:3).

But if postmodernist critics have taught us to detect orientalist tendencies in western representations of non-western peoples and cultures, and heightened sensitivity to textual devices by means of which these subjects are depicted, they provide few guidelines as to how we might relate the character of *specific* works to the particular circumstances of their creation and the historical location of their creators. The need to move beyond the current predisposition to regard virtually all writing about 'others' as amenable to the same kinds of analysis has encouraged recent explorations of the impact of regional influences on ethnographic writing in anthropology (see Fardon 1990). A similar disaffection with the tendency to conflate and thus essentialise European representations of non-European others underlies the present essay. The stylistic traits and rhetorical features which characterize Gurkha texts can only be adequately appreciated if interrogated in their particular historical and socio-military contexts.

Britain's colonial armies were largely shaped by her imperial dispositions, and the Indian army, in which the Gurkha regiments played an important part, was the principal instrument of her Eastern policies (see Burroughs 1986). Subsequently, India's Independence (which brought the division of Gurkha regiments between the armies of Britain and Independent India), the collapse of Britain's empire, and the flowering of Cold War had a profound effect on the role of the British army in the post-war period, as on its Brigade of Gurkhas. Here, for a start, are some of the significant political formations and transformations in which the Gurkha texts were produced and against which they must be examined.

Moreover, it is vital to understand the nature of the 'extra-textual' relationship between British military authors and their Gurkha others. The contrast with both travel writers and anthropologists of yesteryear is worth noting. In the case of the former, contacts with those they wrote about were generally fleeting, so that they remained, in Wheeler's term, 'raw' (1986:53). Anthropologists, however, tended to spend lengthy periods living as participant-observers among 'their people'. While seeking a warm and easy relationship, which frequently resulted in close identification with the persons they studied, they adopted an attitude of professional distance from, or noninterference in, the daily lives of their subjects (in order better to observe or experience their culture as it 'really' was).[2] The British officers who served with Gurkhas, however, were neither raw nor detached. Many spent long years in their regiments. These officers recruited, absorbed and instructed their subjects into a military system which they had themselves created; shaped and controlled the environments in which the Gurkhas lived and worked; and lastly, *commanded and led* them in both war and peace. I should make it clear that throughout virtually the 175 years of Gurkha history, the officers have been British. The Gurkhas themselves have, until very recently (the last twenty-five years or so), served only in subordinate ranks. Unlike both travel writers and anthropologists, therefore, the European officers from whose ranks these military authors emerged, by and large exercised personal dominance over the subjects of their discourse, a relationship moreover instituted for purposes other than the pursuit of knowledge, or of a career as academic or journalist/writer. In the context of a hierarchical military system in which these officers exerted comprehensive control over virtually every aspect of the (usually lengthy) working lives of their subjects, it appears jejune to suggest that the overriding concern of these Gurkha texts is to assert dominance, as a crude orientalist argument seems to assume is the goal of all literature by westerners about non-western others.

The literary devices employed by these authors to characterise the relationship with their Gurkhas raise general issues of representing what Burke (1969) calls the 'mysteries of courtship' between persons of unequal class or rank, and the appropriate styles for transcending these inequalities. Such a relationship, which is marked by both dominance and affection, suggests a special exercise of power which has the effect of transforming inferiors into cherished 'pets' (see Tuan 1984). Thus, the nature of the officer-Gurkha bond has to be understood and explored in the process of analysing the texts.

In commenting on anthropological writing about non-western peoples, some critics imply that it tends to overemphasise difference, and thus to exoticise these others (Keesing 1989). Fabian, for example, has referred to the assumption of distance between the 'knower and the known' (1990:754). Travel writers from the West have also been accused of identifying and emphasising only those elements of the distant cultures they encounter which are at odds with their own lifeways. Thus, both travel writers and anthropologists, Wheeler suggests, are 'strangers who deliver the exotic to [their] audience ...' (1986:58). Representations of the Gurkhas by their military authors do not lend themselves to such a simple analysis. Rather, we are invited by these writers to consider that the exotic qualities of their soldiers are to be found precisely in those endearing and romantic characteristics which, in spite of being 'Orientals', they share with their British officers: they are *warrior gentlemen*. At the same time, the Gurkha is contrasted with his Indian alter, who represents for these European writers otherness in the most negative sense of violating the values and sensibilities of the West.

To appreciate the manner in which these authors represent the Gurkhas compels us also to inquire into the social and cultural settings from which the officers themselves emerge and to which they are attuned. Vagts, in his history of militarism written over thirty years ago, drew attention to the role played by military historians in the process of 'militarising minds', preserving reputations, and more generally confusing 'history as experience' with 'history as authority' (1959:23-27). While such claims may be to some degree applicable to certain writers who have created the Gurkha literature, by and large their ambitions are more parochial and their functions more circumscribed. As part of the Indian—in its time considered a secondary and subordinate force—and later the British army, they were anxious to carve for themselves a place in the military pecking order, and the Gurkha discourse undoubtedly served this purpose. As part of an officer class—if a somewhat economically-pinched sector of that class—educated in the country's public schools, raised on a diet of imperial adventure and certainty in the superiority of their 'race', they imbibed the attitudes and ideologies of their times, which not surprisingly, were reflected in their writings. So that, as students of various kinds of works dealing with non-western peoples have noted, western authors frequently document themselves through their depictions of others (Clifford 1986:10; Kabbani 1986:10; Walker 1991:32). In this essay, therefore, I attend to the range of circumstances—ideological, socio-cultural and politico-military—in which these authors who create the texts are enveloped, the discursive formations in which they are located (see Kapferer 1988:97; also Foucault 1979:148).[3]

The Gurkha Literature

Publications on the Gurkhas are of four main kinds. Firstly, there are regimental histories. At the peak of its peacetime strength the Gurkha Brigade comprised ten regiments, each of which had its own history, which was updated periodically. Regimental Associations tended (and still tend) to commission or provide the subsidies needed to publish these.[4] Secondly, there are personal memoirs, diaries and autobiographies by officers who commanded Gurkhas, and these usually include accounts of particular campaigns or battles in which they took part with Gurkhas. Thirdly, and of more recent vintage, are coffee-table picture books with splendid photographs of Gurkhas in various settings. These books always include a commentary or introductory text on the Gurkhas, their history and exploits, by an officer with the appropriate Gurkha experience. Finally, there are books, probably the majority, which attempt to tell the Gurkha story in a general and popular way. I include in this category the handbooks and manuals produced by the Indian army and other official bodies mainly to assist recruiting staff to identify potential military talent and new officers to familiarise themselves with Nepal and the Gurkhas. Authors were not infrequently involved in the production of more than one kind of publication, so that, for example, a regimental historian might also write a popular book about the Gurkhas, publish a personal memoir, or provide the text for a book of photographs of Gurkhas. I should perhaps refer to these publications as 'core' writings, since there is also a derivative literature—newspaper and magazine articles, and books—by non-military writers, which draws on and replicates the work of these officer-authors (see below).

Who reads this literature? Certainly anyone who has served with the Gurkhas—and there are many hundreds if not thousands of former officers who have such experience—is likely to have a library containing some of these works. At the very least, serving officers are encouraged to know or would want to learn the history of the Brigade and especially of their own regiment. In the recent past, and to some extent even today, this literature served to attract officer recruits. Virtually every officer I have talked to about his reasons for joining a Gurkha regiment mentioned a particular book or several books as having had an important, if not decisive influence. John Masters' *Bugles and a Tiger* (1956) was mentioned most frequently. One retired officer told me that he learned about Nepal and the Gurkhas from the 'Masters' side'. Another recalled that while he was at cadet camp some twenty years ago he was loaned *Bugles* and another Masters book and after reading them decided he wanted to officer Gurkhas. In his words: 'Masters writes about the Gurkhas in a moving way. They're something different. Crack troops. *Bugles* was the story of [Masters'] own development in the 4th Gurkha Regiment. It fired my imagination.'

But there is a much wider audience for this literature than the catchment of prospective, current and former British officers. A lot of men who served in other parts of the army want to read about the Gurkhas because they may have fought alongside them in some campaign or know of their reputation. Finally, there is a large audience among the general public for 'militaria', and the Gurkhas have a colourful and appealing image in Britain and elsewhere.

The officer in charge of public relations at one of the Gurkha camps in the UK told me that this is one of the easiest jobs he has ever had. There is no trouble placing items in the newspapers, or getting coverage. 'The Gurkha image sells. Exposure has really taken off since they first came here in 1971. Their naive, fresh looks, make them popular with people here.' Every December he is apparently inundated with requests to take a Gurkha home for Christmas. So books on Gurkhas sell many hundreds of copies, and are in libraries all over Britain, and other parts of the world.

As with most travel and anthropological writing, the audience does not, by and large, include the subjects of the discourse themselves. In the case of the Gurkhas, it is not simply that these books are linguistically and economically beyond their reach—or were until very recently—but that these texts are written for a particular assembly of (mainly European) readers who can be presumed broadly to share a range of cultural and political attitudes, and collectively to anticipate certain literary conventions—in terms of content, style, metaphor, imagery, etc.—which the military authors who write about the Gurkhas feel bound to take into account. Thus, in so far as this literature implies certain expectations on the part of the audience, 'against and with which the writer works' we can speak of a 'genre' (Green 1980:54).

Gurkhas have been written about, i.e. mentioned in numerous writings, since the early nineteenth century when the East India Company went to war against Nepal and discovered the fighting qualities of these men. Indeed, during much of the century, military campaigns in which Gurkhas participated were reported in newspapers and books, and were apparently the stuff of popular frontier non-fiction which appealed to 'Victorian armchair followers of daring deeds' (Bishop 1976:62).[5] But the genre really only developed fully in this century, and most profusely in the post-World War II period. It has flourished since the division of Gurkha regiments between the Indian and British armies, at the time of India's Independence in 1947, and grown especially from the mid-1960s when the British Brigade of Gurkhas was drastically cut and its very existence felt to be threatened. Up to this time the Gurkhas had been intimately involved in most of the military actions which the Indian and thereafter the British armies had undertaken, mainly in extending and defending the empire, and of course in both world wars. Campaigns in South East Asia involved the Gurkhas in almost continuous jungle warfare between 1948 and 1966, but with the conclusion of these actions the regiments were reduced in strength from over 14,000 to barely half that number, and the Brigade was transferred to Hong Kong, where it undertook border duties. It was around the time of these changes that a substantial number of books on the Gurkhas were published, and some of the writers acknowledge that their aim was to draw the attention of the British public and especially the 'military community' to the Gurkha predicament. The authors of one book were entirely frank about their reasons for turning to print: in their Preface they noted that the motivation for their book was the decision to reduce the size of the Brigade, and its uncertain future (Adshead and Cross 1970:xv).

Although these works are by no means all alike, they have very obvious affinities. Some books are simply reproduced over and over again with only minor amendments, like an official handbook first produced in 1883, which has gone through five editions, the most recent one published for Britain's Ministry of Defence (see Leonard 1965).[6] Others have acquired an authoritative stamp, and, like some anthropological works which serve as 'exemplary texts' (Fardon 1990:26), influence what is written in future. The conventions of western military writing also tend to set limits to what can or should be said and the manner of its saying, including the appropriate style and rhetoric.[7] So a number of themes consistently recur; they are the Gurkha literature's equivalent of what Appadurai calls 'gatekeeping concepts' in anthropology—which 'define the quintessential and dominant questions of interest' (1986:357).

The reiteration of these key topics in the military literature had, by the early part of this century, served to convey to the western reading public a stereotyped image of Gurkhas which was distilled and reproduced in many newspapers and popular magazines of the period. Thus, for example, the *Empire Annual for Boys*, 1917, condensed the core themes of this discourse into a three-page article entitled 'Who are the Gurkhas?'. Here are a few excerpts (the italics are mine):

> Gurkhas are *brave to reckless ... faithful to their officers ... terrible little fighters,* [with their] *fearsome national weapon, the kukri* ... The Nepalese are *proud and independent,* maintaining their *political freedom* through long centuries ... While fighting fiercely ... Gurkhas showed a most generous *spirit of courtesy,* worthy of a more enlightened people ... they d*espise the natives of India,* but have a great *admiration for the British* ... [they possess] *faithfulness, high spirits, and love of humour* [and are] *fond of sports* ... [8]

The article includes a full-page drawing of a Gurkha unit 'charging the German trenches, with the deadly kukri drawn', as the caption states.[9]

These are stirring images, which capture—if in somewhat exaggerated form—the dominant motifs and style which permeate the military literature on Gurkhas. These themes will be discussed in some detail in the course of this essay (see especially Chapters 4 and 5). Parts of the discourse are repro-duced almost verbatim over many years, and in many different texts, recent publications borrowing freely from those which have come before. To quote Padel about writings on Indian tribal populations, they have a 'formulaic quality', in that 'certain formulas, stock phrases and ideas are repeated time and again' (1988:2). Moreover, numerous stories—Des Chene calls them 'Gurkha tales' (1991:85)—keep reappearing in the literature. Even jokes tend to be recycled. Like the early Arab travel writers studied by Kabbani, authors of the Gurkha literature have consistently 'breathed new life into old stories that would otherwise have passed out of currency' (1986:2). As a result, reading this literature sometimes generates a sense of 'déjà-lu', as Barthes has put it.[10]

Some British officers who served with Gurkhas are aware of, and even embarrassed by, the recourse to hyperbole in these writings. During an inter-view one senior officer described some of the recent literature as 'based on myth and legend, feeding on itself without any originality ... anecdotal and stressing only the glamorous'. Indeed, many of the same images of Gurkhas seem to recur despite fundamental transformations during this century in the national and international contexts within which the Brigade has func-tioned, in the size, constitution and role of the Gurkha regiments them-selves, and in the Nepalese state from which the soldiers emerge. A question which must underlie the discussion, therefore, is why a discourse developed in the colonial setting should endure so tenaciously into the post-colonial period, notwithstanding these changes in the wider political environment, and considering the awareness on the part of many who sustain the dis-course of the somewhat dated images which inform it.

In this literature, there is little evidence of a debate, of different readings of the Gurkha contribution to Britain's military history. Burroughs has referred to the unappealing character of much traditional military writing, with its emphasis on campaigns and battles, badges and buttons. 'They rarely raise [...] their sights above the smoke of gunfire or the design of uni-forms to analyse warfare in its wider historical context' (1986:56).[11] To be fair, writers on the Gurkhas have never claimed to be military historians or analysts, but only to be recording the achievements of and thereby Britain's debt to its Gurkha soldiers. Smith, in a popular account of his battalion's role in the Italian campaign during the Second World War, insists that he is not attempting to write a history, but only to set down 'thoughts, impres-sions, and memories of a young subaltern as he learnt how to lead Gurkha soldiers in times of stress and peril' (Smith 1978: Preface).

In consequence, we look in vain for any but positive assessments of the Gurkhas by these military authors. Unlike the orientalists of India discussed by Inden (1986), where on one side he finds utilitarian-minded *disapprovers* of everything Indian, and on the other, romantic-idealist *approvers* of everything Indian, in this discourse on the Gurkhas there are only romantic approvers. The (non-military) author of a recent publication on the Gurkhas remarks that in his perusal of the British military literature of the past 165 years he found only one disparaging word about these soldiers, and that by the 'eccentric' Orde Wingate (Farwell 1984:14).[12] Reading this literature, therefore, one gets a very strong sense of consensus and continuity; it comes across as monolithic and timeless, relying heavily on stereotype, and with little political or historical context.

Geertz suggests that the ability of anthropologists to persuade others to take what they say seriously depends largely on their capacity to convince readers that they have 'been there' (1989:4-5). The European officers who write about the Gurkhas also occasionally indulge in what he calls 'incorrigible assertions', which underline the number of years they have spent commanding Gurkhas in war and peace.[13] Generally, however, their credentials are not self-advertised, but set out in a Foreword, written invariably by a superior officer—the Colonel of the regiment, the Commander of the Brigade of Gurkhas, or an even more illustrious military figure who at one time had enjoyed an association with Gurkhas. Like the 'Acknowledgements' which begin anthropological monographs, and refer to mentors and colleagues in an attempt to establish the ethnographer's intellectual lineage (Ben-Ari 1987), the Foreword imports a legitimating outsider to verify the author's right and authority to speak for and about his subjects. So for the officer writing about Gurkhas, it is less a matter of having to insist that he has 'been there' than of a superior officer attesting to that fact. Thus in his Foreword to Major H.R.K. Gibbs's *Manual on the Gurkhas* (1947), Colonel G.C. Strahan (his superior recruiting officer) writes 'I can vouch for the fact that no one is better equipped to launch a book on the market as the author himself with his lengthy and detailed experience among the … Gurkhas' (1947:iii). Captain Denis Sheil-Small's competency to write about Gurkhas is affirmed in a Foreword by General Walter Walker, his former battalion commander, who cites from his own report on an action in which Sheil-Small was involved and which led to the latter's award of the Military Cross (Sheil-Small 1982). This constitutes a way of defending genre boundaries (Baxter and Fardon 1991) and makes it extremely difficult for someone who has no background in the Gurkhas to write about them, or to be taken seriously by the 'Gurkha community' (as one British officer put it) when they do.

Recent postmodernist critics have sensitised us to literary devices by means of which authors establish their authority to speak for and about their subjects, or leave little room in their accounts for any but their own voices (Rabinow 1986). Certainly in the Gurkha literature the military authors control completely the writings they produce: there are no dialogic or polyphonic texts here. But the political character of this literature is not simply or primarily to do with asserting control over textual constructions (see Sangren 1988). This of course takes us to the heart of the debate between those who, on the one hand, are persuaded by Derrida's (or at least his imitators') much-cited pronouncement that nothing exists outside the text,[14] and, on the other, those who bemoan the 'literary turn' in anthropology, and see it as drawing a *cordon sanitaire* around the interpretation of politics and society (Scholte 1987:44). My own inclination is to see this as a spurious divide. This essay attends to the textual strategies and devices employed by military writers, while constantly referring them to the politico-military settings in relation to which they are produced and reproduced, and in the contexts of which their meanings become more readily understood. To do otherwise, as Mani and Frankenberg remark, is to convert political issues into textual ones (1985:176) or, as Parkin implies in his critique of certain postmodernist writings, to confuse power and style (1990:183; see also Nugent 1988:84).

Who are the Gurkhas?

The collective attachment to common cultural and social perspectives on the part of both military writers and their audiences—and the interplay between authors and readers implied in the notion of genre—raises a host of questions about the nature of the Gurkha reality which this literature purports to describe. To the extent that these authors endow the phenomenon they represent with their own meanings and understandings, they tend to constitute the Gurkhas in the very process of writing about them (see Holy and Stuchlik 1983:109). The Gurkha can thus best be understood as a fiction. This is not to imply that Gurkhas do not really exist, or that those who write about them are deliberately fabricating lies and fallacies. Rather, these writings—like anthropologists' ethnographies—can be labelled fictions in the sense of something 'fashioned' (Clifford 1986:6). The 'other', Fabian observes, is 'never simply given, never just found or encountered, but *made*' (1990:755, Fabian's emphasis). Gurkhas exist in the context of the military imagination, and are thereby products of the officers who command and write about them; outside that setting, it can be argued, there are no Gurkhas, only Nepalis.[15] Besides, in Nepal, no group or category of people refers to itself or is referred to by other Nepalis as 'Gurkhas'.[16] The term most commonly used for a soldier who serves or has served in foreign armies is *lahure*, a corruption of Lahore, the city in Punjab where, even before they took service with the British, many Nepalis were enlisted into the Sikh army of Ranjit Singh (see Singh 1962:119).

Nepal was, for a time, in the eighteenth and nineteenth centuries referred to by the British as the land, territory or Kingdom of the Gurkhas, Goorkhas or Gorkhalees, since the dynasty which conquered the Valley of Kathmandu around 1768, and has provided Nepal's monarchs ever since, had originated in a small territory called Gorkha situated in the hills west of the Valley. But while the term Gorkhalee gradually fell into disuse in political circles, the military continued to employ the term (variously spelled) and since 1891, the official version employed in British service has been 'Gurkha' (Chapple 1985:1). Its use by the military, however, has been somewhat inconsistent. Occasionally it referred to the country or its people as a whole (see Spaight 1941). More commonly it was applied to selected sections of the population whom the British wished to recruit into the army. In this sense, the term referred to all the 'martial races' of Nepal (Chapple 1985:4; Davis 1970:103-4; see also Chapter 4). In this second connotation, 'Gurkha' conflated several ethnic or 'tribal' communities, speaking various Tibeto-Burman languages, who inhabited the middle hills of the country long before these areas were penetrated by high-caste Hindus fleeing the Muslim invasions of north India in the twelfth and thirteenth centuries. While possessing differing languages, beliefs and practices, these various indigenous ethnic groups did share many features of culture and history, but most of all came to experience a common political subordination to the high-caste latecomers, who in almost every respect grew to dominate the government and bureaucracy of the country from the time of its unification in the late eigtheenth century under the House of Gorkha (see Chapter 2). These high castes did not become the primary targets of British recruitment, and were not usually included under the generic 'Gurkha' rubric, although a number were eventually enlisted into a high-caste regiment, and so came to be labelled 'Gurkhas' in yet a third sense of the term, i.e. those who actually serve or have served in the Brigade.

The creators of this discourse saw the Gurkhas as the descendants of the fighting men of Gorkha who had conquered the Valley of Kathmandu and created the modern Nepalese state. Pemble observes that this 'misconception' still persists, and suggests that while the Gorkha leadership eagerly recruited the 'Mongolian hillmen' into the army of the state, it was also their policy to keep these tribesmen distinct and subordinate (1971:26). One British military writer who appears also to have entertained this 'misconception' describes his disappointment at discovering on his visit to the town of Gorkha in the early 1960s that it looked 'no different from any of the smaller towns in the Nepal Valley', and is 'now no more than a backwater, with scarcely a man of those we know as Gurkhas living in it' (Forbes 1964:29).

The Gurkha, then, is a fiction in the sense that he is a creation both of the military ambiance in which he assumes his persona, and of the military authors who represent him. Should we argue for a Gurkha 'reality' to set alongside this portrayal? In Anglo-Indian novels written during the colonial period, Mannsaker tells us, there is a constant two-way traffic 'between the romance and the actuality, so that at times it is difficult to sort them out' (Mannsaker 1983:26). Sorting them out is precisely the problem, and brings us face to face with fundamental issues regarding the relationship between representation and represented (see Rorty 1982; Fabian 1990). Said has been criticised for his ambiguity about the desirability or relevance of invoking the 'real' Orient to set beside the constructions of the orientalists (see Crapanzano 1980:135; Mani and Frankenberg 1985:181). But Clifford argues that orientalist 'inauthenticity is not answered by any authenticity' (1980:209).

In this essay, constructions of the Gurkha by military authors are regarded as authentic—despite the fictional nature of their subjects—and are shown to be so by constant reference to the contexts in which they have arisen, and the circumstances of their persistence. This avoids both the attachment of truth values to these depictions as well as the ultimately pointless search for what the Gurkhas are 'really like'.[17] But the attribution of authenticity to these representations need not imply acceptance of the viewpoints therein expressed, nor prevent consideration of alternative discourses. Anthropologists and historians of Nepal—both indigenous and foreign—offer different and at times contradictory perspectives on the Gurkha project, providing both a contrast to and a deepening of our understanding of the military narratives. Nepalis who are serving or have served in the Gurkhas and their families provide yet another outlook, although their voices are almost never heard in the literature produced by European military writers, nor are they much represented by or among the Nepalese intellectuals who increasingly comment on the employment of Gurkhas in foreign armies. Finally, there are compelling historical conditions— economic, social and political—in the mountains of Nepal from which the soldiers originate and to which they return, which provide a non-discursive context for the exploration of the Gurkha literature. By attending to these various (and disparate) discourses, I attempt to dissolve the polarities between rigidly text-centred approaches and those which, in privileging context, downplay or dismiss the character of the texts.

In the next section I consider the circumstances surrounding Britain's first encounter with the Gurkhas.

Encountering the Gurkhas

In the view of Ramakant the two major objectives of Britain's Nepal policy during the colonial period were free trade and the recruitment of Gurkhas into the Indian army (1968:327). An abundance of evidence suggests that from as far back as the eighth century there was an active trade between India and Nepal, and even before that, Nepal under the Newar kings was an important intermediary in the commerce between India and both Tibet and China (see Sen 1977:16-18). It was also the route followed by Indian pilgrims and scholars to preach the doctrines of Buddhism to the Chinese and Tibetans (Dasgupta 1930:379). The East India Company merely utilised and extended these long-standing links. By the middle of the eighteenth century there was a brisk trade between representatives of the Company and the Newars in the Kathmandu Valley. Nepal was regarded by many English merchants as a region of opulence, and they wanted its rice, butter, spices, oil-seeds, forest products, drugs, dyes and gold (which was actually Tibetan gold). In turn, the Company sold English and Indian-made cloth, sugar, salt, tobacco, and other produce to Nepal. In this period Nepal enjoyed a favourable balance of trade with India, the balance paid for by India in silver, enabling the Gorkha king to purchase arms for his troops as well as luxury items for the nobility (Sen 1977:26).

In 1767 the Company, anxious about its trade with the Newars, had sent an expedition under Captain Kinloch to assist one of the Newar kings (Jayaprakash) in his battle against the invading armies of Gorkha, whose growing power threatened an economic stranglehold on the Valley (see Prinsep 1825:56). The expedition failed, and thereafter, the House of Gorkha, which soon became the ruling power in Kathmandu, remained suspicious of the Company and sought to keep it at arm's length. Trade sharply declined as the markets of both Nepal and Tibet were closed to the direct accession of the British traders (Stiller 1973:327-8). Eventually, the Company was able to exploit internal dissensions and Nepal's tenuous hold on its own feudatories to impose a treaty, signed in 1801, which established a British Residency in Kathmandu. By this means the Company hoped to regenerate the trade which had been lost in the wake of the Kinloch expedition, and to create a more pliable regime in Kathmandu.[18] The Resident remained for only a year, however, leaving in disgust at the Nepal government's delays and prevarications, and the Treaty was formally dissolved in 1804.

In the decade which followed the abandonment of the British Residency at Kathmandu, relations between Nepal and the Company deteriorated. As in the past, the King of Nepal continually sought to establish his proprietory rights over the territories of other petty principalities and there was a steady Gorkha expansion towards both the west and south. The Gorkhalis occupied Kumaon in 1790, and parts of Garhwal in 1803, and between 1787 and 1812 more than two hundred villages in the *terai*—the fertile strip of plains between the Company's territories and the hills—were appropriated by the Nepalese rulers. These were activities which the English, with their concept of fixed and immutable political boundaries—a concept alien to the Nepalis[19]—saw as encroaching on their own territory or that of their neighbours and allies (see Stiller 1976:220-1; Burghart 1984:114-15).

The Company could probably have invaded Nepal at any time but was reluctant to do so because in this period it was committed in the Maratha country, and was also fearful of antagonising the Chinese (Chaudhuri 1960:140), since it 'was generally assumed that Kathmandu was in some form of political subordination to the Ch'ing Emperors' (Rose 1961:209), an assumption which Kathmandu did little to dispel.

However, the British were concerned about a possible alliance between Nepal and the Sikhs, so if the Nepalis could be expelled from the bordering *terai* region they would be contained in the mountains and no longer pose a danger. Declaring a 'principle of limitation', the Governor-General insisted that all *terai* lands were the Company's prerogative, and that Nepal should withdraw to the hills, thus establishing a clear boundary, and removing the threat of further incursions (Stiller 1973:328). But the nobility and political leadership of the country were paid from *terai* lands, and its alienation 'would not merely deprive some officers ... of their excess wealth ... [T]he unity of the state depended on the continued loyalty of these officers and on their fulfilling their duties to the state' (Stiller 1976:19). It is no surprise that the Nepalis resisted such pressure. The British therefore decided on a military solution, and the Governor-General, Lord Hastings, declared war on Nepal in November, 1814.

Several south-Asian historians suggest that the British assumed a rigid attitude on border disputes—thus precipitating the war—because the Governor-General had decided to contain the Gorkhas, and to bring their expanding Himalayan state under British influence (see Sanwal 1965:211; Ramakant 1968:21-24). Rana takes a broader view of events, acknowledging that the uninhibited growth of two regional powers led inevitably to a military confrontation (1970:28), while Stiller concludes that the collision had been inevitable 'from the time that the Gorkhali advance to the west had placed them squarely athwart the trade routes through the Himalayas' (1973:332). British military writers on the Gurkhas, however, taking their cue from earlier British accounts (e.g. Fraser 1820; Smith 1852), and from each other, place the entire blame for the war on Nepal. Vansittart, for example, states that 'From 1804 to 1814 the Nepalese carried on a system of outrage and encroachment on the British frontier' (1915:31). For Forbes 'the root cause of the war ... was the desire of the barons of Nepal to extend their sway over the zamindars [the landlords] of the plains ...' (1964:46-7). Northey also writes that 'the Gurkhas pushed steadily southwards into British territory ...' (1937:57). This is apparently still the accepted view of military writers on the Gurkhas (and the official British position), in as much as it is repeated in Leonard's Ministry of Defence-sponsored handbook on the Gurkhas (1965:30).

The Anglo-Nepal War

The Anglo-Nepal war of 1814-16 is a critical reference point for the discourse to which I am referring, since it was during this war that the British 'discovered' the Gurkhas.

By the late eighteenth century there were two distinct bodies of armed soldiers in India. The first consisted of detachments of the Royal or King's army, which were British throughout. These were mainly regiments of the British Home army which took it in turn to have a spell of duty overseas. The second, approximately three times the size of the King's force, was the Indian army, until the mid-nineteenth century the army of the East India Company. This was divided into three separate establishments, one at each of the three Presidencies of Madras (in the south), Bombay (in the west), and Bengal (in the east). These regional armies were composed of a small proportion of British troops and a very much larger native contingent. The latter consisted of soldiers (sepoys) and NCOs who were mainly Indian, while the officer corps—at least from the end of the eighteenth century— was British, although for a whole variety of reasons, the Company's officers were made to feel inferior to officers of Royal regiments (see Chapter 3). The armies of Madras and Bombay were administered by the governments of those Presidencies, while the much larger Bengal army—which garrisoned the area extending from the Bay of Bengal to Afghanistan—was under the direct administration of the Government of India (Saxena 1974:56). The three armies were ultimately subject to the Commander-in-Chief of the Bengal force (Pemble 1971:90).

The regular Bengal army on the eve of the Nepal war totalled some 68,000 men of all ranks—including a contingent of about 3,000 European troops. There were three battalions of (European) foot artillery, one (European) regiment of horse artillery, and eight regiments of native cavalry. The bulk of the force consisted of fifty-four native infantry battalions (ibid.:91). Between 30,000 and 40,000 troops of the Bengal army were deployed against Nepal in 1814.

The Nepalese army was exclusively an infantry force, numbering an estimated 12-14,000 men during the war, and 'past masters of the art of stockade warfare' (ibid.:29). The organisation of the regular troops had been modelled on the Bengal army, and even its dress imitated Company uniforms. Nonetheless, when Colonel Kirkpatrick visited the country in 1792, he had not been much struck with the appearance of the Nepalese army, and did not think its men superior to the 'rabble ordinarily dignified with the title of sipahis in the service of the generality of the Hindoostan power' (1811:215). Kirkpatrick, moreover, saw only the smartest and best trained of them. The greater part of the field army (as many as two-thirds) consisted of irregular troops recruited locally on the basis of (unpaid) compulsory labour (*jhara*) to boost the permanent garrisons around the country. According to Pemble, 'these tatterdemalion bands were very different from the trim, English-style soldiers [in the regular force]' (1971:28).

The Gorkhalis had learned their tactics from as wide a variety of sources as they had acquired arms. Although in the last decade of the eighteenth century several munitions factories were built in Kathmandu and other parts of the country (Regmi 1971:79), these were unable to produce anything like the quantity of arms required to defend the country against the Company's formidable power. Chaudhuri notes that at the commencement of the war Nepal had only musketeers, archers, men armed with sabres and rocket men, while Shaha estimates that there were about 400-500 guns of all kinds (1986:6).

The Anglo-Nepal war has been much studied and analysed by historians (for example, Pemble 1971), and numerous writings on the Gurkhas by military authors include an outline of its key battles (see Pearse 1898; Northey and Morris 1928; Tuker 1957; Forbes 1964). There is, therefore, no need here for another summary of hostilities between the Bengal and Nepalese armies. It is enough to note that after some initial successes against the Company's forces, the war resulted in the defeat of Nepal. Pant (1978:155) suggests that among other things, the Company's superior technology, financial resources, and military intelligence proved too much for the outnumbered Gorkhalis. Nepal lost most of the *terai*, approximately one-third of its existing territory. Some 7,000 square miles were ceded to the English by the Treaty of Sagauli, which concluded hostilities. As I have already noted, the *terai* was a major source of government revenue and provided the lands granted in pensions and rewards to military leaders and administrators for loyalty and service to the monarch. The Company's appropriation of this land was thus a direct threat to the future of Nepal's noble families and the unity of the Kingdom (Stiller 1976:49).[20]

The Anglo-Nepal war was a turning point in several ways: geo-politically, it halted the expansion of Nepalese power, and reiterated (if this was still necessary) Britain's pre-eminent position on the sub-continent; militarily, it demonstrated and justified the strategy of employing artillery against forti-fied mountain positions, such as those assumed by the Nepalis, while in terms of the Royal-Company hierarchy it marked a significant success for an Indian army officer. General David Ochterlony 'emerged from the war in a blaze of glory', was decorated by the Governor-General, and told that he had at last 'obliterated a distinction [between themselves and officers of the Royal army] painful for the officers of the Honourable Company' (Pemble 1971:339). And since Ochterlony was of comparatively junior rank, it was a refutation of the Company's cumbersome system of military promotion (ibid.:357).[21]

For military writers on the Gurkhas, the most conspicuous feature of the war was the discovery of Nepalese fighting qualities (see the epigram at the commencement of the chapter). The Nepalis had obviously acquired some-thing of a reputation for military skill even before the war. Kirkpatrick pro-nounced them 'brave, sufficiently tractable, and capable of sustaining great hardships ...' (1811:215), while the Sikh Maharajah Ranjit Singh is said to have praised their agility in the 1809 war against his Punjab army (Singh 1962:119). General Rollo Gillespie, who led Company troops against the Nepalis in the ill-fated battle at Kalunga, is purported to have written prior to the engagement that 'the Gurkhalees are a very active, warlike people ... I fear disaster' (Wakeham 1937:249). But the celebration of Nepalese valour in the Anglo-Nepal war probably has its origins in contemporary military reports of the early encounters in which the Bengal army acquitted itself so poorly. Pemble hints at the tendency among certain officers to excuse the army's initial failings by praising the military might of the Nepalis. The Governor-General was apparently annoyed that the Indian army's own 'shy-ness' in battle was 'vindicated ... by expatiating on the unexampled courage shown by the enemy ...' (1971:161). William Fraser, the Political Agent, was similarly vexed, and moreover concerned lest the idea of Nepalese invincibility take hold and sap the morale of the Bengal army. In the midst of the war he wrote: 'I could wish that the general impression in their favour was less prevalent ... [on the grounds that the] boldness of the enemy [will] increase in proportion we fail in confidence' (ibid.:203).

However much these military qualities may have been exaggerated by their British opponents, the Nepalis undoubtedly acquitted themselves commendably well in the face of superior forces (see Stiller 1973:291-2; Shaha 1983:3). Campbell, the Assistant Surgeon at the British Residency in Kathmandu, writing shortly after the war, praised the Nepalis as 'naturally spirited, fierce and brave' (see Hasrat 1970:lxix). Even before hostilities had concluded, men who had been taken prisoner or deserted in response to invitations from the British, were fighting for the Company. Military authors reckon that over 4,500 men sought service, and were formed into several battalions (the 'Nasiri' and 'Sirmoor') commanded by British officers. While these soldiers had impressed the British as being of potential value in their employ, there was some reluctance to trust the new recruits, since it was deemed that they would not 'so soon fight against their brethren of Nepaul'.[22] But as Enloe notes, those who seem at first to be the least reliable often turn, in time, into the most reliable (1980:27).[23] Rathaur insists that these 'deserters' were not 'pure Gurkhas' as the British may have assumed, but Kumaonis, Garhwalis and others whose loyalties were elsewhere (1987:35; see also Forbes 1964:54; Whelpton 1983:93).

This implies, of course, that 'real Gurkhas' would have been loyal to their leaders and country, and would not have deserted to the enemy. A concern to deny that Nepalese soldiers would turn against their own country, or could have been guilty of the heinous act of desertion and treason is understandable. But it projects modern ideas of the state and of loyalty due from citizens and soldiers back two centuries, to a time and place where the very notion of nation-state was in its infancy (see Burghart 1984). In the absence of any concept of fixed political boundaries, ordinary villagers gave tribute or paid taxes to the most powerful rajah and, in the course of time, as one replaced another, village loyalties shifted and changed. Even when the Gorkha king gained supremacy over a wide territory, his influence in various parts of the kingdom, and especially away from his capital, was by no means uniform (see Caplan 1970). Thus, at least until well into the nineteenth century the very idea of 'desertion', with its strong moral undertones, would not accurately reflect the kinds of shifting allegiances which characterised the relations of villagers with external powers, whether as taxpayers, political followers, or soldiers. Thus, Des Chene suggests that the dependence of most regular Nepalese troops on their commanders for remuneration[24] meant that when the officers' possessions of land (*jagirs*) had been lost to the British 'it was a natural step to offer their services to those who now ruled over their jagirs', while irregulars who were compelled to serve the state without reward 'crossed over on the assumption that there were better prospects elsewhere' (1991:52-3).

Recruiting Gurkhas

The Treaty of Sagauli which concluded the Anglo-Nepal war expelled the Nepalis from their *terai* lands, gained for the Company several hill districts which enabled it to build sanatoria for its European officers and civilians, and established a British Residency in Kathmandu to keep a 'careful and controlling watch on all the moves and intrigues of the Nepal durbar [government]' (Sanwal 1965:211).

Although many writers on the Gurkhas attribute the right of the Company to recruit Nepalis to the Treaty of Sagauli, there is in fact no mention of recruitment in the Treaty (see Cavenaugh 1851). This right derived, it would appear, from a convention agreed with the Nepalese commander in the western region (Amar Singh Thapa) in May 1815, i.e. before the war had ended (see Ramakant 1968:269; James and Sheil-Small 1965:17).

As already noted, several battalions of Gurkhas were raised before the war ended. But these early Gurkha soldiers seem not to have been highly regarded, according to the historian Landon (1928/1:96), and 'did not command for a long time the general admiration which the British later gave them' (Mason 1974:308). They were small irregular units and it was, in fact, nearly fifty years before the British brought these Gurkha battalions into the regular Indian army, at which time the whole force was organised on a permanent regimental basis (Hunter 1896:258-9).

Nonetheless, shortly after the war ended there was a campaign orchestrated at the British Residency in Kathmandu to enlist Nepalis on a systematic basis into the Company's forces. Edward Gardner, the Resident, apparently with the approval of the Nepalese *durbar*, urged the Government of India to consider attaching to their own forces a portion of the regular Nepalese army (with its own officers). He felt this would prevent any further invasion of British territories by the Nepalis. But this offer was turned down by the Company on the grounds that it was opposed to the recruitment of separate bodies of foreign mercenaries (Hunter 1896:107; Landon 1928/1:97).

Hodgson, who was for a time Assistant Resident and later Resident in Kathmandu during the third and fourth decades of the nineteenth century then proposed that the Company recruit Nepalis directly into the Company's service as individuals on the grounds that 'they are by far the best soldiers in India [with] unadulterated military habits' (1833:221). But at the time that he wrote—hardly fifteen years after the end of the Anglo-Nepal war—Hodgson suspected that the Nepalis might turn against the British again, and it seemed to him wise to employ Gurkhas in the Indian army. Campbell, the Assistant Surgeon at the Residency, echoed this view, arguing that 'the enlistment of Gurkhas would tend to thwart the war policy of Kathmandu' (see Hasrat 1970:229). Stiller suggests that Hodgson (and probably others at the Residency) was obsessed by the size of the Nepalese army, and by the fear that it might turn against the British again (1976:249).

Indeed, the Nepalese *durbar*'s suspicions of just such British motives led to persistent resistance to the enlistment of its subjects. As early as 1815, rights to collect rent on lands assigned as *jagir* to Nepalese soldiers who had gone over to the British were confiscated and transferred to others.[25] Until very nearly the end of the nineteenth century the expansion of Gurkha numbers occurred in the face of measures by successive Nepalese governments to thwart these recruitment efforts—although at times 'this opposition was veiled under profession of cooperation' (Mojumdar 1973:162). Their attitude to the enlistment of Gurkhas was one of consistent hostility, so much so that the British had to carry on the recruitment *sub rosa*.

Jang Bahadur Rana, the Nepalese prime minister at the time of the Bengal army's rebellion of 1857 (the 'Mutiny'), viewed the interest of the British in the Gurkhas as a sinister design to denude the country of its fighting population and weaken it. He had strong reasons to suspect that the Gurkhas served the British as suppliers of military and other information which he wanted to keep secret. When he inspected the Sirmoor battalion he is reported to have called the Gurkhas there 'deserters'.[26] Jang Bahadur thus sought to restrict the flow of these men to India. Nepalis were legally unable to leave the country without the authority of the government, and this would of course not be given to allow anyone to enlist in the Indian army. Moreover, there was a ban on families leaving the country to join their soldier husbands/fathers, and, for a time, Gurkhas were prevented from returning home on leave (Mojumdar 1972:162-5). The *durbar* also threatened to execute recruiting agents sent by the British (Rathaur 1987:57). But while the government was set against recruitment, it was no doubt aware of its economic benefits in the hills, and its 'safety-valve' effect through exporting energies which might have been turned against the government, especially in the aftermath of the Anglo-Nepal war when Gorkhali expansion was halted.

Even after the death of Jang Bahadur the Nepalese regime expressly for-
bade men to leave the country for army service and threatened dire punishments if they did so (Husain 1970:241). However, succession quarrels after
Jang Bahahdur's death gave the British the leverage they needed to press the
Nepalis to ease their restrictions. According to one historian 'a deal was
struck by which the British undertook to supply the Nepalese government
with modern arms in exchange for unrestricted supply of Gurkha recruits
for the Indian army' (Mojumdar 1973:10). But even then Jang Bahadur's
successor Ranodip Singh maintained an obstructionist policy. Matters only
really improved for the British in the last quarter of the nineteenth century
when the regime of Bir Shamsher took over in Kathmandu. The British
threatened to support his rivals for power, the sons of Jang Bahadur, and
faced with such an alternative, Bir Shamsher 'reluctantly gave in' (Rose and
Fisher 1970:147). After 1884 the Nepalese government's increasing dependence on the British for arms (to say nothing of the Ranas' growing appetite
for European luxury goods) and Britain's dependence on the Nepalis for
Gurkhas led to friendlier relations.

This history of British pressure and Nepalese resistance, however, has little place in the military discourse on Gurkhas which ignores the *durbar's*
opposition and/or stresses the harmony of purpose between the British and
Nepalese regimes since the end of the Anglo-Nepal war, and especially since
the rise of the Ranas to power in 1846. Thus, James and Sheil-Small note
that 'For 150 years Gurkha recruits have made the journey down the mountain to join the British Army. And all this time there has been a strong
allegiance between Nepal and Britain' (1965:14). Similarly, Masters
acknowledges no problems between the two governments when he notes
that the rulers of Nepal 'agreed to allow their Gurkha subjects to enlist ...
in the East India Company's service' (1956:90). Another author asserts that
the Ranas, as part of their policy of friendship with Britain, 'continue[d] to
allow Gurkha soldiers to be recruited into the Indian Army ... ' (Edwards
1979:225) Indeed, Bishop specifically identifies Jang Bahadur Rana as one
who had 'whole-heartedly' encouraged British recruitment of Gurkhas
(1976:49), while Northey suggests that he 'actively assisted in their recruitment' (1937:77). The tendency on the part of these writers to ignore or even
misrepresent the historical and political realities surrounding the immediate
post-Anglo-Nepal war period seems explicable mainly in terms of a refusal
to acknowledge that there could be any opposition to the Gurkha project,
especially from such a key player as the Nepalese *durbar*.

Gurkhas in the Twentieth Century

Despite these obstacles, the numbers of Gurkha units in the Indian army grew steadily during the latter part of the nineteenth century. At the beginning of this century there were five Gurkha Rifle Regiments (1st to 5th GR) in addition to several regiments in the Bengal army and one in the Madras army which were composed entirely of Gurkhas. In several reorganisations of the Indian army during the first decade of this century the latter were brought into the Gurkha 'line' so that by 1908 there were ten Gurkha Regiments each with two regular battalions (Chapple 1985:17). This remained the basis of the Gurkha Brigade until its division at the time of India's Independence, and was the structure with which most writers on the Gurkhas were or are personally familiar.[27] Alone among the constituents of the Indian army, each Gurkha regiment was established at a permanent home cantonment in the hills or foothills of the Himalayas, although battalions of the regiment would frequently be away from their home base during exercises or when on active service.[28]

During the two world wars each regiment was allowed to raise additional battalions.[29] Between 1914 and 1918 some 200,000 Nepalis are reported to have served in the Indian army, while from 1939 to 1945 a quarter of a million men are said to have been recruited into approximately fifty-five battalions of Gurkhas (Tuker 1957:145).[30] A number of regimental histories and other accounts describe in great detail the participation of Gurkhas in both world wars, their heroism and sacrifices (see, for example, Woodyatt 1929; Poynder 1937; Mackay 1952; Smith 1978; Sheil-Small 1982).

With the end of the Second World War and the approach of Indian Independence, it was decided that Gurkha regiments would be divided between the British and new Indian armies. After hurried and often rancorous discussion and debate, it was agreed to transfer four regiments—the 2nd, 6th, 7th and 10th—to the British army, to form the Brigade of Gurkhas. A unit of Gurkha Engineers and Signals, and a Gurkha Transport Regiment were later established. The remaining six regiments went to, or rather remained in, the Indian army. Several writers expressed dismay at the division. Tuker, angered that several of the oldest regiments had been assigned to India, predicted that they 'will one day have their numbers changed, later be deprived of their titles, and will have lost their identity' (1950:638). On the contrary, the Indian army has not only retained the old regimental numbering, and many of their customs and traditions, but has expanded the number of their battalions, and recruited several new regiments (see Das 1984).[31] Today there are an estimated 100,000 Gorkhas in some forty-two battalions of the Indian army.[32] After India's Independence a Tripartite agreement was signed with Nepal which allowed both Britain and India to continue to recruit Gurkhas. The literature which I will explore in this essay refers only to the Gurkhas under British command, whether in the pre-Independence Indian army or in the post-1947 Brigade of Gurkhas in the British army.[33]

At the time of the division, regiments of the British army moved from their bases in India (and what came to be Pakistan) to Malaya and Singapore, which were at the time the nearest to India and Nepal of Britain's remaining colonial possessions. Within months the Brigade was caught up in the Malayan 'Emergency' which went on for nearly twelve years, and involved the Gurkhas in jungle warfare against the guerilla forces of the Malaya Communist Party (the Malayan Races Liberation Army), many of whom the British had trained to harass the Japanese occupation during the Second World War. This was followed several years later by the Brigade being called in to help suppress a rebellion against the Sultan of Brunei, and shortly after that, to take part in the four-year 'Confrontation' with Indonesia, which was anxious to prevent the British colonies of Sarawak and North Borneo from being incorporated into Malaysia.

India's Independence and the division of regiments marked a turning point in the history of the Brigade. But the decision to reduce further its size was delayed until the end of Confrontation in 1966, when numbers fell from a post-war high of 15,000 to approximately 7,000 men. At first it was announced that each of the four regiments was to be reduced to a single battalion, but when the Sultan of Brunei agreed to a renewal of the existing treaty with Britain, and to meet the costs of a Gurkha battalion to be stationed there, a fifth battalion was deemed necessary. The 2nd GR was thus able to retain both of its battalions, and the Brigade's strength settled at approximately 8,000 men. In 1971, the headquarters were moved to Hong Kong, and it was also decided that one battalion would be permanently stationed in the UK.

Several officers to whom I spoke recalled the period of cutbacks as a traumatic time. During these immediate post-war years the Brigade of Gurkhas had made its mark in the British army (just as it had previously made its mark in the Indian army). It was the only branch of the military which at this time was almost continuously in action (and for this reason alone, the envy of officers throughout the army). The Gurkhas were regarded as *the* experts in jungle warfare, and officers with other regiments looked on secondment to the Brigade as good for their careers in terms of broadening their experience, and of course as an opportunity to live for a time outside Europe. One officer to whom I spoke thought that the Gurkha role throughout this period was not much different than it had been prior to and during the war: 'it was very much a colonial type of existence; long periods in the jungle hunting down [the enemy]'. But with the end of these 'insurgencies' in South East Asia, and the dramatic cutbacks in the size of the Brigade, British officers with the Gurkhas began to apprehend that their 'finest hour' had passed, indeed, that the very existence of the Gurkhas was at issue. Many also came to realise that the kind of soldiering on which the Gurkhas had built their reputation was rapidly being superseded, and that the unit was in danger of becoming a 'backwater'.

A majority of the authors of the texts I am discussing served with the Gurkhas during the Second World War and/or in South East Asia during the period of almost continuous military activity. They thus experienced the dramatic transformation of Gurkha fortunes, as numbers were drastically cut and the very existence of the Brigade clouded in uncertainty. They also became aware of the changing evaluations of the Gurkhas within the British army, and the growing doubts about the benefits of such service for an officer's career prospects in the modern military. Moreover, they clearly appreciated the romantic appeal of the Gurkhas to the British public at large, and how this appeal would have been enhanced by expatiating in print on the unrivalled qualities of these troops. It is thus possible to identify a political and military context out of which a great deal of the recent literature on the Gurkhas has emerged, and within which many of the authors of that literature spent their formative years.

The Brigade of Gurkhas today represents about ten per cent of British army infantry units and about fifteen per cent of infantry manpower. In addition, since 1949, there has been a Gurkha contingent in the Singapore Police Force (numbering about a thousand men), and the Sultan of Brunei employs a Gurkha Reserve Unit (of some 2,000 men) as part of his armed forces, which is recruited from those who have retired from British Gurkha service. A Gurkha unit also serves in Belize.

However, as I write these words the future of the Brigade looks very uncertain. In June, 1994, in keeping with the British government's plans to decrease the size of its armed forces, the four existing regiments were officially amalgamated into the Royal Gurkha Rifles. In the next few years this will be reduced to two battalions, and the Corps regiments—transport, signals and engineers—to squadrons. This involves a reduction in strength from 8,000 to 2,500 men in all—in the opinion of some officers, not a viable proposition.

The next chapter examines the ecological and historical conditions in the mountains of Nepal where young men who entered the pre-Independence

Indian and later British armies grew up, the circumstances encouraging their enlistment, and the socio-political implications of military service in the villages to which they return. This is followed by a consideration of the British officers who commanded (and created the texts about) Gurkhas. It touches on their educational and social backgrounds, the military structures in which they were located, the regimental cultures they elaborated, and the ideological influences to which they were subjected, all of which contributed to the formation of their images of Gurkhas. The next two chapters then turn to how the Gurkhas are represented in the military literature. Chapter 4 examines their depiction as a 'martial race', and the related virtues of masculinity and loyalty. The latter arises from what is regarded as a natural affinity between British officers and their Gurkhas, although a discourse emerging from the ranks of Nepalese intellectuals is examined for an alternative perspective on the Gurkha project. Chapter 5 first explores the notion of courage in Western military thought, finding in it hierarchical connotations, and thus differentially applied to Gurkhas and their officers. The discussion then turns to those textual images which on the one hand portray the Gurkhas as mirroring their officers' gentlemanly characteristics, and on the other, render them as perpetually juvenile, and thereby in need of a controlling hand. The concluding chapter draws together the various themes of the essay and argues for an approach which relates text and context while retaining the integrity of each.

Notes to Chapter 1

1. Chapple's *Bibliography of Gurkha Regiments and Related Subjects* (1980) lists approximately 320 items on Gurkhas, and while many are brief articles or 'in-house' publications, probably half are substantial texts.

2. Contemporary anthropologists are less certain of the viability of 'distance' as a fieldwork technique, certainly more aware of the impact of their presence on the communities they study, and more likely to become involved in advocacy on behalf of the latter.

3. From a somewhat different perspective, literary and cultural theorists increasingly consider the importance of history in shaping perceptions and interpretations of texts, and stress the dialectic between language and reality (see Collier and Geyer-Ryan 1990).

4. In Perkins's *Regiments of the Empire* some sixteen pages of text are devoted to listing the histories of Gurkha units (1989:208-24).

5. Burroughs notes that generally in this period there was an 'intense popular appetite' for distant battles and military exploits in the cause of empire. Englishmen could thereby 'vicari-

ously share the excitement and glory of conquering foreign lands and upholding British civilization in remote, exotic places' (1986:72)

6. These works also utilise an extremely limited range of references. A prominent Nepalese scholar (and one with Gurkha 'connections') observes that the bibliography in Leonard's 1965 Gurkha text had only twenty-seven items on Nepal, although Wood's authoritative bibliography of 1959 already ran to 103 printed pages (Gurung 1991:20). The bibliography attached to the recent House of Commons Report on the future of the Gurkhas (in which former and serving officers had a large input) lists only forty-one references, the majority published prior to the Second World War (House of Commons 1989:lxxxi).

7. Asad and Dixon (1984) point to the limitations imposed by the metaphors current in the writer's culture on his or her ability to portray the concepts of alien cultures.

8. Danvers Dawson (1917:119-121). I am grateful to Dr Helen Kanitkar for drawing this article to my attention.

9. The *khukuri* is a curved knife which serves as an all-purpose implement in the hills of Nepal. See also Chapter 5.

10. Despite these remarks, it must be said that most of the Gurkha texts are very informative.

11. Dandekar (1989) asserts that military history (like the sociology of the military) occupies a marginal position in the profession.

12. Wingate criticised the Gurkhas, among other things, for being 'mentally unsuited' for the role given them in the first Chindit expedition in Burma during the Second World War. But Wingate himself is accused by one military author of failing to understand that Gurkha soldiers 'need a different type of leadership to the British soldier' and so of failing to 'exploit their best qualities' (see Smith 1973:126).

13. In his review of *The Gurkhas* (1984) by Farwell, who had never served in the Brigade, Cross (who has himself authored several books on Gurkhas) begins with the comment: 'In this review I shall endeavour to compare what the author has written with what I know to be true, having myself served with Gurkhas for 38 years' (1985:168).

14. Norris has attempted to argue against what he sees as the widespread popular distortion of Derrida's position (1990).

15. Fox makes a similar distinction between the Sikhs as a religious or ethnic category, and the martial 'Singhs' (Lions) constructed by the British (1985).

16. Their reputation as fearless and honest has led to an ironic situation whereby in Indian cities nowadays the term 'Gurkha' usually refers to a watchman (usually but not necessarily a Nepali) who guards office blocks, factories, building sites and the houses of the well-to-do (see Dixit 1990:10). Of late, it has also assumed political significance with the rise of the 'Gorkhaland' movement (see Subba 1992).

17. With sardonic insight, some feminists have observed that the postmodern discovery of the contingency and multiplicity of truth comes just at the time when women and other previously muted groups have begun to challenge the dominant male monopoly of truth (Mascia-Lees, Sharpe and Cohen 1989:15).

18. Chaudhuri comments that the Company's assistance was sought by hill rajahs in their quarrels with one another and with the Gorkha rajah, and it intervened when it saw opportunities for increasing its trade (1960:51).

19. Stiller points out that the notions of 'boundary' and 'boundary lines' were foreign to the Nepalis, who were 'concerned with the control of villages, which waxed or waned according to the military strength and vigour of the ruling dynasty ... boundary lines followed from the

history of western diplomacy and drew their meaning from maps and lines drawn on maps' (1976:220-1).

20. Some of these lands were in fact returned to Nepal soon after the conclusion of hostilities, since 'their value did not justify the expense of maintaining British authority there' (Stiller 1973:332). Others were given back to Nepal as reward for the government's loyalty and assistance during the Mutiny.

21. Promotion in the Indian army—unlike that in the Royal army where until 1871 commissions could be purchased—was strictly by seniority. This meant that promotion was extremely slow, especially in peacetime, and men who were 'unfitted by age or physical infirmity or even military incompetence [were able] to attain senior rank' (Heathcote 1974:32). One early-nineteenth century observer remarked that 'every individual who has entered the army and happened to live, is alike qualified to fill the upper ranks ...' (Badenach 1826:23).

22. *Digest of Services, 1st Battalion, 2nd King Edward VII's Own Goorkhas (Part 1, 1815-1898)*, p.2.

23. Enloe also suggests that 'ethnic soldiers' are often first encountered in hostile circumstances, impressing their adversaries with their potential value to the state (1980:27).

24. At this time the Nepalese army 'paid' its officers and some of its regular troops by assigning lands (*jagir*) from which they received revenue.

25. See *Regmi Research Series*, 1974.

26. Letter from Major C. Reid, Commander of the Sirmoor Battalion to Major Norman, Deputy Adjutant General of the Army, 25 January, 1858. (*Letter Books of the 2nd K.E.O. Goorkhas 1853-1884.*)

27. The notion of a Brigade usually has specific military connotations in terms of magnitude and command structure. However, despite changes over the years in the size and composition of Gurkha units, they have, since about the beginning of this century, been organised and integrated into a single organisational entity, referred to as the Gurkha Brigade, and latterly, the Brigade of Gurkhas.

28. The 1st Regiment of Gurkha Rifles (1GR) were quartered at Dharmasala, the 2nd and 9th at Dehra Doon, the 3rd at Almora, the 4th at Bakloh, the 5th and 6th at Abbotabad, the 7th and 10th at Quetta, and the 8th at Shillong.

29. In peacetime, each regiment consisted of two battalions of approximately one thousand men each. It was only after 'Confrontation' in South East Asia that most regiments were reduced to a single battalion.

30. Chapple's figures, drawn from official sources, suggest that a much lower number—possibly half these totals—actually served (1985: 18-21).

31. Only the former British royal titles, not surprisingly, have been removed. So what was the King George's Own 1st Gurkha Rifles is now the 1st Gorkha Rifles, what was the Queen Alexandra's Own 3rd Gurkha Rifles is now the 3rd Gorkha Rifles, and so on (see Das 1984).

32. The Indians have chosen to use this form of spelling, i.e. *Gorkha.*

33. As far as I have been able to ascertain, apart from keeping regimental histories up to date (see Proudfoot 1984; Sharma 1988; Palsokar 1991), Indian officers have hardly written about 'their' Gorkhas.

CHAPTER 2

GURKHAS AT HOME

The Ecology of Military Service

> Each valley, in the seclusion of its surrounding mountains,
> was self-sufficient. The chiefs dispensed justice, but they
> could not ride roughshod over their people. The clansmen
> would not tolerate it. By and large people owned their
> own land. They were freehold yeoman farmers.
>
> Major D. Forbes *Johnny Gurkha*, 1964.

Introduction

This chapter introduces the reader to the home environment in which the great majority of men who have served or are at present serving in the Gurkhas have grown up. It attends, albeit briefly and therefore superficially, to certain historical developments in Nepal during the past several centuries, and seeks to identify certain of the ecological, economic and social contexts within which decisions to serve in foreign armies were made. Finally, the implications and effects of military service on the local communities from which soldiers migrate are considered. The chapter relies heavily on the work of historians and anthropologists, including my own study of a cluster of settlements in east Nepal.

Populations of the Middle Hills

The overwhelming majority of Gurkhas originate from the villages and townships situated within the middle hills of Nepal (the *pahar*), a territory roughly 500 miles in length (from west to east) and 80 miles in depth (from south to north). These hills, broken by deep river valleys, lie between the *terai*, a narrow belt of low-lying plains bordering India, and the high Himalayan ranges. The bulk of their inhabitants—who comprise perhaps sixty per cent of Nepal's population today, and a much higher proportion until relatively recently[1]—reside at altitudes between 3500 and 9000 feet.

The people at present living in the mid-montane regions of Nepal have entered these areas over many hundreds of years. Linguistic and other evidence suggests that the earliest migrations originated from areas to the north of the kingdom, from the mountains of China, Burma, or Tibet. These 'Mongoloid' peoples spoke a diversity of what are now classified as Tibeto-Burman languages, some virtually indistinguishable from one another, others mutually unintelligible. Certainly, by the early middle ages, when new migrations from (mainly north) India began, these ethnic, or, as they are frequently labelled, 'tribal' groups, had long been settled throughout the middle hills of what is now Nepal Himalaya.

Although the middle hills have for many years contained many Tibeto-Burman-speaking ethnic populations, recruitment into the Gurkhas has concentrated on only four of these groups, namely the Magars, Gurungs, Rais and Limbus.[2] While these communities were sometimes regarded and portrayed by British military authors as a uniform category—they might describe 'Gurkha weddings' or 'Gurkha funerals'—and at other times as culturally distinct, ethnographic evidence suggests that there are wide overlaps both within this category of recruitable groups, and between them and others not generally enlisted. Macfarlane points to similarities between the Gurungs living in the Annapurna region of central Nepal and certain Magars living to the south and west (1991:1). Ragsdale even suggests that some Gurung communities may have absorbed Magar lineages (1990:2). Both these groups, according to Macfarlane, share a great deal with local Tamangs, Thakalis and inhabitants of lower Manang and Mustang. The Bhotiyas and Tibetans to the north are also 'culturally like the Gurungs' (Macfarlane 1991:1), while according to Grierson, the Gurung language is 'closest of all Himalayan tongues to Central Tibetan' (quoted in Ragsdale 1989:42). Similarly, Macdonald (1991) remarks on the affinities between Gurung and Tamang speech, but also demonstrates the wide divergences existing within apparently homogeneous communities such as the Rai and Tamang, suggesting heterogeneity within as well as between primary named ethnic groups. This is supported by Hitchcock's finding that Magar groups were often culturally very different from one another (1970:184-5). What is thus apparent is that cultural, social and linguistic boundaries in the middle hills have all along been fluid, and the labels attached to people (by anthropologists, as by British recruiters and military authors) are, as Macfarlane puts it, to some extent 'random and recent' (1991:1).

Depending on local ecological conditions, these communities gained a livelihood in various ways: by pastoralism, long-distance trade, soldiering, and (principally) forms of shifting and settled cultivation on land held mainly by lineage groups. In the country of the Limbus in what is now east Nepal, for example, land was deemed to belong to the group of agnatic kinsmen who cleared the forest and brought it under cultivation. The individual household had rights to land by virtue of membership in kin groups of ascending order—sub-lineage, lineage, clan, etc. Since the key resource was labour (and not land, which was in plentiful supply) the principle of agnation was not marked. Rights to use land within the group's territory were granted to kin and political followers who were not necessarily agnates. Such grants were made in the context of a non-commodity or 'clan-based' economy, characterised by an absence of private property (see Gregory 1982; Caplan 1991:309). This tenurial system, and others like it among the Tibeto-Burman populations in the middle hills, were later to be designated by the rulers of Nepal as *kipat.*

Migrations from the south into the territories of these Tibeto-Burman communities had profound effects on their ways of life. The immigrants introduced new crops and patterns of agriculture, forms of social organisation based on ideas of caste, and a literary culture previously unknown in these regions. They also imported Hindu orthodoxies into communities which had adopted and evolved syncretic ideas and practices based both on neighbouring Buddhist and local religious traditions. The rise of the Gorkha power in the mid-eighteenth century, under a royal house with purported ancestral links to north India, led to the establishment, by conquest and alliance, of a 'Hindu kingdom' between Garhwal and Kumaon on the west, and Sikkim on the east. The Tibeto-Burman populations occupying the middle hills were, within several decades, absorbed into this alien Gorkha polity.

The demands of the immigrants for land to cultivate increased in the wake of the Gorkha conquest, and the original Tibeto-Burman populations were urged to settle these immigrants on their lands. Since tribal holdings were extensive and there was a need for settlers to provide labour, land grants were conferred on the newcomers, who recognised their dependence by both tributary and ritual offerings. These grants were regarded as inalienable gifts, since in the clan-based economies of the period, lacking private property, there could be no concept of alienation. In this respect the Tibeto-Burman populations of Nepal shared a conception of land as held by countless indigenous or tribal peoples around the world, for whom 'membership in the community generates an attitude to the land which is antecedent to the working of it' (Hart 1982:46). Limbus, for example, insisted that their forebears had cleared the forests and worshipped the deities who thereby were witness to their rights to these lands. *Kipat* was thus more than a system of land tenure; it was the basis of their identity as a people. The grant of Royal Orders (*lalmohar*) by the first Gorkha king was seen as state confirmation of this legacy.

In time, however, the state introduced legislation and administrative procedures which in effect encouraged these immigrants and their descendants to hold the lands they had been granted and acquire others in the form of private property, thereby freeing them of economic and political dependence on their Tibeto-Burman hosts. There is abundant evidence that during the course of the nineteenth century the existing social hierarchies based on traditional modes of land holding were replaced by inequalities grounded both in new forms of landed wealth (as private property) and in the caste system introduced by the Hindu newcomers. Within the latter scheme most Tibeto-Burman groups became *matwali jat* ('drinking castes'), and for a time several of them (including Rais and Limbus) were categorised as enslaveable (see Höfer 1979).[3] The Brahmans, Thakuris and Chetris, as sacred-thread wearing castes (*tagadhari jat*) were placed at the apex of the hierarchy.

Almost everywhere in the middle hills of the country where immigration had created heterogeneous populations, the local economic elite came to be drawn mainly and often exclusively from these *tagadhari* castes. In one area south of Pokhara in west Nepal, 'less favoured groups, including many [Tibeto-Burman] Magars, [had become] dependent on the Brahmans for labor opportunities, and for loans of cash or grain' (Hitchcock 1963:79). Höfer found a similar situation in a district in central Nepal, where members of high castes had entered the area of the [Tibeto-Burman] Tamangs, and this led eventually to the emergence of significant differences in status and wealth between them. The greater wealth of Brahmans and Chetris, he reports, 'derives partly from the fact that they cultivate fertile, lowland rice fields on which irrigation is possible, and partly from the privileges the government accorded them in the past' (Höfer 1978:180). Referring to far-east Nepal in the late 1960s, Jones and Jones point out how most [Tibeto-Burman] Limbus were 'hopelessly in debt to high-caste Hindus' (1976:36), and I have traced the growth of upper-caste dominance in another part of east Nepal initially settled by the Limbus (Caplan 1970).

While it has to be stressed that not all members of these high castes were well-to-do, or powerful, they were disproportionately represented among

Nepal's dominant class. Members of such groups came virtually to monop-
olise the national and district political and administrative structures following the creation of the Nepalese state, excluding the traditional
Tibeto-Burman leadership from this network of power. The latter came to
exercise a much reduced influence within their local ethnic communities,
indeed, were themselves often the creation of the administration, seeking
instruments for collecting taxes, organising forced labour, and maintaining
security in the villages (see Höfer 1978:180; Sagant 1985:170). This situation has certainly continued into the present century. Hitchcock, who studied an area south of Pokhara in west Nepal, notes that 'there have always
been many Brahman officials in local district offices. Twenty years ago, at a
time when no Magar held a post above the thum [local administrative] level,
five Brahmans from the thum held such office' (1966:105). In one study it
is noted that '[b]eyond the Chetri-Brahman-Newar "establishment", other
groups in Nepal's population remain uninvolved in national politics ...'
(Gaige 1975:162).[4] Blaikie, Cameron and Seddon showed that in 1972
these groups held approximately ninety-three per cent of all higher civil-ser-
vice and political posts, although they represented only twenty-two per cent
of the population (quoted in Macfarlane 1990:25; see also Bista 1991:2).

These nineteenth-century transformations were occurring alongside a
steady increase in the population of the middle hills. By the latter part of the
century, however, there was little new land to bring under cultivation, so
that many inhabitants of the region began to experience severe land problems.[5] Since there were no local alternatives to pastoralism or agriculture,
large-scale migrations began—mainly to the south and east—in search of
land or employment, for example, in the newly established capitalist timber
and tea plantations (see Mishra 1985/6:157). Approximately one-quarter of
a million people of Nepalese origin were recorded in the Indian Census of
1901 (see Blaikie et al 1980:37). The first migrations to Darjeeling began
with the appointment in 1839 of Dr Campbell as Superintendent, and by
1891, over half the population of Darjeeling was of Nepalese origin, and
one-third had been born in Nepal (O'Malley 1907:43). One visitor to
Sikkim remarked that '... it is because every bit of the land in their country
is taken up that there is such a steady emigration into Sikkim' (Donaldson
1900:208). Indeed, Nepalese immigration into Sikkim reached such pro-
portions that the authorities attempted (unsuccessfully) to check the flow by
legal means (Nakane 1966:260).

The notion of 'land shortage' is, of course, an ambiguous one, but it suggests either an overall insufficiency for the population of an area, or—and
this is the more likely in the changing conditions described above—an

increasingly unequal distribution of existing land resources as these moved out of the control of Tibeto-Burman groups. There is evidence that a disproportionate number of nineteenth-century emigrants from the hills belonged to tribal populations. But land shortage was not the sole motive for emigration. Hill dwellers left their homes to avoid excessive (and often unofficial) taxes, high rents on agricultural tenancies, extravagant rates of interest, or onerous forced-labour exactions. The government frequently castigated local bureaucrats, headmen and village notables for failing to prevent these emigrations, or for bringing them about in the first place. Thus, in an Order to Limbus dated June, 1850, the authorities wrote:

> We have received reports that you are leaving your kipat
> lands and going abroad because of the pressure of
> moneylenders and the oppression of amalis, revenue col-
> lectors, and government officials ... . [You] should come
> here and represent [your] grievances to us, and we shall
> redress [your] legitimate grievances. With due assurance,
> observe your customs and usages and remain on your
> kipat lands and homesteads.[6]

Needless to say, it was the more disadvantaged members of these communities who most felt the burden of exploitation and took flight in search of a better life.

Becoming Gurkhas

It is against such a background of increasing impoverishment, land shortages, political marginalisation and official harassment that we can better understand the attractions of enlistment in the (British) Indian army, but it would be wrong to assume that this would be the first time Tibeto-Burmans from the middle hills had served in foreign armies. We know that men from these communities (particularly Magars and Gurungs) had a history of service in the armies of the Newar kings and of the various warring principalities in the Himalayan regions prior to the establishment of Gorkha pre-eminence (Stiller 1989 [1968]:44). We know also that members of such groups were among the 'Gurkhas' who are said to have fought in the army of the Sikh leader Ranjit Singh prior to as well as following the Anglo-Nepal war of 1814-16 (Sinha 1933:157). Indeed, as I have already noted, the term *lahure*—which is the common Nepali term for a Gurkha—was in vogue before the British raised their first Gurkha battalions, and referred to a hillman 'who sought his fortunes in the armies of states to the west of Nepal' (Pahari 1991:7). Moreover, the success of the East India Company in halting the expansion of the Nepalese army might very well have contributed to the tendency for Tibeto-Burmans to seek employment in the British Indian army. Pahari suggests that following the Anglo-Nepal war, the high-caste officer corps began to prefer soldiers 'of their own kind', so that the Nepalese army became 'the monopoly of nineteenth-century Nepali elites', encouraging Tibeto-Burman men to look elsewhere for military employment (ibid.).[7]

But there is no evidence to suggest that military service was widespread among hill people, or that such an occupation was regarded as the only one worthy of a young man, as various British observers of the Nepalese scene asserted in the course of the nineteenth century (see Hasrat 1970), and European military authors writing on the Gurkhas have reiterated time and again (see Chapter 4). The overwhelming majority of inhabitants of the middle hills were, as already suggested, cultivators and pastoralists, although, as has also been noted, attempting to be so in a rapidly diminishing economic environment.

However compelling the pressures to enter the East India Company's army, the Nepalese *durbar* was strongly opposed from the beginning to British attempts to recruit its citizens, and devised a veritable obstacle course for both recruiters and potential recruits, thereby ensuring that as few as possible actually entered service (see Chapter 1). Certainly, there is evidence that the *durbar*'s policy over the years had a deleterious effect on recruitment. The Commander of the Sirmoor Battalion (one of the first contingents recruited from Nepal) at the time of the 'Mutiny', Major C. Reid, complained in a letter to the Deputy Adjutant General of the Indian Army how difficult it was to obtain 'real Gurkhas' in any number, and how he had found this a problem since joining the battalion six years previously.[8] By 'real Gurkhas' he meant members of Tibeto-Burman groups from the middle hills.

Even when the *durbar* liberalised its policy in the last decades of the nineteenth century to allow Nepalis to join the Indian army, the initial response was muted. The Prime Minister Bir Shamsher apparently had to offer money to lure recruits, and when this failed to attract sufficient numbers, a regulation was promulgated compelling villages to supply candidates (Rathaur 1987:70). For a time, some senior government officials were only appointed on condition that they meet recruitment quotas.[9] According to Husain, young men were 'pressganged' by the authorities, and many deserted (1970:246). These measures made enlistment unattractive to villagers and the British Resident in Kathmandu reported that it was seriously affecting the popularity of Bir Shamsher's regime (ibid.: 245-6). It took some time for the *durbar* to reassure the population, and encourage young men to volunteer of their own accord.

This change of attitude in Kathmandu, alongside the introduction by the British in 1886 of a centralised recruiting system to replace the previous one whereby regiments made their own arrangements, had the desired effect. Gurkha numbers began to expand rapidly. Whereas in 1879 there were five regiments with a total of just over 4,000 men, by 1886 the addition of second battalions in each regiment had doubled the total strength of the Gurkha infantry, and on the eve of the First World War there were some twenty battalions.

Even then, the numbers were unevenly spread among hill communities. Because the Indian army based its recruitment policies on the conviction that only certain groups were martial and therefore suitable for army service, many sections of the population were deliberately excluded (see Chapter 4). This meant that large areas such as the far-west, the north-west and the north-east never became important recruiting grounds (see P. Caplan 1972:40; Fisher 1986:69; Ortner 1989:217). Particular Tibeto-Burman groups, as I have noted, were especially favoured by recruiters. Macfarlane suggests that, from before the beginning of the present century, but more intensively since the First World War, the Gurungs became a society based on military service with the British Indian army. He points out that in 1969 (when he first spent time there) over fifty per cent of men between the ages of twenty-one and fifty-five in a Gurung settlement north of Pokhara had spent a year or more in the army (1976:288). Ragsdale discovered that a similar proportion of Gurung men in the village he studied had taken such employment (1989:77). And despite the fact that Ilam district in east Nepal had never been a prime source of recruits, I too found that (in 1964-5) nearly forty-four per cent of *all* living Limbu males over eighteen years of age in the settlements I knew either had served or were at the time serving in the army (Caplan 1970:114-15).[10]

Recruitment was highly concentrated even within those areas with fairly high percentages of eligible ethnic groups. Thus Blaikie and his colleagues, in their study of west-central Nepal, which contains large populations of Tibeto-Burmans, found that some villages and even some districts within the region had very low recruitment rates (1980:282). Moreover, certain groups within the general 'martial' category would sometimes be missed out by recruiters in a region of otherwise heavy enlistment. Dahal found that in a population of approximately 4,000 Athpahariya Rais in the Dhankuta area, only five were drawing military pensions and not one was serving at the time of his study (1985:72).

It was not until the First World War, when Nepali men were recruited into the Indian army from all parts of the country, and from a variety of Tibeto-Burman groups, that the implications of Gurkha service began to be felt more widely. The Second World War drew even larger numbers of hill people into the army, and there would have been few areas of the hills which were not affected by the outflow of young men. Hitchcock observes that in the two generations between the wars the number of Magar soldiers and pensioners had tripled in the western Nepalese administrative division he studied (1966:104). This pattern of growth seems to have characterised most parts of the country and sections of the population from which the British recruited soldiers (see also Jones and Jones 1976:37).

The Economics of Gurkha Service

Nepal reaps significant economic advantages from Gurkha remittances, which were, until the comparatively recent development of tourism, the country's largest earner of foreign currency. The total annual pay for British Gurkhas is currently some £22m and a large part is remitted to Nepal. In addition, the annual cost of Gurkha pensions is approximately £5.6m a year for just under 21,000 pensioners, so that the value to Nepal of British Gurkhas alone is about £30m annually (House of Commons 1989:xxvi). The figures were no doubt much greater before the reduction in the Brigade's strength at the end of the 1960s (see above). In addition, the Gurkha Welfare Trust, set up in 1967, spends up to £1m annually to 'alleviate distress and destitution, and improve conditions in the hills' (ibid.:xxxix).

Nepal is also thought to benefit from an annual British government sub-sidy for being allowed to recruit Gurkhas. Pahari is only the latest to insist that in recognition of the 'service rendered by her people and her rulers dur-ing World War I' Nepal was granted an annual payment of Rs 1m in per-petuity and that this was raised to Rs 2m after the Second World War (1991:9; see also Bolt 1967:97; Rose and Fisher 1970:148). Official British sources sometimes deny such claims, at least in respect of the period fol-lowing India's Independence (see Cross 1985/6:164).

Turning to the middle hills, while seasonal and long-term migrations to India for various kinds of menial employment have been a significant feature of life for some time (see McDougal 1968; P. Caplan 1972), ethnographers are generally agreed that these sources of cash were minor in comparison to army service (see Hitchcock 1966:17; Messerschmidt 1976:36). Indeed, many Tibeto-Burman communities became dependent on army pay and pensions for what little economic viability they enjoyed. 'It is the principal alternative source of employment to farming in [areas that suffer] badly from overpopulation and land shortage, while the pay and pensions of the servicemen are often the major source of capital for their home areas' (Rose 1971:258). Sagant remarks that when three Limbu servicemen returned to their village in the Taplejung area of east Nepal after the First World War with Rs 4,400 between them, these were 'colossal sums in the valley at that time' (1978:158). His figures suggest that military service continued to bring large inflows of cash into the area. Further south, in the Indreni cluster of settlements in Ilam, I estimated that in 1964-65 annual earnings from pensions and army salaries far outweighed any other single source of cash income and roughly equalled the total of income from all other sources put together (see Caplan 1970:122). Moreover, I reckoned that approximately sixty per cent of soldiers' earnings reached the settlements, a substantial amount, and had a significant impact (ibid.:117). When I revisited the Indreni settlements in 1988, I learned that a family which had been extremely poor at the time of my first stay, had in the intervening years acquired several substantial paddy fields. When I asked members of the household how this good fortune had transpired, I was told by the senior woman in the group that her son had joined the army a few years after I had left the area. 'The money to buy the land came from *des* (i.e. the army). How else could we have made it here? You can't earn Rs 27,000 by portering loads, don't you know that? You've lived here before!'

For many poor families, therefore, army service represents their only chance of alleviating hardship. As an Indreni man told me in 1988, 'one of my boys has gone to *lahur* [the army]—we have only that hope'. In a recent report on the future of the Brigade of Gurkhas, the Defence Committee of the British House of Commons suggested that 'a British Gurkha is a rich man', with an annual salary (in 1986-87) 'about 100 times the average income in the hills from which he came' (House of Commons 1989:xxv). Deciding to join the Gurkhas was not, of course, a guarantee of recruitment. During both world wars selection criteria were considerably loosened, and many thousands of men who would not otherwise have been chosen were taken into the Indian army, only to be discharged immediately hostilities concluded. But in peacetime the standards demanded were much higher and a young man would have to meet the army's minimal qualifications of age, physical fitness, good health and, latterly, education. In addition, there were in any year limits on the numbers recruited (since the late 1960s the numbers have fallen steadily), so only a small proportion of hopeful candidates would be accepted. One man in the Indreni settlements told me how he had tried to get into the army in the mid-1970s.

> The year I went 326 boys came to meet the recruiter, but only eighteen were taken to Dharan [the British induction centre for eastern regiments, where they would undergo further tests]. In the physical tests I did well, but I think I failed in my reading and writing.

The highest incomes were earned by those who spent long enough in the Gurkhas to earn a pension.[11] One recent report on the British Brigade of Gurkhas suggests that virtually all Riflemen (ninety-five per cent) serve for at least fifteen years, sufficient to qualify for a pension (House of Commons 1989:xxx).[12] But this was not always the case: several village studies indicate that a significant proportion of soldiers left before qualifying. A number of factors could conspire to prevent a man from completing the requisite number of years of service. In many instances the men's careers were cut short by the army itself (acting on the policies of the British government). After both world wars, large numbers were discharged as the additional battalions raised during hostilities were disbanded. Moreover, as already indicated, when 'Confrontation' in South East Asia came to an end in the late 1960s, and British military commitments were revised, several thousand Gurkhas were again dismissed as the number of battalions in the Brigade was reduced (see Chapter 1). Only a minority (approximately one-quarter) of ex-servicemen in the Indreni settlements in Ilam had earned a pension, mainly because many had been recruited during the First and Second World Wars, or soon after the latter, and therefore had been dismissed long before completing the required number of years' service.

Even where Gurkhas were not directly affected by these policy decisions, personal circumstances could influence the length of military service. Pignède notes that some men left because they could not abide military discipline or regulations (1966:251). The period immediately following enlistment was the most difficult, and I found that desertions or resignations occurred most frequently in the early years (Caplan 1970:116). Des Chene argues that prior to the 1960s, in the Gurung area she studied, the young men were *discouraged* from enlisting by their elders, who stressed 'not the glory and honor of being a soldier', but the hardship (1988:8). Only recently, she insists, have they been urged to enlist, for the economic benefits and the prestige of having a 'Hong Kong Gurkha' in the family (ibid.:12).

In the Indreni settlements, most abandoned their army careers for family reasons, for example, due to a parent's death and the need to divide an estate, or because of property quarrels (Caplan 1970; see also Pignède 1966). But everyone in the villages was fully aware that a pension could transform a family's economic circumstances, and most soldiers only left the army voluntarily for what they considered very pressing reasons. Messerschmidt suggests that servicemen from wealthier Gurung households tended to remain in the army longest and thus would be more likely to earn a pension (1976:42). Before 1886 pensions were payable after forty years' service, but this was reduced to twenty-one and more recently to fifteen years. The rewards of staying on were substantial. 'Even a small pension is a useful asset, and the larger ones ... represent comparative munificence' (Hitchcock 1966:17). The 'larger ones' were those earned by men who had risen out of the ranks to become what are now termed Queen's Gurkha Officers (QGOs).[13] As the Joneses remark, the pensions they bring back 'have a significant economic impact' (Jones and Jones 1976:38).

Most ethnographers who have recently worked among Tibeto-Burman populations sending men to the army seem to agree that economic hardship was and continues to be the dominant motive for seeking to join the Gurkhas. Pahari suggests that already by the early nineteenth century large sections of the hill population were destitute and turned to (Indian) army service (1991:7). In the late 1950s Hitchcock cited the 'pressure of indebtedness, and, ultimately, the increasing pressure of population upon a difficult and unproductive environment' as the main reason for enlistment (1961:19). The explanation I was most often given by both former and serving soldiers in the Indreni settlements in Ilam was economic hardship (*dukha*). In one ex-soldier's words (echoed by numerous others): 'I went to the army for my future. If I had stayed here, I could not have improved myself. So because there was *dukha* in my house I went' (see also Caplan 1970:114; Pignède 1966:43).

Alternatively, a low incidence of army service could reflect economic viability of a community or of particular households (McDougal 1979:49). Macfarlane found that in the Gurung village of Thak, 'the wealthier landholders of the 1920s did not send their sons into the army; there was plenty for them to do at home. But the poorer families who were recruited then have now profited and increased their wealth' (1976:194).

Messerschmidt, however, studying another Gurung village, found that it was mainly the wealthier households who could afford to allow sons or brothers to enlist. The poorer households needed their men on the land (1976:42-3). My own study seems to indicate a slight shift of emphasis over time. In the Indreni Cluster in Ilam, it was the most depressed sections of the population which first turned to Gurkha service. These were mainly members of lineages and households without traditional rights to *kipat* land. They had left their original areas (and ancestral lands) in Limbuan to marry uxorilocally and settle in the Indreni hamlets, and had been given small plots of land to cultivate by their in-law hosts. But their sons or grandsons found these lands insufficient and having no traditional rights to property in the village, turned to army service. To give just one example, Bhage Sur's father had come to the Indreni area to marry the sister of a resident, and was given a small plot to cultivate. The two sons of the marriage found the plot too small to divide, so Bhage Sur joined the Gurkhas, and died in the First World War. His son and grandson both spent a period in the army (see also Caplan 1970: 115).

Subsequently, however, members of comparatively well-to-do households whose viability was largely due to army service, also began sending sons to enlist. Gurkha service came to be seen not simply as a way of alleviating hardship, but as a means to maintain a favourable economic position.

While I was constantly reminded of the dire economic circumstances fuelling decisions to enlist in the Gurkhas, I was never told by a serving or former Gurkha soldier that he had joined because he wanted to follow his father into a regiment, although several of them did in fact do so. But this was in part because there were only two regiments (7GR and 10GR) enlisting men from east Nepal, so the chances of serving in the same regiment as a close forebear were comparatively high. Furthermore, the induction centre, learning that a new recruit had family links to a regiment would likely have placed the young man in that regiment. One Indreni Limbu family, with a long record in the Gurkhas, served as follows: the first man to enlist was in the 2/10GR and was killed at Gallipoli.[14] Two of his sons saw service in the same battalion of the regiment, although both transferred to an Indian unit (11GR) when the Gurkha regiments were divided between the British and Indian armies at the time of India's Independence in 1947. A third son was in a different battalion (3/10GR, raised during the war). In the succeeding generation, only one man joined the army (also 2/10GR). Two of his sons are presently serving in the 7GR. However, the fathers of most of the Indreni men who were in the British army at the time of my visit in 1988 in fact had no record of Gurkha service.

It is not surprising that a significant proportion of income from army service was invested in land. Messerschmidt, writing of a Gurung village in the early 1970s, observed that army service was directly related to landed wealth: with pensions and salaries regularly invested in land (1976:942). This was equally true for the (Gurung) villages studied by both Pignède and Macfarlane. The latter gives several examples of how Gurkha service resulted in a dramatic increase in land holding within a generation. The money was 'used to alter the land-owning pattern at each generation' (1976:196). Similarly, several of the wealthiest households in the Magar settlement studied by Hitchcock in 1961 were headed by British Gurkha pensioners, one of whom had used his earnings to increase his landholding six-fold (1961:16). A retired Subedar in the Indreni settlements in Ilam reckoned that he had inherited one-quarter of the lands he possessed (in 1964)—his father had been a Gurkha—procured a further one-quarter while he was in the army, and acquired the remaining half with his pension after retirement.

In Limbuan, savings and pensions from Gurkha service often allowed Limbus to repay debts and retrieve long-mortgaged lands (Jones and Jones 1976:37). In the Indreni settlements and elsewhere in east Nepal most of these lands had previously been pledged to members of high castes, who had enjoyed their usufruct for generations (see Caplan 1970:118-20). Thus, in some areas of the hills, army service had contributed to a partial realignment of the economic hierarchy, based on land, which had been established in the course of the nineteenth century.

Soldiers, of course, could and did use their income for purposes other than repaying loans and purchasing land, although for the most part there were few alternative opportunities for investment. Some became money-lenders themselves, invested in cattle and/or a younger brother's marriage, spent on rituals which the household had long neglected, or built large houses. Indeed, pensioners' houses are frequently conspicuous by their size and tin roofs. Macfarlane notes that one ex-Gurkha spent Rs 12,000 'on buying the biggest and smartest house in the village to which he retired ...' (1976:65). Soon after his retirement from the army in 1951, the highest-ranking pensioner in the Indreni settlements built a large, three-storey house at a cost of Rs 8,000, a considerable sum in those days. It remains one of the largest and most prominent dwellings in the area.

Unmarried servicemen usually saved for their own weddings, which were often costly affairs, involving major expenditure on entertainment, bridewealth, and gifts to affines. In anticipation of these occasions, they would purchase good quality gold abroad to be made into jewellery, which constitutes an important item of marriage exchanges, and to sell for profit (see Macfarlane 1976:108). Following India's Independence, and the movement of the Brigade of Gurkhas to the Far East, soldiers had access to a variety of consumer goods (radios, tape recorders, cameras, watches, etc.) which they were able to purchase relatively cheaply—in Malaysia, Hong Kong or Singapore—and bring back to Nepal where such items constituted popular gifts, or could be sold to traders for very high prices (see Blaikie et al.

1980:163). When I went to Kathmandu airport in 1988 to clear some unaccompanied luggage, virtually all eyes (of employees and clients) were on the
open courtyard outside the Customs Shed where officials were examining
the contents of perhaps a dozen large wooden crates belonging to a Gurkha
soldier recently arrived from Hong Kong. The contents, which were strewn
over the ground, included a wide range of consumer items, from basic
household goods to large and expensive electronic appliances.

But an exclusive stress on the direct recipients of these salaries and pensions overlooks the way in which these benefits tended to be dispersed in the
local setting. Sagant, writing of a region of north-east Nepal without banks
or roads (the first motorable road only reached Taplejung in 1988), has
shown how the return of the Gurkha from his regiment either on leave or at
retirement was always fraught with danger and uncertainty, as he sought to
avoid the thieves, prostitutes and gamblers whose principal purpose was to
relieve him of his money en route to home. But even the successful negoti-
ation of this obstacle course brought him face to face with the innumerable
demands of relatives and neighbours for gifts, loans, and assistance in alleviating financial problems; creditors wanting him to repay loans, his own
and those of close kin; village leaders seeking donations to community projects; Limbu headmen insisting on a variety of ritual and traditional payments; and many other supplicants making diverse claims. Sagant suggests
that while some of these could be resisted, if the soldier was to retain his
position in the community he was compelled to acknowledge many of these
demands—to recognise village values—which could seriously erode the
amounts he had left for his own purposes (1978:179).

The Social Implications of Gurkha Service

Service in the Gurkhas did not only have economic consequences. There
were in addition certain obvious demographic implications. During two
world wars and in the innumerable 'peace-time wars' in which they were
involved, the Gurkhas lost many thousands. The number of Gurkhas killed
during the two world wars alone is estimated at 30,000, with countless
more wounded (Pahari 1991:8-9). Nonetheless, death in foreign armies did
not constitute a particularly high proportion of total fatalities in the middle
hills. Macfarlane found that while it was the second highest cause of mor-
tality among those aged ten to forty-nine years (exceeded by tuberculosis),
it represented only five per cent of all deaths, and this in a village where a
majority of men had experience of army service (1976:266). He also suggests that army recruitment had 'very little general effect in lowering

Gurung fertility'. While it encouraged men to wait longer than they might otherwise have done to marry, and delayed the birth of first children, this was probably offset by improvements in maternal health which accompanied better standards of living (ibid.:233-4).

There is also the matter of those who left for the army and never returned to their villages. In the middle hills there are numerous stories of young men who went off to join the army, and when they were unsuccessful in their bid, were too humiliated to return. But a surprisingly high proportion of those who did succeed never came back to their villages at the end of their service. Blaikie et al. quote figures suggesting that one-third of those who were discharged at the end of the First World War failed to return to Nepal (1980:37). Sagant found that half of the ex-soldiers in the Taplejung village he studied did not return to their ancestral homes (1978:177).

The absence from the villages of a high proportion of males at the peak of their productive years undoubtedly had serious implications for village agriculture, as for the general demographic balance of the society. In 1958, when he did his study of Mohoriya, Pignède found comparatively few men aged forty to fifty years of age, since these were of the generation who had spent the war years in the army. He also found far fewer children aged ten to twenty years because of the men's absence (1966:51). Macfarlane echoes Pignède in pointing to a society (in an era and area of high recruitment) 'in demographic disequilibrium, composed of children, women, old people and a small number of men aged over 30 years' (1976:289).

Tibeto-Burman communities with such demographic imbalances necessarily had to depend more heavily on female labour. The Joneses, writing of the Terha Thum area of east Nepal in 1969, argued that such imbalances had altered family structure, in the sense that

> ... much of the day-to-day decision making fell to the women. Many Limbu homes had no adult males, and so women did *all* the decision-making—when to plant, when to harvest, when to perform important household rituals. They made decisions about the marriages of their sons and daughters, handled the business affairs of their husbands' *kipat* lands, collected and paid taxes or interest on loans, even mortgaged *kipat* land in time of need. They took to the fields to perform many of the tasks once allotted to men ... (1976:47).

While in many parts of the middle hills absent servicemen (and their wives) could rely on the assistance of senior agnates (fathers, fathers' brothers, brothers) to maintain a watching brief over the affairs of their households, and to protect their interests, the Joneses are right to stress the enhanced and crucial part played by women in all aspects of family life during the absence of their husbands. But increased reliance on women during the absence of men does not necessarily imply greater autonomy of the former. Mikesell and Shrestha point out that in Nepal, as in many developing societies, the expansion of wage labour and capitalist relations can result in 'increasing powerlessness of the women to an even greater degree than the men' (1985/6:151).

For many women, the separation from soldier husbands, fathers and sons imposes a considerable emotional strain. In a series of interviews with such women, Aryal was told of long periods of 'waiting and worrying', especially during years of conflict and danger (1991:18). It is difficult to gauge the precise effect of these lengthy absences on the stability of servicemen's marriages, since historically many Tibeto-Burman communities practiced forms of union which differed markedly from those of the high castes and which members of these latter groups regarded as unorthodox (see Sagant 1970; McDougal 1979; Allen 1987).[15]

At the time of marriage, new brides might be specifically urged to remain faithful to their *lahure* husbands. During the ritual blessing (*asik*) of a Gurkha's wedding by a low-caste Damai (Musician/Tailor) in the Indreni settlements in 1988, the latter reminded the bride that she was marrying a 'Malaya' soldier (i.e. a British army Gurkha) and if she would be patient and true, he would make her life comfortable and happy. However, young brides generally spend a great deal of time at their natal homes (*maiti*) while their new husbands are away in the army (and before there are any children), and these are the most dangerous years for the marriage (see Macfarlane 1976:228). Among the Limbus, there are few constraints on a young woman in her natal home, and she is free to associate with young men at the *dhan nac* ('rice dances') which are held regularly. On such an occasion she might decide to form another relationship. While her family would attempt to dissuade her from such a course of action by reminding her that marriage to a Gurkha could mean a life of comparative wealth and position, in the end, if she was determined, they would have to accept her decision and pay compensation (*jarikal*)—or ensure that her new partner did so. Soldiers, of course, might have sexual encounters while they are away from home, but here as elsewhere they do not threaten the marriage.

The movement of a woman to her husband's household (her *ghar*) and/or the birth of children reduces considerably the likelihood of such extra-marital liaisons, but would not eliminate them altogether (see Jones and Jones 1976:116-17). In what had achieved the status of a folktale in the

Indreni settlements in Ilam, people recounted the story of Ombar Bahadur, who had married a woman from Panchthar and brought her to his home.

> He went to the army and while he was in the army Jasahang, a man from Panchthar district, took his wife after a dance. She became pregnant and had a child. When Ombar Bahadur came home on leave and heard that his wife had gone off with someone else, he went to Panchthar to claim compensation. Jasahang heard that Ombar Bahadur was coming and fled in fear. His wife went to her natal home. When Ombar Bahadur arrived at her father's house the woman and child were hidden upstairs. His father-in-law asked why he had come, and Ombar Bahadur answered that he had come for compensation because his wife had gone off with another man. The elders of the village asked why he wanted compensation since his wife was still pure, and he had heard only wicked rumours. Then Ombar Bahadur asked to see his wife and when he saw her again, he fell in love with her (*dekhne bittikey maya lagihalyo*). He asked her if she still wanted to live with him, and she said she did. He gave her some gold which he had brought with him from the army, and they celebrated with millet beer (*jar*) and spirits (*roksi*). Then they showed him the child. 'Whose child is this?' he asked. 'He is given by god, you must accept him' they answered. He didn't say it, but the beer and spirits said that it was Ombar Bahadur's child, and he agreed to take him.

In the past, there were significant spinoffs (other than economic ones) from Gurkha service, not the least of which was access to literacy. From the end of the nineteenth century the British Indian army had made a point of recruiting from the most isolated mountain regions, from among young men who had definitely not been exposed to whatever few educational facilities existed in Nepal at the time. British recruiters and officers in general, disdained especially the 'line boys' who had been brought up in the Gurkha family cantonments surrounding the regimental headquarters, and thereby exposed to the negative effects of schooling, which was believed to diminish their fighting abilities (see Chapter 4). Until the 1970s, therefore, by which time a fairly comprehensive system of primary schools had been established in Nepal, most potential recruits to the Gurkhas were effectively illiterate. Yet, perhaps paradoxically, it was only through military service that a significant proportion of soldiers learned to read and write, since there were both formal and informal mechanisms available for them to do so.[16] Hitchcock reports that in the Magar village of Banyan Hill nine of the ten men who had served in the British army learned to read and write in the course of their service (1963:80). Ragsdale was told by over 100 men in the Gurung village he studied that they had become literate in the course of such employment (1989:51-2; see also Höfer 1978:183; Russell 1992:313-14). A significant number of ex-soldiers in the Indreni settlements told me that they had not been able to read or write before joining the military. Indeed, several suggested that the acquisition of literacy was a principal reason for enlisting—a point noted by Vansittart nearly a century before (1894:247).

Moreover, on their return to the hills, many of these ex-soldiers infused their local communities with a positive attitude to schooling, and played a vital part in setting up schools around the country.[17] Pat Caplan reports that a village school in the far-western district of 'Belaspur' was founded by a former Magar serviceman in the early 1950s, and that in 1969, at the time of her study, the teachers at the school were all ex-servicemen, as was the headmaster (1972:48). Similarly, in the Indreni settlements in Ilam the first primary school was established and run principally by ex-Gurkha soldiers (Caplan 1970:178). Ragsdale, whose study focuses largely on education, reports that (in the 1970s) a high proportion of teachers in the Kaski district's schools (in western Nepal) were ex-servicemen (1989:77-8).

For some time now Gurkhas of appropriate seniority have been able to apply to have their wives join them in Hong Kong or Brunei for the length of a contract (usually three years). This 'family permission' entitles the children to attend British Gurkha schools which now follow the Nepalese curriculum and enjoy good facilities and high academic standards (see House of Commons:xxxiv). Indeed, to be accepted into the Brigade nowadays young men must have at least eighth standard of schooling, which is a far cry from the earlier preference for unlettered recruits.

The Political Implications of Gurkha Service

It is quite clear that those servicemen who succeeded in obtaining promotion and in earning a Gurkha officer's pension acquired the wherewithal to enhance dramatically their own economic standing in the rural areas when they eventually returned.[18] We have seen how they were able to repay old debts, purchase land, build fine houses and provide loans in the local community. They became known by their titles ('Havildar', 'Subedar', etc.), as did their wives ('Havildarni', 'Subedarni'), and acquired reputations far beyond their immediate localities. Hitchcock reports that the Magar settlement he lived and worked in was known as 'the Captain's village' after its highest ranking officer (1966:107). On one occasion in 1964, when I was recording a genealogy in a Limbu household, the man I was interviewing told me, without feeling any need for further elaboration, that his wife was the daughter of 'the German Captain' (so named because he had been taken prisoner by the Germans during the First World War). When people in Ilam or other parts of Limbu country who did not know me would ask where I was residing, I had only to mention that I lived near 'Loftan' (a former Gurkha Lieutenant) and they knew immediately how to locate me.

Many pensioners, then, and especially those who had risen above the ranks, earned considerable reputations, and in the view of some ethnographers, became part of a new elite in the hills, thereby challenging the high-caste monopoly of local political structures. Höfer found that pensioners in Dhading district had returned from the army to assume an active part in local affairs. He reports that the presidents of many village councils (*pan-chayats*) are ex-soldiers, and that initiatives such as the building of a new school, the construction of a waterpipe, or the introduction of fertilisers 'would be unimaginable without the initiative of the soldiers' (1978:182).[19] Moreover, because of their experience in the army, these Gurkha pensioners—unlike the majority of their co-villagers (and fellow Tamangs, in particular)—acquired a 'national orientation', a sense of Nepal as a nation (ibid.:185; see also Pignède 1966). Ragsdale argues that the Gurkha Brigade, through its policy of imposing a common 'Gurkhali' (i.e. Nepali) language on the soldiers, and by promoting Hindu caste and ritual norms, effectively cooperated with the Kathmandu government in fostering a 'Nepalese consciousness' (1989:49-50).

These developments certainly echo those in many parts of east Nepal. In Ilam, where Tibeto-Burmans have long been in a minority, ex-Gurkha officers played an active part in local organisations set up for the benefit of ex-servicemen (see above), and took an interest in whatever system of government obtained during and immediately following the end of Rana rule. In the case of the most recent system of *panchayats*, established in 1962, they expected to be consulted on most important decisions. However, they were careful to avoid being too closely associated with its policies, since until they were abolished in 1991, the *panchayats* were dominated by members of high castes, and so suspect in the eyes of most ordinary Limbu villagers. Thus, long service, promotion from the ranks, and a good pension encouraged the emergence of a new elite within the Tibeto-Burman populations of the middle hills. But while these ex-soldiers enjoyed some respect and influence in the wider society, there is no evidence to suggest that the structures of dominance which became established towards the end of the nineteenth century were significantly affected. Members of high castes continued to enjoy preeminence in the government and in the senior echelons of both the national and local administrations. This, as Des Chene suggests, is somewhat at odds with the portrayal by British writers of retired Gurkhas as village leaders with immense prestige and power (1988:6).

The emergence of a new elite of ex-Gurkha pensioners raises questions about their relationship to traditional Tibeto-Burman headmen. There are suggestions that the former usurped the respect and prerogatives previously reserved for the latter. The headmen were appointed by the administration to collect taxes, resolve disputes, recruit forced labour (*begar*) for the government, and so forth, all of which responsibilities gave them special privileges *vis à vis* their lineage or village followers. In most areas containing Tibeto-Burman populations, therefore, these headmen were acknowledged—both within and outside their ethnic groups—as the leaders and spokespersons for their communities, and as such were consulted on a variety of official and personal matters. But these leaders by and large did not escape the general impoverishment of the Tibeto-Burman populations during the nineteenth century, and with the return to the villages of wealthier, better-educated and more articulate Gurkha pensioners, the position of the traditional notables was obviously threatened. In the mid-1960s, the Limbu headmen (*subba*) in the Indreni settlements continued to exercise a few official duties, but it was clear that most Limbus had come to regard the former Gurkha officers as their natural leaders, and the latter were constantly looked to for advice, assistance and mediation.

Yet the *subbas* were not completely ignored or downgraded by their own people, who made a point of honouring them on appropriate occasions such as during the festival of Dasein. These headmen continued to enjoy prestige and some influence in the settlements, despite the considerable diminution of their wealth and powers. I could only explain this situation in terms of their earlier and continuing struggles to preserve ancestral land under a traditional system of tenure (*kipat*). Because the *subbas* had led the movement to protect rights in *kipat* they were regarded by the Limbus as symbolising the unity and continuity of the group. As the Limbus saw it, the *subbas* were defending not only a form of land tenure, but a whole way of life (see Caplan 1970:180-195).

Referring to a more distant and ethnically homogeneous part of Limbuan (Taplejung), Sagant offered a different explanation for the reluctance of wealthy and important ex-Gurkhas to subvert the authority of the headmen.

It is partly that in this area the latter seem to have held on to many of their historical prerogatives, and Sagant identifies a variety of ways in which the Limbu headmen had retained their hold as political leaders and community notables. Indeed, if anything, it was the *subbas* who benefited most from the return of Gurkha soldiers. However, Sagant also implies that any such challenge to the traditional leadership would have threatened the order and undermined the values of what was still a remote and tightly-knit village (1978).

Höfer offers a somewhat similar explanation for the reluctance of influential ex-soldiers in Dhading district to supplant the traditional Tamang headmen. He suggests that they were 'neither able nor willing to risk a complete break with the traditional values upon which the authority of functionaries of the old system rested'. There was, moreover, a belief in 'an intimate or mystic link between the person of the village ... headman and the deities which are thought to be responsible for the fertility of the soil' (1978:184).

The emergence of a category of comparatively well-to-do and respected ex-servicemen must be seen in the context of a hierarchical society which has traditionally accorded Tibeto-Burman communities—from which the overwhelming majority of Gurkhas are recruited—a caste status below that of the Brahmans, Thakuris and Chetris—who wear the sacred thread. In the hill villages from which these soldiers originate, they have traditionally been viewed and treated by these high castes as social, economic and ritual subordinates. It is little wonder that the men who sought to escape or alleviate such a position by joining foreign armies—and earning something of an international reputation for military prowess—were still regarded by the dominant groups at home as social inferiors. In Ilam's Indreni settlements, soldiers on leave and ex-servicemen were often resented for their new-found wealth. They were accused of driving up the price of land, of upsetting long-standing tenancy arrangements, even of monopolising scarce agricultural labour. Their wealth might earn them grudging deference but not necessarily respect from erstwhile economic superiors belonging to high-caste groups. Nor have Gurkhas been seen in a more favourable light by the educated urban elites, most of whom are members of high castes. During a seminar on the Gurkhas held in Kathmandu in 1991, one participant recalled that even in Rana times the *lahure* was 'not respected within Kathmandu Valley'.[20] Referring to more recent times, Hutt points out that enlistment in foreign armies raises some 'disquiet' among Nepal's educated classes. He examines the ways in which Gurkhas are represented in modern Nepali literature, and concludes that while there is a certain amount of sympathy and grudging admiration, there is also a tendency, especially among Nepali poets, to 'despise and resent' these soldiers (1989:29). This antagonism is partly a hostile political judgement on the Gurkhas' role in Britain's colonial and neo-colonial past and present (see Chapter 4), and no doubt an expression of the artist-intellectual's disdain for militarism—especially in the service of foreign armies. But it is no doubt also to do with a feeling that these members of a traditionally subordinate stratum in Nepalese society have somehow subverted the hierarchical order by gaining access to desirable resources outside of the local system. One military author rightly concludes that 'the name and the fame of Gurkhas is more widespread outside Nepal than in it' and that they enjoy little prestige outside their own [Tibeto-Burman] 'social enclaves' (Cross 1985/6:175).

Ex-Gurkhas in Town

It is difficult to predict with any certainty how the projected further reductions in the size of the Brigade of Gurkhas (from its current 8,000 men in five battalions to 2,500 men in two battalions by 1997) will affect Tibeto-Burman communities in the middle hills. Fewer opportunities for army service will obviously increase economic hardship for countless families who might have relied on this source of income to ameliorate their conditions. It is likely that the Gorkha regiments in the Indian army will continue to recruit young Nepalis, and possibly increase their intake to make up the numbers no longer enlisted in the British forces. But even if they did so, it would be unlikely to benefit many of the poorest elements of the population who have virtually no access to schooling beyond the elementary levels. The Indian army now demands educational qualifications (School Leaving Certificate) which only a small proportion of Tibeto-Burman hill villagers can acquire. When I was in the Indreni settlements in 1988, a young man whose father had earned a pension in the British Gurkhas (7GR), presented himself—along with eighty-seven other young men—to a British army recruiter but was not selected. When I asked him if he would try to enlist in the Indian Gorkhas instead he replied: 'I can't go to the Indian army because they take only tenth class [graduates]. India demands a lot of education. No one here [in the settlements] can meet their requirements'.

What is easier to predict is that certain trends already evident among ex-servicemen will probably continue and possibly intensify. I am referring to the tendency for returning Gurkhas to invest their savings and pensions in land and houses in towns where they can educate their children and enjoy an 'easy' life (Macfarlane 1991). This has meant that valuable capital is being diverted from productive agriculture (or simply redistribution) in the villages towards mainly unproductive consumption of (largely imported) goods and services in rapidly expanding urban centres. There are now colonies of Gurkha and ex-Gurkha families in Kathmandu, and larger concentrations in key urban centres outside the Valley.

Few soldiers from the Gurung area studied by Des Chene (1991) who are currently serving in Hong Kong expect to return to the village after completing their tour of duty. Macfarlane (1991) reports that thirty retired soldiers from the village of Thak are now living in Pokhara, one of the fastest-growing towns in Nepal, with road and air links to Kathmandu. Ragsdale also found that (by 1974) seven Gurung households from 'Lamnasa' village (all but one headed by ex-Gurkhas) had moved to Pokhara permanently, and twice that number had houses and business interests there, although they were still officially listed as resident in the village (1989:80). According to Ragsdale, these ex-Gurkhas live in 'close-knit and neighbourhood-specific' colonies, and are involved in a range of business ventures, including tourist lodges, small 'hotels', taxis, and various shops—selling auto parts, cloth and ready-made garments, general goods, or foreign manufactures. The latter ('Fancy Stores') rely on army contacts in South East Asia and the Far East for their supplies (ibid.:78-83). He notes, however, that despite their prominence in the economic life of Pokhara, these ex-Gurkhas had not 'gained entry into the town's numerous bureaucracies' which were still monopolized by Brahmans and Newars. Many also admitted that without their army-derived income as well as access to farm produce from home villages, they would be unable to afford to live in the town (ibid.:83).

But not all those who have left their villages become involved in new economic ventures. Referring to ex-Gurkhas from Thak settled in Pokhara, Macfarlane suggests that one-third are 'doing nothing in particular, other than living off pensions and invested capital' (1991). They have simply chosen to settle where the 'action' is. In Ilam, a similar trend is evident, even though it is far more remote from Kathmandu than Pokhara or other towns popular among ex-Gurkhas. Ilam Bazaar, the district capital, is now linked to the east-west highway in the *terai* (and to Kathmandu) by an all-weather road which extends north through the Indreni settlements to the districts of Panchthar and Taplejung. A number of ex-servicemen from other parts of Ilam or even from outside the district altogether have begun moving to Ilam Bazaar. Others are buying plots of land and building houses beside the road running north from the district capital, thereby situating themselves within easy reach of its administrative offices, schools, banks, hospital and other amenities.

British officers who keep track of former soldiers after their return to Nepal have noted such a tendency with dismay, although it appears too recent a development to be cited in the literature. One officer told me that one of his former orderlies retired at the age of thirty-five years and returned to Phidim, the district capital nearest his village home in Panchthar, in north-east Nepal.

> He does nothing there. It's awful. He has two houses in Phidim, lives in one, and rents out the other. I don't think we ever thought that this sort of situation would arise. But if you ask them 'why don't you do something for your country?', they say, 'what's the point, sahib, these [high castes] are all corrupt and will take everything we have.'

Conclusion

The 'Gurkhas' are not a homogeneous category in Nepal, nor yet a series of totally discrete social groups. Linguistic and cultural boundaries dividing those ethnic units recruited into the British colonial and post-colonial military forces are both flexible and permeable, as are the lines separating them from other Tibeto-Burman groups not regarded as 'martial'. What all these groups share is a marginal position vis à vis the state, whose structures have been dominated since the establishment of the Kingdom in the late-eighteenth century by a ruling class composed almost entirely of members of high castes. As one participant in a recent seminar on the Gurkhas observed, there was and is an inverse relationship between the number of recruits from (Tibeto-Burman) ethnic groups and their representation in national politics.[21] Drawn from such a peripheral category of the population, the Gurkhas have become, in Enloe's phrase, quintessential 'ethnic soldiers' (1980).

Political subordination, the gradual loss of their land to high-caste immigrants in the middle hills, and the absence of alternative economic opportunities conduced to encourage a tendency among members of Tibeto-Burman communities towards both long-term and temporary emigration. The latter included employment in foreign militaries from at least the latter part of the eighteenth century, although service in the Indian army reached a scale previously unexampled. The realities of these precarious economic circumstances provide a stark contrast to the claims by some military authors that it was the Gurkhas' 'natural' inclination for military activity, or their desire to serve Britain's causes, which weighed most heavily in their decisions to seek enlistment. (Pignède (1966:43) is adamant that young men did not enlist out of a 'spirit of patriotism'.)

There is room for debate about the overall impact of such employment. One view, for example, suggests that far from aiding the Nepalese hill economy and society, army service impoverished it, and that it was only Britain's imperial designs which derived any real benefit from Gurkha arms (see Mikesell and Shrestha 1985/6:147). But most ethnographers who have spent time in Nepalese villages are agreed that at the level of the individual family or household or even settlement, the financial benefits of a spell—especially a lengthy one—in the military could be significant.

While the political repercussions might also be far-reaching in terms of the challenge to traditional leadership within Tibeto-Burman societies posed by wealthy and influential Gurkha pensioners, the inflow of considerable resources into the middle hills over a period of one hundred and fifty years appears not to have led to any significant change in the existing state and local political hierarchies. Recent trends among ex-Gurkhas to gravitate towards towns, in keeping with national population movements, portends a diversion of significant resources away from rural investment and redistribution, and into urban housing, education, and to a lesser extent commercial activity. It is too early to ascertain if these contemporary strategies succeed—where others have failed—in gaining for these ex-Gurkhas, and especially for their children, access to Nepal's hitherto impregnable citadels of power. In the meantime, although soldiering in the British and other foreign armies may be seen by Tibeto-Burman residents of the middle hills (and by most of their ethnographers) as the most important, if not the sole means to gain financial independence, respect and enhanced status for members of their communities otherwise excluded from internal sources of wealth and influence, it continues rather to be stigmatised by articulate voices from within the dominant groups—as it was for a time by the Rana rulers—as a betrayal of national honour.

Notes to Chapter 2

1. The *terai* was thinly populated until the 1960s when the government of Nepal undertook a major programme of malaria eradication.

2. A small proportion of soldiers was also recruited from other Tibeto-Burman populations, as well as among the 'Khas', or 'non-tribal' Chetri and Thakuri inhabitants of the hills (see Chapter 4).

3. By 1861 members of these two groups could no longer be enslaved, although others could. The system of slavery was finally abolished in 1924.

4. The inclusion of Newars in the political-elite results mainly from their residence in the nation's capital, and their long history of literacy. But the Newars themselves have a complex caste hierarchy of their own, so that only members of a few high castes tend to be so privileged.

5. Not all parts of the mid-montane region were equally affected. Macfarlane notes that many Gurung areas did not experience chronic land shortages (1976:239).

6. Regmi Research Series, Vol. 64, pp723-24. *Amalis* refers to members of a moot or local court (*amal*) responsible for settling disputes among Limbus.

7. A somewhat similar development occurred in the Bengal army following the East India Company's 'de-militarisation' of much of the Indian peasantry which 'radically reduced the employment opportunities for the military labour force ...' and resulted in a much narrower caste-base for recruitment (Kolff 1990:187).

8. *Letter Books.*

9. See *Regmi Research Series*, Vol. 67, pp. 139-41.

10. All three authors mean service in both the British and (pre- or post-Independence) Indian armies.

11. According to figures given by Cross, between 1948 and 1986, some 37,000 men had served in the Brigade of Gurkhas, and some sixty per cent of these were on pensions (1985/6:169).

12. By contrast, the British private soldier serves an average of only five years (ibid.).

13. To earn a QGO pension a man would have to serve a further length of time (see Heathcote 1974:111).

14. Regiments are generally referred to as 1GR, 2GR etc. The battalion precedes the regimental number: thus 2/10 GR implies second battalion of the 10th regiment; 1/7GR, first battalion of the 7th regiment, and so on.

15. In the late 1950s and early 1960s anthropologists were much taken with definitions of marriage, and with ways to measure its stability (see Gluckman 1950; Leach 1961).

16. For years, British 'Gurkhali' (i.e. Nepali) speakers used and taught Romanised script instead of the *devanagri*, in which the language is written in Nepal.

17. This was effected through an organisation of District Soldiers Boards (see Hitchcock 1963:80). More recently, the Government of Nepal introduced a policy of universal primary education, and assumed responsibility for the provision of schools throughout the country.

18. It is important to reiterate the distinction between a Gurkha officer and a British officer with the Gurkhas. Until very recently, the former always ranked below the latter (see Chapter 3).

19. Tamangs were not at first labelled a 'martial' group, so many enlisted in the Gurkhas as 'Gurungs' (see Chapter 4).

20. The seminar was sponsored by and reported in the Nepalese English-language magazine *Himal* under the heading 'To fight or not to Fight: Nepalis in foreign uniform' (Vol. 4 (3), 1991).

21. See note 20.

CHAPTER 3

················

OFFICERING GURKHAS

The Culture of Command

The old Indian Army was a British institution and the
frame that held it together was the British officer ...

Field Marshall Sir William Slim *Courage and Other Essays,* 1957.

Introduction

In the recent proliferation of reflexive writings in anthropology, a prominent target for criticism is the tendency in traditional ethnographies for
writers, after briefly establishing their credentials, to withdraw from their
texts in the interests of a spurious scientific objectivity. The military writers
who I am examining are certainly not absent from their accounts of
Gurkhas, in as much as they are evident participants alongside the troops in
both peace- and war-time activities, being seen to share, indeed to control,
the everyday working lives of their subordinates. With few exceptions, however, an authorial vacuum is apparent when, as readers, we ask about the
personal backgrounds and outlooks which led these officers to settle with
the Gurkhas, seek any kind of evaluative comment on the wider military
and particular regimental cultures in which they spent the greater part of
their adult lives, or inquire about the ideologies shaping officers' attitudes to
and the nature of relationships with Gurkhas. Des Chene found the 'task of
getting close to the thoughts, views and aspirations of British Gurkha officers [a] daunting one' (1991:1).

In short, there is little or no reflexivity in these texts, although this is not to suggest that the officers are not capable of it. Such commentary tends to emerge in their (usually unpublished) diaries and letters, and certainly was forthcoming in the informal interviews and conversations which I had with British officers of various ranks and experience, both serving and retired. In this chapter I draw on all this material, as well as on published studies, to develop a profile of the British officers who opted for Gurkhas in the Indian and later British army, constructed and sustained regimental rituals and identities and, latterly, have been forced personally to confront changes in Gurkha fortunes occasioned by post-war global political re-alignments. By attending to the social, cultural and ideological contexts within which these officers are situated we can better appreciate and comprehend the manner in which they have represented Gurkhas.

Royal and Indian Officers

The existence in India from the middle of the eighteenth century of two armed forces (sections of the Royal army alongside the much larger Indian army) created awkward relationships between their officers. Because Company officers advanced by seniority, whereas those in the Royal army could (until 1871) buy promotion, it was not uncommon for a Royal officer with a few years of service to order about an Indian army officer with many years' experience, even one who held similar rank, since the former took precedence over the latter (see Palsokar 1984:165; Cohen 1971:9–10).[1] This and other anomalies rankled with the Company's officers who felt that, in the words of one, they were 'the very life and soul of the Indian army and, consequently, the main prop of our Eastern Empire ...' (Anon 1849:iii).

There was also a widely acknowledged (though probably exaggerated) social distance between them. Officers in the Royal army considered themselves a cut above their Indian colleagues. Pemble notes that the 'Company's officers [were made] aware of the panache, the mystique, the prestige attaching to the King's army, and left in no doubt that the military service of a mere trading corporation was decidedly inferior' (1971:93). While the Royal army was dominated by sons of the aristocracy and the gentry, the large majority of Indian army officers came from middle class and professional families.[2] Indeed, the Company's Court of Directors was at first opposed to the appointment of 'well-born' men as officers 'for fear they would resent being ordered about by merchants ...' (Bryant 1978:204). Razzell suggests that the aristocracy viewed the 'Indian' officers with 'social contempt' (1963:257), and this attitude did not change significantly when the Crown assumed control of the Indian army after the Mutiny, and the divisions became less marked. Even well into the present century Royal officers would sometimes not allow the Indian officers to forget the distinctions between them. Masters reports how shocked he was at the shabby treatment British regiments often meted out to Indian army subalterns who were temporarily attached to them before assignment to their Indian regiments. 'One [British regiment] even made them sit at a separate table in Mess' (1956:23–4).[3]

Despite the disdain in which they were sometimes held, officers with the Indian army were still 'anxious to grasp the social cachet which marked royal service', and eagerly emulated the King's officers (Peers 1991:557). Anderson comments wryly that the colonial empire 'permitted sizeable numbers of bourgeois and petty bourgeois to play aristocrat off centre court: i.e. anywhere in the empire except at home' (1983:138).

The Indian army thus allowed 'lesser lights' to 'quench their thirst for social status' (Razzell 1963:259). According to John Morris who transferred from a British to a Gurkha regiment after the First World War, 'most officers in the Indian Army came from undistinguished professional families without the private income needed to exist in a British regiment' (1960:192). Many of these officers were from military families, and after the armed forces, the largest paternal occupation represented was the church (Heathcote 1974:124; see also Razzell 1963). What little information exists on the backgrounds of officers serving with the Gurkhas suggests that they were not untypical of the generality of British officers in the Indian army. The *Register of Officers* who spent time in the 2GR (going back to the early nineteenth century), though by no means complete, suggests that the highest proportion came themselves from military families. Less frequently, the fathers of these 2GR officers were clergymen, civil servants, businessmen, and—latterly—professionals.[4]

While service in India was apparently popular among ordinary British soldiers, since they were comparatively well housed and fed, and were relieved of many menial tasks undertaken by native servants (see Saxena 1974:257), officers in the Royal army were not universally enamoured of an Indian posting. Many were able to evade such a billeting by going on half pay or exchanging (at a price) into another regiment while their own was overseas (see Razzell 1963:256). Even those who condescended to accompany their regiments to India might exchange or sell out if it was ordered to a 'disagreeable station ... up-country' (Turner 1956:227). Heathcote remarks that the numbers who resigned or transferred rather than accept an

Indian appointment 'was rather a joke in the army' (1974:117), although the situation altered somewhat towards the end of the nineteenth century. Those who went to India often did so to alleviate temporary financial hardship.

To be a British army officer in the nineteenth and first half of this century, it was necessary to have private means, since army salaries certainly did not cover the expenses of regimental life. This, according to Otley, was 'deliberately contrived ... in order to ensure that only men of means entered the officer corps' (1970:215). Referring to the officer class in the early part of this century, Baynes suggests that they thought of the British army as a way of life which they were prepared to pay to share, rather than as a 'profession from which they hoped to earn their livelihood' (1967:31).

By contrast, officers in the Indian army could manage (if sometimes only just) on their salaries, which were significantly higher than those in the Royal force.[5] Referring to the inter-war years, John Masters, whose family had served continuously in India for well over a century, and whose father had retired as a Lieutenant-Colonel in the Indian army, writes that 'while it was just possible for a young man without private means to exist as a subaltern in some of the more undistinguished British regiments, it was not comfortable. The Indian Army got more pay, and living on one's pay was not only possible but feasible.' (1956:39) This sentiment is echoed repeatedly by other officers in their diaries and memoirs. In the words of one diarist who served in the 2GR between the wars: 'For those who possessed no wealth India offered a splendid and spacious life. There is no other country which can offer such attractions as polo, shooting, fishing and other luxuries which, in England, would require an income of at least £5,000 per annum. In India any average young officer could enjoy them all on no more than his army salary and most of us did so.'[6] Moreover, although promotion was slow—nine years for a Captaincy and another two and a half years for a Majority—it meant the officers could count on steady advancement and improved incomes.

Officers in India could also afford to employ a number of personal servants. Lieutenant-Colonel Mains of 9GR records that when he was at the Infantry School in Mhow after the Second World War, he and his wife had a staff of nine—a 'bearer' (a 'cross between a valet and major-domo'), cook, *khitmagar* (waiter), *chokra* (odd job boy), sweeper, two syces (grooms) and two *malis* (gardeners)—to look after two adults, two horses and four dogs. When their daughter was born they added an *ayah* or nurse-maid (1990:83–4).[7]

British Officers and the Public Schools

For centuries British army officers required no formal education, were in fact 'singularly ill-educated' (Otley 1973:192). In the mid-nineteenth century, with the introduction of entrance examinations for the army, which were purposefully based on the syllabus taught at the public schools, prospective officers were required to look increasingly to these schools for their educational qualifications. The army/public school link grew stronger during the course of the century as the latter provided educational assistance for army candidates in excess of the normal curriculum, and made special provision (in the way of reserved places, designated scholarships or reduced fees) for the sons of officers (see Worthington 1977; Otley 1970, 1978).

From the 1860s virtually all officers were recruited from the public schools and at times during the course of the next century army cadet college entry was monopolised by public school boys (Turner 1956:252; Otley 1973:194, 203).[8] Razzell quotes figures from the War Office to show that as late as the 1950s, eighty per cent of Sandhurst Commissions went to public school boys, in spite of the fact that only about ten per cent of the relevant age group attended these schools. A number of these schools, including those established only in the mid- to late-nineteenth century—Marlborough, Wellington College, Cheltenham and Clifton, for example—had a particularly strong attachment to the military (Worthington 1977:187; see also Green 1980:399). Ellis reports that in the second part of the nineteenth century the latter two schools alone contributed about half their pupil output to the forces (1981:101). But whereas a century ago only a small number of institutions provided all the Royal Military Academy's cadets, by the middle of this century the number of feeder schools had grown six-fold (Razzell 1963:259), and the majority would be regarded as of lesser status.

Indian army officers, including those attached to the Gurkhas, were likewise products of the public schools. The Regimental *Register of Officers* for the 2GR provides information on schooling for fewer than one-quarter of the names listed, so only very tentative observations are possible. Between 1815 and 1965 some eighty-four public schools are mentioned as having been attended by 212 officers; an additional four grammar schools are noted. Several of the original nine 'Clarendon Schools' appear in the record of institutions attended up to the First World War, but the most frequently cited are other schools which established prestigious reputations after the Royal Commission Report of 1861 (see Macdonald 1988): Wellington (twenty officers); Marlborough (thirteen); Clifton (thirteen); Haileybury (twelve); Cheltenham (eight); Blundells (seven); and Fettes (seven).[9] But following the First World War the institutional spread widened, and the greater part of those entering the regiment had been to less well-known schools. Indeed, it is likely that the overwhelming majority of those for whom no record on education was available had attended minor public schools, since the collective memory, as anthropologists have often discovered when taking genealogies in the field, is invariably selective of the more prominent members of the group.

One former officer who entered the 10GR at the beginning of the Second World War, recalled during an interview that the Indian army concentrated its recruitment on the minor schools, since the British army 'filled up automatically with [boys from] all the "big schools" [which] poured people into their family and county regiments'.

Army officering, observes Otley, has been 'markedly hereditary' (1970:233), and a high proportion (forty to fifty per cent) of Sandhurst cadets since the beginning of the nineteenth century have been the sons of military officers (ibid.:230). I have already noted how many public schools went out of their way to accommodate the children and orphans of officers. Conversely, great sacrifices would be made by Indian army officers without much wealth to ensure that their sons could attend a public school. Masters reports that his father, a retired Indian army officer, had had to 'commute his small pension in order to give my brother and me the education essential to a young gentleman' (1956:39). The recipients of such education were, in turn, anxious to provide the same opportunities for their own children. The schooling of his only son was a constant worry for a young officer (later a Brigadier) serving with the 3GR, and the topic featured in numerous letters written to his mother in England between 1921 and 1937. In one, he approves of a local (primary) school for the boy, and reassures his mother that young John will soon lose any 'Norfolk accent' he acquires as soon as he gets to Shrewsbury (his old public school and the one he wants John to attend). In another he expresses the desirability of his son being sent to a school where the 'corners can be rubbed off' by older boys, and where he 'would get discipline all day'. He notes that many schools make reductions in fees for the sons of officers, and when John is finally accepted into Shrewsbury, he writes about finding money for the 'extras' which John may want to do—'OTC or boxing, perhaps'.

Although considerable emphasis was placed on public school attendance, British officers—or rather the British army—attached virtually no importance to a university education. Only about ten per cent of officers with the 2GR about whom information is available had attended university, and a number of these were in fact graduates who had received short-term commissions during the Second World War. Among career officers the proportion would undoubtedly have been much lower, and officers with the 2GR would not have been untypical. Unlike its American or French counterparts, which provided a university degree, the military institution which most British officers attended (Sandhurst) offered only a military education (Farwell 1989:99), and Greenhut remarks that academic performance there throughout the Victorian era was 'low' (1984:15). Indeed, during this period, military college was regarded essentially as a kind of 'finishing' academy for the public school boy. The eighteen year-old who went on to Sandhurst or Addiscombe, Keegan tells us, 'was treated when he arrived there as someone already formed in character and attitude and only needing tactical training to take his place in the regiment' (1976:279).

Since the public schools educated virtually the whole of the English upper and upper-middle class throughout the colonial period, it was assumed that only the public schools could produce the right kind of officer, socially and morally (Mason 1974:458). The rise of the British empire was attributed by the Victorians to 'the distinctive racial attributes of the English people' (Street 1975:19), and from the middle of the nineteenth century imperialism was the dominant national ideology (Richards 1989:2). The public schools educated boys to share the assumptions prevailing throughout this period about the Anglo-Saxon destiny as a governing race. To perform this latter task, these schools were compelled to undergo profound changes. Whereas up to the middle of the nineteenth century they encouraged an independence of spirit and individuality of thought,[10] after about 1860—in response to the growing demands of an outside world—they were increasingly geared to the molding of 'forceful, but obedient and well-indoctrinated officers and apostles of imperial orthodoxy trained to govern the empire' (Chandos 1984:340). They had become, by the end of the century, 'manufactories for the production of a serviceable elite ...' (ibid.:346).

At the heart of Victorian imperial ideology was an image of manliness which combined chivalry, patriotism and sportsmanship (see Mangan and Walvin 1987). The nineteenth century has been seen as the new age of chivalry which bred an updated image of the English gentleman to engage especially the growing (non-propertied) middle and professional classes being educated in the public schools, who were being called upon to staff the outposts of empire. The chivalrous gentleman, Girouard suggests, was 'brave, straightforward and honourable, loyal to his monarch, country and friends, unfailingly true to his word ... a natural leader of men, fearless in war and on the hunting field ... [etc. etc.]' (1981:260). This ideology of the chivalrous gentleman was vigorously promoted in the public schools, and provided the dominant image of masculinity for generations of British officers. It was accompanied by an outpouring of what Chandos refers to as 'tremulous sentimentality and bellicose patriotism' (1984:344).[11]

Baynes, in his account of the Second Scottish Rifles during the First World War, devotes an entire chapter to the topic of patriotism. He suggests that most people in Britain prior to the war were intensely patriotic, by which he means 'they had no doubt that Britain was the greatest country in the world, and the finest' (1967:218). One reason they felt this way, he suggests, was because at the time Britain was the most powerful nation in the world, with a far-flung empire. Furthermore, people genuinely believed in the obligations attaching to such power (ibid.:224).

This kind of patriotism flourished because it was 'driven home in almost everything that people [i.e. people of the upper and upper-middle classes] read or were taught' (ibid.:220). Baynes examines the kinds of fiction a young officer at the turn of the century would have been likely to read, either at home or at school: authors such as Henty, Scott, Kingsley, Haggard, Doyle, and of course Kipling.[12] The character of the literature to which young public school boys were exposed underwent significant alterations in the nineteenth century. Green suggests that the new boys' adventure literature of this period was 'training their imaginations in the ways of the military caste' (1980:115). He argues that during the course of the century adventure took the place of fable in books written for children, and this new boys' literature focused attention on empire and frontier. These adventure tales constituted the 'energizing myth of English imperialism' (ibid.: 3; see also Moore-Gilbert 1983:93). As far as Baynes is concerned, this literature 'reinforced the future officer's ideas of the importance and value of Britain, her way of life, and her influence in the world' (1967:222). He even suggests (no doubt, somewhat unfairly) that most officers would have done their reading for life by the time they joined the army, so that they were already 'well doctrinated with patriotism' (ibid.:222–23).

British officers who served with and wrote about the Gurkhas during the late-nineteenth and first half of the twentieth centuries emerged from the same social backgrounds as the officers discussed by Baynes. They attended the same schools, read the same adventure stories as well as the same poets of imperialism, and generally were subjected to similar kinds of cultural influences, thus sharing these feelings of patriotism and empire. This occasionally surfaces in the Gurkha literature. One former officer with 2GR recalls that

... those who did not experience what it was like to be a
son of a 'Service Family' cannot understand the mood in
the country in the early years of this century. [As boys]
we learnt that our main duty was to the Empire and if
necessary we must die for it (Forteath 1991:2–3; see also
Masters 1956:329).

More commonly, such sentiments revealed themselves in private diaries.
One officer serving in the same regiment just prior to the Second World
War confides that:

There was, moreover, the indescribable feeling of being
the rulers in a foreign land with all the subtle implications of romance and adventure which such a position
implies. In my generation we did not decry imperialism
and were not ashamed of possessing colonies ... we
accepted them as ours by conquest and we recognised
that we were there to defend them.

Sporting Officers

The transformation of the public school ethos during the nineteenth century was effected largely through the encouragement of sport. Seen not simply as the avenue to physical strength and fitness, games were reckoned the
best means of training character, and the 'supreme test of moral excellence'
(Chandos 1984:340). Playing games came to be regarded as the mark of a
gentleman. Hughes's *Tom Brown's Schooldays*, published in 1857, which
went into at least fifty editions and reprints during the remainder of the century, suggested that physical prowess was far more important than intellectual achievement in the formation of a gentleman. This attitude—which
was termed 'muscular Christianity'—soon came to permeate the public
schools, and many in which the country's future officers were educated—
including several attended by those serving with Gurkhas—were actually
founded in the last half of the century deliberately to foster this ideology. By
the late 1870s, compulsory games were the rule in public schools (Girouard
1981:166–69).[13] Public school ideologues—including those who expressed
their views in verse—frequently represented the playing field as a metaphor
for the battleground and the imperial mission (see Mangan 1988).

Officers educated in the public schools thus came to regard games as an
integral part of their identity as gentlemen, and officers with the Gurkhas
were, not surprisingly, avid sportsmen. Indeed, according to one writer: 'An

officer's life in the British army, probably more than in any other army in the world, was a life of sport and games of every description ... What officers in other units did, British officers with the Gurkhas always seem to have done more often and more energetically' (Farwell 1984:120). Several regiments had their own polo grounds and tennis courts, others their own squash courts and at least one (the 2GR) its own golf course (Mains 1990:90), so that prospective officers not unnaturally took account of sporting facilities and reputation in games when applying for a regiment. One Brigadier records how, as a newly qualified officer, he had considered choosing a cavalry regiment, assuming that life would be ideal in a world of horses and polo. But without private means it was out of the question. However, he soon discovered that officers of two Gurkha regiments did play polo, so as his first choice he applied for the 9GR (Bristow 1974:22). Alternatively, an individual's sporting ability was an obvious attraction for a regiment considering a potential officer colleague for inclusion in its ranks. General Twiss recalls how his appointment to the 9GR was not especially popular with its Commanding Officer, until the latter saw Twiss play in a Civil vs Military cricket match, and was won over (1961:21).

Officers' diaries and letters are full of accounts of sporting activities.[14] In his reminiscences of life in the 5GR prior to the First World War, Palit recalls that good polo was played in almost all stations, and even as a junior officer he had been able to maintain a polo stable (1954:57). During peacetime officers had little to do, and Morris notes that in his regiment, since afternoons were generally free, most officers 'spent the time playing tennis or squash or watching the men play football' (1960:10). One officer who served in the 3GR between the wars constantly refers in his letters home to the tournaments he plays in—billiards, hockey, tennis, football, polo, squash and golf. Another recounts how even in a remote outpost there was trout fishing in the mountain streams, and some skiing. Even during wartime they would not be denied their sport. One officer with the 2GR near Quetta wrote home in 1942 that he continued to ride, swim, play tennis and squash. In his published memoirs, another officer (serving in 9GR) also notes that Quetta offered a variety of sporting facilities, even a nine-hole golf course (Pickford 1989:139).

If officers enjoyed playing games, they were keener still on hunting game. In letters written to his wife between 1891 and 1896 a young officer in the 2GR refers constantly to the shooting he enjoys, wherever his posting: quail, duck, spotted deer, black buck, and larger prey. Another in the same regiment recalls shooting large turtles and crocodiles, while an officer in the

9GR, in his unpublished autobiography, notes that there were 'picnics and shoots galore!'

The commander of one regiment, in addition to a thick volume on the Gurkhas, produced a 500-plus page account of *Sporting Memories in India*, which he sub-titled '40 years with note-book and gun' (Woodyatt 1923). Heathcote comments, with an equal measure of repugnance and amazement, on the 'vast quantities of large mammals and birds [which] were slaughtered by military sportsmen'. Mess ante-rooms and private bungalows were 'vast hecatombs containing the skulls, horns, and stuffed heads of victims of British marksmanship' (1974:150).

Indeed, hunting (*shikar*) occupied a special place in the mystique of colonial India. Bennett suggests that to understand the British raj fully we need to appreciate the significance of *shikar* (1984:73).[15] It was seen as the test of a man's moral qualities, and so an extension of 'muscular Christianity' to the colonies (ibid.:78). Similarly, MacKenzie regards hunting as closely bound up with the symbolism of imperialism, 'a mark of the fitness of the dominant race, a route to health, strength, and wealth, an emblem of imperial rule, and an allegory of human affairs ...' (1989:170). He points out, moreover, that it required all the most virile attributes of the imperial male: courage, endurance, individualism and sportsmanship (1987:179).

An officer's sporting abilities might be recorded and praised in regimental records as his most abiding virtue. Thus, in the 2GR's *Register of Officers* we read, beside one man's name, only the following: 'a keen polo player ... a very good shikari ... keen fisherman ... played cricket, golf and tennis well'. In his portrait of an ideal British officer, Baynes suggests that he excels at field sports, is an excellent shot and skillful fisherman, an accomplished horseman and plays ball games well. Still, however gifted, he never takes games too seriously, and 'is a very good loser' (1967:124). Needless to say, these are also the characteristics of the 'chivalrous gentleman'.[16] Discussing colonial fiction, Ridley remarks how in the nineteenth century, the love of sport and hunting emphasised the 'racial health and strength of the English' (1983:92). This stress on physical and moral fitness as superior Anglo-Saxon virtues might also have been related, suggests Burroughs, to the growing rivalry after 1870 for imperial influence among European powers (1986:63).

The Gurkha Regiments as an Elite Corps

The modern regimental system developed in the course of the nineteenth century. At its beginning officers were still 'independent gentlemen, holding rank by cash purchase ... and swapping regiments almost at whim' (Keegan 1976:193). By the end of the century the officer's loyalty was to his regiment, which was an extension, in a sense the creation, of the Victorian public school system. The military code of rewards and punishments which the officers administered, like the games they organised for the men, mirrored the system in which they had been brought up themselves (ibid.:78–79).

The Indian army was organised on a regimental basis, and in the course of time, there emerged a complex array of distinctive regimental cultures. A number of units vied for recognition as the premier service, but there seems to have been no commonly agreed hierarchy of regiments,[17] as there apparently was within the British army. According to Baynes, who served in the Second Scottish Rifles during the First World War, his own regiment would come about half-way up (or down) the army's 'status ladder'.

> Above them in popular reckoning would be the Household Brigade, the cavalry Regiments, the Green Jackets and the Highland Brigade. Below them would be the bulk of the English county Regiments, artillery other than Horse or Field, engineers and the few corps and services which then existed. On roughly the same level in general estimation would be the Light Infantry, the R.H.A. and the Field Artillery, and the best English County Regiments.

Yet these things were never discussed. 'At a certain level in society everyone knew the nuances and ramifications of the system ...' (1967:32). Garnier was surprised at the persistence of this hierarchy, which still obtained when he spent part of 1967 at Sandhurst conducting a study of officer recruitment (1977:83).

In the course of the nineteenth century the Gurkhas came to regard themselves as a unit apart from the rest of the Indian army. The Brigade was deemed an elite corps and its officers took every opportunity to emphasise the superiority of their men to those of other Indian regiments. In 1855 a young ensign with the then 66th Gurkhas wrote his parents that 'there is not a more celebrated corps in the world ... I fear you will be quite tired of hearing their praises sung ...' (Quoted in Petre 1925:47). Nearly a century later, Morris was still 'infected with the distinctly superior attitude that officers of the Gurkha regiments adopted towards the rest of the army ...' (1960:216). In the view of one Indian army officer on the receiving end of this attitude the British officers commanding Gurkhas 'adopted an air of condescension' towards other regiments including those whose 'fame and glory were the pride of the Indian army' (Proudfoot 1984:27). Masters recalls that while a few other (non-

Gurkha) regiments of the Indian army were barely tolerated, the British army 'lock, stock, and barrel, was [considered] useless' (1956:103).

The Gurkhas thus acquired a certain reputation, and Gurkha regiments were much sought after, with several applications for each vacancy.[18] From the viewpoint of a young subaltern without family ties or good connections, these vacancies appeared to be reserved for sons of distinguished Indian Civil Service (ICS) and military officials, or the 'relatives of other great men' (Woodyatt 1922:62).[19] Certainly, a number of officers report having obtained a place in a Gurkha regiment through friends or relatives in high places. In the memoirs of one senior officer with the 5GR at the end of the nineteenth century, he attributes his Gurkha appointment to the military secretary to the Viceroy, 'who had been written to by Lady H [...], a distant relation ...' Another officer, who came out to India in the 1930s and served for a time—as was the custom—in a British regiment before applying for an Indian regiment, records in his diaries that his CO (in the British regiment) 'was an old school friend of the Colonel of the 1GR, so I got to go to [that] Regiment.' I was told by a retired officer that utilising personal connections was quite common even when he joined at the beginning of the Second World War. 'I went to the 10GR because my father was working with the sister of the adjutant of the regiment and he put in a good word'. Davis records that he deliberately chose the 3GR because his cousin was an officer in the regiment: 'I trusted to nepotism. It worked' (1970:11). Without some influential contacts, the chances of a Gurkha posting were much reduced, but not entirely out of the question. For at least one aspiring (and successful) officer—who ended up in the 9GR—the solution was to pass out of officer cadet training 'higher than my rivals' (Bristow 1974:22).

The most desirable and valued claim on a place in the officer cadre of the Gurkhas was to have a family link to a regiment. The British military establishment, until this century, like that in many western European countries, was the preserve of a very small elite, which maintained its continuity of dominance through generations—with fathers, sons and grandsons passing through the same regiments (Ellis 1981:175) It is doubtful whether the same degree of continuity characterised the Indian army regiments, including the Gurkhas, although British officers sometimes write and speak as if this was the case. There is a widespread feeling that in the past sons followed fathers into the regiment with regularity, but that this practice has diminished of late. Certainly all Gurkha regiments contained (and still contain) a few officers with close kin ties to previous members of the regiment, but even a superficial perusal of records makes it clear that they were in a distinct minority. The *Register of Officers* in the 2GR lists only some forty men whose fathers or other close relatives (brother, grandfather, uncle) served in the same regiment. Probably half this number again had close links—both of kinship and affinity—to officers in other Gurkha regiments. This is a small proportion of the 900-odd officers listed in the *Register*. While the compilers were unable to obtain information on family ties for most of these names, my guess is that they would have successfully discovered virtually all those with such links to other officers in the same or different Gurkha regiments, so that those about whom no information is available were less likely to have had such family ties.

Despite their comparative rarity, sons of the regiment are a focus of attention in a regiment's portrayal of itself, and give it a sense of continuity. Every regimental officer knows of the existence of such lineages, can trace their genealogies, and takes pride in their recitation.[20]

British Officer—Gurkha Officer

The theory persistently propounded by the highest British authorities in India during the nineteenth century was that Indians were incapable of exercising military command. Although a few voices refuted such assertions, Lord Roberts of Kandahar, who was Commander-in-Chief of the Madras and later the Bengal armies in the last two decades of the nineteenth century, probably expressed the general British view in his insistence that 'eastern races ... do not possess the qualities that go to make leaders of men ...' (1897:444; see also Saxena 1974:270–71). What had been forgotten was that as late as the beginning of the nineteenth century Indians could hold higher commissions (Gutteridge 1963:39). It had simply been assumed that only their own officers could comprehend the ways and thoughts of the native sepoys, which were 'completely undecipherable to Europeans' (Mason 1974:172). It was only with the reorganisation of the Indian army in 1796 that this old system of command by native officers was phased out and direct command by British officers put in its place.

The reason sometimes given for the elimination of Indians from higher ranks was that whereas the latter might have been competent to command irregular corps, only Europeans could train and officer regular units operating on a western military model (see MacMunn 1932:345). Contemporary Indian army historians argue that the theory 'falls to pieces' when it is remembered that native officers have always progressed when given the chance to do so (Saxena 1974:270). Mason suggests that the officer 'was judged by social as well as professional standards, by delicate distinctions in

behaviour difficult to define in writing and hard for a foreigner to learn'
(1974:458). Whatever the reasons, from the early nineteenth century there
was a 'steady decline in the prospects for an Indian officer' who was 'firmly
in place as junior to the youngest of British officers' (ibid.:173).

It was not until the end of the First World War that the King's Commission would be open to Indians and ten places a year reserved for Indians at
Sandhurst.[21] In 1922 the Indian military academy at Dehra Dun was established, to provide an education on English public school lines, and men
commissioned from there became Indian Commissioned Officers (ICO). So
there were three classes of commissioned officers: British Officers holding
the King's Commission, ICOs and Viceroy's Commissioned Officers (see
below), which commissions were held by all Indians until 1918, and which
the majority continued to hold even after Indians were allowed to attend the
military academies at Sandhurst and Dehra Dun (see Gutteridge 1963;
Bristow 1974:24).

Indianisation, when it came, did not affect Gurkha units, which were
specifically excluded from the scheme. Neither the Sandhurst-trained officers
nor those graduating from the Indian Military Academy were sent to them.
In the opinion of one (Indian) historian of the Indian army 'the obvious fear
was that the Indian officers might subvert the Gorkha's loyalty to the British'
(Proudfoot 1984:127). But the more common view among British officers
was that Gurkha soldiers would not agree to be commanded by Indian officers. The reasoning was that as hillmen the Nepalese soldiers had the high-
lander's usual aversion to the men of the plains so that the 'idea of military
service under Indians [would be] unacceptable [to the Gurkhas]' (Tuker
1950:626). This view was belied by the considerable numbers of Gurkhas
who, at the time of the 'opt' in 1947, chose to serve in the army of independent India under Indian officers rather than move to the British army.[22]

Gurkhas in the British army were allowed to earn full commissions from
the late 1950s by attending the Royal Military Academy, Sandhurst, and in
1989, these officers represented approximately eight per cent of the Brigade's
total officer establishment (House of Commons 1989:25).[23] Nonetheless, in
Gurkha regiments of the Indian army until independence, and in the British
army's Brigade of Gurkhas until the 1960s, the only officers who held the
sovereign's commission were British. Nepalis could hold the rank of what in
the Indian army were termed Viceroy's Commissioned Officers, and from
1947 King's/Queen's Gurkha Officers.

The relationship between British officers and their Gurkha soldiers was
by and large mediated by these Gurkha officers.[24] VCOs in the Indian
army—such as Jemadars and Subedars—commanded platoons and, more

rarely, companies, duties which would be performed by a sovereign's commissioned officer in the British army (Forbes 1964:77–8).[25] The VCO/QGO was the second-in-command of a company, and the British officer was advised and expected to rely on him to provide an invaluable and indispensable conduit to the ordinary Gurkha riflemen. Many British officers readily admit the extent to which they relied on their Gurkha officers, especially when new to the regiment. One retired battalion commander pointed out that since as many as one-third of British officers in a Gurkha battalion would be away on leave or courses at any one time, the Gurkha officers were regularly called on to do their jobs.

The senior VCO was the Subedar-Major (later 'Gurkha Major'), usually a man of long and distinguished service. The officer commanding a battalion always deferred to his judgement on all matters concerning 'Gurkha custom and religion', and frequently on a host of other issues as well. Des Chene notes the vital role these Gurkha officers played in dealing with conflicts arising in relationships among soldiers from the same ethnic group or locality where kinship ties prescribed one kind of behaviour while differences of military rank demanded another (1991:300–11).

Junior British officers, Davis recalls, were very respectful of the Subedar-Major, and were careful not to offend him (1970:25). I was told by a former commanding officer that he would always listen to what his Gurkha Major told him, even if it was to express an adverse opinion about one of the British officers. 'I'd have been silly not to listen to him, and he was unfailingly right, too'. Another remarked that a British officer was 'only as good as his Gurkha Officer', and owed any success to him. But however experienced and capable—and most were promoted from the ranks only after fifteen to twenty years of service—the VCO/QGO ranked below the most junior British officer holding the sovereign's commission.

Regimental Cultures

By the end of the nineteenth century, the Indian army officer's primary loyalty was to his regiment. The fact that the Indian, and especially the Bengal force was organised on the basis of caste or ethnic units probably encouraged stronger regimental attachments here than in the Royal contingents.

Gurkha regiments grew by fits and starts as a consequence of the Nepalese *durbar*'s initial hostility to recruitment, British concern to prevent the growth of a large (and potentially hostile) Nepalese army (see Chapter 1) and, following the Mutiny, the wish to replace certain categories of Indian sepoy by what were assumed to be more loyal Gurkhas (see Chapter 4). By the beginning of the twentieth century the Gurkhas had become a fairly distinctive force, with twenty battalions in ten regiments, having assumed the shape with which most officers who later wrote about Gurkhas were personally familiar.[26]

In the course of time, each regiment elaborated its own distinctive traditions. It acquired its 'own very personal possessions and habits: its Badge; its Band and Pipes and the Days it commemorates. There are its Trophies, its Silver, its War Memorials; and other almost private things important only to itself' (Mackay 1962:360). Invariably, certain battle honours were incorporated in the collective memory and corporate identity. Thus, as a reward for their sacrifices in the battle of Delhi during the Mutiny, the Sirmoor Battalion (later 2GR) was granted the 'exceptional honour of carrying a third special Colour on which the word "Delhi" was to be inscribed ...', and the siege of Delhi came to be observed as Regimental Day on the 14th of September every year (see Smith 1973:26). Later, in place of the colours the regiment was presented with the Queen's Truncheon. All recruits are sworn in by touching it at a special parade.[27]

Additionally, the sovereign would honour a regiment by appointing him or herself, or another member of the royal family, to be its Colonel-in-Chief, and their names would be permanently incorporated into the title of the regiment. The first royal title conferred on any regiment in the Indian army was that granted the 2GR in 1876 by Queen Victoria who appointed the Prince of Wales (later King Edward VII) as Colonel and the regiment came to be called 'the 2nd King Edward VII's Own Goorkha Rifles'. In time, all Gurkha regiments were granted royal titles; thus, the 'First King George's Own', the '3rd Queen Alexandra's Own', the '4th Prince of Wales' Own', and so forth. In addition, each regiment appointed an honorary Colonel, usually a senior officer (often retired) who did his early soldiering with a battalion of that regiment.

Each regiment, partly to reflect these honours, developed its own particular insignia which might appear on buttons, headdress, mess jackets or collars, and these were spelled out in regimental *Orders of Dress*,[28] and periodically listed in army Regulations (see Nicholson 1974:34–39). Even ties became emblems of identification (see Laver 1968). There were meticulous rules for employing the regiment's title in an officer's official and unofficial correspondence, on personal name plates and calling cards, etc.

Informally, too, regiments developed distinctive symbols of differentiation: thus, only the 5GR had the 'privilege' of keeping arms in the barracks (Maxwell 1986:263); the 7GR alone among Gurkha regiments flew the national flag of Nepal on special occasions; it was also the only regiment to employ the term 'commandant' to refer to the C.O. (Mackay 1962:362,364). While other regiments used the *khukuri* as their badge in a variety of ways, only the 10GR combined it with the bugle horn of rifle and light infantry regiments ('thus embodying the two ideas of "Gurkha" and "Rifles"') (Mullaly 1957:439); the regiment's pipers also enjoyed the 'unique distinction' of wearing the Hunting Stuart tartan (Mullaly 1950:16); 2GR wore red behind their badges and brown boots when other regiments wore black, and retained the spelling 'Goorkha' in their title;[29] and so on.

Official histories became an important means not only for keeping a detailed record of regimental accomplishments, but for maintaining links between the past and present, and providing regimental cultures with the sacred stamp of tradition. The first regimental history appeared early this century (see Shakespear and Stevens 1912) and since that time every regiment has commissioned its own history to be written and periodically updated. The reality of a regiment's past could be extremely complex and confusing, since Gurkha units were in a constant state of flux, with transfers, amalgamations, incorporations, re-numbering, and changes of status, composition and title.

To take one example, according to Nicholson, the 1GR 'rejoiced in no less than ten changes of title between 1858 and 1936' (1974:11). The other Gurkha regiments underwent only slightly less frequent transformations (ibid.: 22–24; Chapple 1985). This very complexity, of course, gave some scope for 'creativity' in making claims to a distinguished lineage, hence richer traditions. One regiment might claim to be the oldest by virtue of being the first Gurkha battalion raised, another the most senior by virtue of being the first regular unit, a third most venerable through tracing its lineage back to an older Indian regiment. Thus, 10GR (after a lengthy advocacy) recently had its battle honours earned prior to 1890—as part of the 10th Madras Infantry—'restored' by the Queen, and thereafter allowed by the Army Dress Committee to wear a new arm badge to commemorate this service. 'With the restoration of our old battle honours', proclaimed the regimental magazine, 'we can rightly claim to be the oldest regiment in the Brigade ...'[30]

These were matters of some importance to any regiment, and an elaborate set of rituals usually surrounded and symbolised them. One former officer who had served for many years with the 2GR told me: 'The 2GR is different, that's not reputation, that's fact. That is because it is the senior unit, the premier battalion. The Prince of Wales is the Colonel-in-Chief, we have the Queen's Truncheon which is the emblem others don't have [one officer in another regiment referred to it scathingly as "their holy pole"], and so on.'

The officers' mess was a principal site for evolving and policing regimental customs. It was the social body to which all officers belonged, the corporation holding their property, the custodian of their tradition, and a tangible focus for their *esprit de corps*. There were elaborate rules detailing appropriate etiquette, dress, the behaviour of officers towards one another, the treatment of guests, even permitted topics of conversation. Lady Wilson found exasperating the refusal of officers to talk about anything other than 'polo, polo ponies, dogs and sport' (1984 [1911]:140).[31] There were even rules about where and when to smoke. On Regimental Guest Nights in the Queen's Gurkha Engineers, no officer was permitted to smoke between 'Officers Dress Call and the Loyal Toast'.[32]

In virtually all Gurkha units, the most elaborate ritual was reserved for Regimental Guest Nights, held once or twice a month, and detailed procedures were usually prescribed in the regiment's mess rules. All officers, including the married men, had to attend, and this was the occasion when officers were 'dined in' or 'dined out' on joining or leaving the regiment. A pre-World War II guest night with the 4GR at Bakloh is described as follows:

> ... We all get up as the C.O. comes in with the Brigadier, who is a regimental guest ... As he leads the way into the dining-room the Band plays 'The Roast Beef.' The C.O. goes to his place halfway down the table with the guest on his right, the President and Vice-President to the head and foot, and other officers where they please ... The table itself has no cloth and reflects the silver under the shaded lights—the Chinese junk in the centre, the war memorial bell and the 1st Gurkhas' figure in front of the President, the Band and Pipe programme stands, the Rifle Brigade hunting-horn, the sedan-chair, the bugle snuff-box and a long line of cups.
>
> Under the eye of the Havildar the servants bring in ... the dinner.[33] At intervals the Band and Pipes outside play ... When dinner is over the orderlies bring in the wine ... the decanters are passed round clockwise. Then the President rings the war memorial bell and everyone stands. The President gives the toast, 'Mr Vice, the King-Emperor'. The Band plays the first part of 'God Save the King'. Mr Vice says, 'Gentlemen, the King-Emperor', and with 'The King-Emperor, God bless him,' officers drink the toast and sit down. Cigarettes are brought in ... Then a chair is set beside the President and the Bandmaster is invited in to have a glass of wine.

> The President asks the C.O.'s permission and the pipers
> are called ... They come in playing a march: after three
> rounds of the room they halt behind the C.O.'s chair
> and break into a strathspey followed by a reel; finally
> they change again to the march, move once around the
> room and go out, to the accompaniment of subdued
> rapping on the table as a mark of appreciation ...

> Coffee and liquers are brought in, and again the Pipe-
> Major is sent for. This time however, he comes without
> his pipes and halts beside the C.O. who gives him a dou-
> ble peg of whisky in a silver quaich ... He tosses off the
> whisky and, to show that there is no deception, turns the
> quaich upside down and kisses the bottom. The wine
> goes round again. We begin to feel that we have had
> enough of the dinner table, but we cannot get up before
> our guest ... (MacKay 1952:586–87).

Even a quick outline of the ritual conveys the sense of rootedness in regimental history and tradition, as well as the emotive potential of the rich
symbolism. General MacMunn mentions his particular pleasure at dining in
the officers' mess of a Gurkha regiment, although the feelings it inspires in
him might be somewhat suspect nowadays: 'When the pipes come in and
the Tartar (sic) pipe-major takes his tot of whiskey ... is to feel that Britain
really does inspire' (1932:198). What is evident from the above description
is that despite the participation of Gurkhas—the pipe-major and pipers are
Gurkhas—the symbolic significance of the ceremony—its sacred trophies,
bagpipes, marches, dances—appeal to and are only meaningful in the context of British officer culture. The strong Scottish flavour in these and other
ceremonials stems from long-standing links between Gurkha and Scottish
regiments, which are usually explained in terms of the natural affinity of
highlanders for one another (see Nicholson 1974:3): hence, the 'mutual
attraction between the Scottish soldier and Johnny Gurkha' (Mullaly
1950:16); their 'similar tastes' (Woodyatt 1922:179); their 'special sort of
freemasonry' (Northey 1937:97); even the comparability between their
clans and kindreds or septs (Neild n.d.:3).

Women were generally not permitted in the mess, except on special occasions, such as the arrival of a bride in the station (Mackay 1952:588). Mains
reports that in the 9GR women could only attend functions—such as tea
parties—held in a marquee or on the mess lawn, but never in the mess
building itself. Special Ladies Guest Nights were only introduced in 1939
(1990:88). When one officer who served in the 5GR before the First World

War found that following the Second World War women attended mess functions, he reports having felt a 'twinge of regret' to see the mess 'used ...like a Club' (Palit 1954:57–8). This was indeed a change from the days when in many regiments a woman's name could not be mentioned in the mess. These taboos, as Macmillan has suggested, may have been part of a code meant to dissociate women from violence, as well as to assert and maintain the masculine character of the regiment (1984:90).

On the whole, mess discipline was strict. A perusal of the mess rules of any Gurkha regiment attests to the meticulous surveillance exercised over details of dress, comportment, decorum, the taking of meals, procedures regarding visitors, etc. Mess rules of the Queen's Gurkha Engineers even prescribed the form of wedding present to be purchased for an officer of the regiment on his marriage. An officer who first served in the 2GR during the First World War reported in his diaries that etiquette and custom were 'laid down by regimental fiat even to the extent of approving the hotels where one stayed on leave', and vetting one's friends. Masters remarks that offences against the code of behaviour were dealt with by informal 'courts martial' (1956:31).

Thus over the years each Gurkha regiment had elaborated a distinctive identity, through shaping its own history, developing exclusive conventions and rituals, acquiring its sacred trophies, competing for the most illustrious royal names as colonel-in-chief, and holding stereotyped images of their own and other Gurkha regiments, to say nothing of other army units. In the course of an interview with a former officer in the 7GR, he remarked:

> You'll get a 10GR [officer] telling you they are the best,
> and the others are rubbish; that the 2GR are so snooty
> they only talk to God; the 6GR are by the book and
> haven't got a brain between them; the 7GR are the great
> unwashed and undisciplined; and so on. It's all made up:
> engenders team spirit.[34]

Introducing the diaries of a 2GR officer, written in 1880, Chapple and Wood note that he makes some 'sweeping generalisations' about the quality of other regiments, and remark that this is a 'trait common to many regimental officers' (1981:207). Exclusiveness was also fostered by the incorporation of officers' families into the definition of the regiment. In his memoirs, an officer who served in the 1GR between the wars remarks on how the regiment was 'very much a family. Officers and their wives visited and stayed with each other's relations when on home leave'. Many years later, after retirement, he returned to India and Nepal as part of a party of thirty ex-officers, their wives and children. 'We were all old friends and acquaintances and we had a strong common bond'. Regimental publications kept (and still keep) abreast of the activities, health and deaths of former regimental officers and their families, and Regimental Associations provide an important context for maintaining old ties.

Although no clear hierarchy of Gurkha regiments emerged, officers seemed to imply that internal status distinctions were recognised. I was told on one occasion that any regiment that included 'Frontier Force' in its title (as did the 5GR) was considered a cut above the rest. But most officers would acknowledge (some more grudgingly than others) that the 2GR had the reputation of being the most prestigious unit. One ex-battalion commander with the 1GR commented that in his day the 2GR was referred to as 'God's regiment', while a former senior officer with the 7GR remarked in the course of an interview that 'there are the 2GR and the rest'. Those I questioned on the matter had differing explanations for singling out this regiment. One suggested that it was because 2GR officers tended to come from the better schools, another that the regiment takes great pride in its age and strong tradition. For a third it was simply a feeling: 'you can tell a 2GR officer a mile off; he is a bit more pleased with himself'.

There were other points of distinction within the Brigade as well. For one thing, 'eastern' regiments (i.e. those recruited mainly in eastern Nepal) were sometimes deemed different in character (and performance) to those whose soldiers originated in the western part of the country. For another, officers with the 9GR occasionally expressed annoyance at the tendency for other officers to regard 'their Gurkhas', who belonged to high castes, as somehow inferior fighters to the Tibeto-Burman soldiers who predominated in other Gurkha regiments (see Twiss 1961:24; also Chapter 4). Finally, all officers in Rifle regiments apparently looked down on those belonging to Ordnance and Army Service Corps, whom Morris reports were regarded as akin to 'tradesmen' (1960:94). As one officer with the 6GR put it: 'Infantry officers everywhere looked down on fellow officers with the signals, transport and engineers, and Gurkhas were no different'.[35]

But it would be wrong to over-emphasise the distinctiveness of regimental cultures or relationships, and to overlook the very real links among officers throughout the Brigade. They were, after all, educated in the same schools and to the same values, and trained and commissioned at the same military academies. Moreover, they were aware of themselves as 'Gurkhas' in opposition to other units of the army, or indeed, other occupational categories within India. Officers are reported to have enjoyed few friendships outside the army, and certainly had little time for 'box-wallahs', the term of derision reserved for European businessmen in India (Farwell 1989:93). Furthermore, officers from different Gurkha regiments were brought together in a variety of official and unofficial contexts: several regiments were neighbours in that they shared the same stations (see Chapter 1, note 28); during wartime close ties would develop among officers from different Gurkha units fighting alongside one another; those belonging to separate regiments met each other on training courses; and officers were frequently promoted from one regiment to command another (in fact, promotion only usually came with a transfer to another unit). As I note below, a substantial proportion of officers moved among regiments and therefore had the opportunity to establish links to and ties in more than one. Officers from different regiments were also brought together at social gatherings both in India and Britain. Masters describes the inter-war June Ball at Sandhurst as 'probably the most colourful function in … England and was annually attended by about two thousand people' (1956:56–7).

They were also drawn together in the Gurkha Brigade Association. The Association included British officers who had served in all the Gurkha regiments, including those which became part of the Indian army in 1948. In this way, officers were likely to meet and come to know virtually all other Brigade officers, at least of their own generation. One officer who served in 6GR told me that he knew all the officers of his own age bracket whatever their regiment. 'When officers came back to the UK on leave they would phone each other up and get together for a drink. We had so much in common, and it was always nice to find out what was happening in other regiments. And of course we invited them to our weddings and vice versa'. Another who was in 10GR remarked: '[The older officers] have known each other for thirty-five or forty-five years or whatever. We have an annual reunion of all the regimental associations [i.e. the Gurkha Brigade Association], and people come from wherever they are if they can.[36] It's a great family. Many are personal friends; we joined up together, or we met on courses in India or Britain. So after some years we got to know them all. And now we attend each other's funerals more and more.'

Finally, not a few officers were linked by kinship and marriage. It was not uncommon for several brothers or cousins to serve in different Gurkha regiments.[37] And marriage frequently linked officers in the same or different Gurkha regiments. In the words of one retired officer: 'We sometimes married one another's sisters or daughters. It happened naturally. They were the people you met'.[38]

The Regimental Officer

For the British officer, the regiment was the object of fierce loyalty, and demanded total devotion. While most officers were expected to marry, there were conventions which ensured that junior officers remained single and thereby attached entirely to the regiment.[39] Even those who were married were often separated for long periods from their families, if wives returned to Britain to remain with school-age children. Such officers effectively returned to their previous bachelor existence.[40] Finally, many officers remained unmarried throughout their military careers, which were thereby devoted utterly to the regiment. Indeed, the ideal of the regimental officer as unmarried was not confined to the Gurkhas. Baynes, in his sketch of the model British army officer in the early part of this century, suggests that he was unmarried, so that the regiment was the 'first love of his life' (1967:124). This carried the implication of protecting the regiment's honour and reputation, and remaining utterly loyal to brother officers, all of whom participated in and were formed by the regimental culture. As one officer with the 6GR phrased it, 'the regiment is almost like a school, in that it has a great capacity for determining the kind of person you are going to be'.

The good regimental officer was thought to be one who dedicated his entire career to the regiment. The 'old codgers', as one former regimental commander put it, 'wouldn't contemplate serving anywhere other than a Gurkha battalion. They might agree to transfer from one Gurkha regiment to another to get promotion, but wouldn't consider transferring out of the Gurkhas altogether. A few men even spent their entire army career in the same battalion'. The 2GR's *Register of Officers* provides some evidence for the widely-held belief that traditionally an officer would spend the greater part of his military life in the same regiment. The *Register* has details on the length of service of over 600 officers, and of these, more than one fifth (137) spent ten years or more in the regiment; fifty-five of them had served it for over twenty years. While these long-serving officers still constituted a minority, there were significant enough numbers of them to create a lasting impression of total regimental dedication.

Although a Staff College was founded at Camberley in the early part of the nineteenth century and another in Quetta, in India, at the beginning of this century, to provide courses in advanced military administration and strategy, neither college was popular. This was apparently a prejudice shared by officers in the British army as well. According to Farwell, 'some of the more stylish regiments considered it smart never to have had an officer who had been graduated from Camberley' (1989:99). This would undoubtedly also have been part of a long tradition of antagonism to 'learning'. In 1852, the army's top brass successfully opposed pressures to introduce tests for officers, which reinforced the pervasive anti-intellectualism characteristic of the military (Vagts 1959:172). The emergence of the cult of games in the public schools which educated the officers, moreover, led, according to Chandos, to a decline in scholarly standards (1984:344). Thus, the ideal British officer was said to 'care little for the theory of his profession' (Baynes 1967:124). But whatever other reasons explained this hostility to attending courses, they were deemed a potential threat to the officer's regimental loyalties.

So, it is not surprising to read that when General Villiers-Stuart took command of the 1/5GR in 1921, he found that with the exception of himself and two others, 'no officer had passed any of the numerous and necessary language and promotion examinations, and none of them had attended a musketry, PT or signalling course. From long experience I knew none of these officers would pass anything unless I took drastic steps' (Maxwell 1990:266).

While attitudes in the rest of the British army seem to have changed as Staff College graduates began to earn promotions and preferment, many officers with the Gurkhas are reported to have resisted professionalisation until well into the 1960s. During interviews with former officers who served during the period up to and including 'Confrontation' in South East Asia, they would invariably refer to the hostility shown by even the most senior officers to 'careerism', perceived as an insidious threat to the regimental focus of the British Gurkha officer. In the words of one: 'At one stage, after the war, you joined the Gurkhas and expected to serve for the whole of your career in the East. There are stories of young officers who, if they asked their commandants whether to put in for Staff College, would be thought to be showing too much interest in a full army career.' According to another: 'In the 1960s we were extremely reactionary. The Company commanders in those days were wartime officers. One told me: "Don't think you're going to staff college, my boy, because that will ruin your career. You're a regular soldier and we don't want you poncing about on courses"—you were distrusted if you went to staff college. If you left the regiment you were either trying to escape the front line, or an ambitious little shit who wanted to become a General'.

Another recalled: 'In the days of Confrontation we never thought of leaving. Nobody went outside his regiment, thought of going away even for career reasons. Not many of us went to Staff College. One of our Generals used to say "If you want to go to Staff College do so by all means, but don't bother coming back". It was only when Confrontation ended that people began getting career minded'.[41]

The Career Officer

The cessation of hostilities in South East Asia at the end of the 1960s was a turning point in several senses. For one thing, the Brigade was drastically reduced in numbers, and not all the officers could continue to serve in their regiments. It was decided to reduce a permanent officer cadre from 180 to 100 over a four year period, and to achieve this level of reduction, twenty per cent were either declared redundant or given transfers out of the Brigade (James and Sheil-Small 1975:239). There were therefore growing pressures to look elsewhere in the army for a career. For another thing, the post-Confrontation Brigade grew increasingly marginalised within the British army. Many officers I spoke to felt that the reputation which the Gurkhas had enjoyed at the end of the Second World War and during the conflict in South East Asia had declined, as the British army became more and more committed to NATO and engaged in Northern Ireland.

The Gurkhas' experience in jungle combat was no longer required; the importance of these skills and the general respect for them consequently diminished. One former officer put it this way: 'The Gurkhas had fought the funny little wars—in the jungle—without heavy arms and tanks, artillery and armoured cars. So we were one of the "funnies". Of course we revelled in it, because we had had the opportunity to fight for real'. At the same time, it meant that the British officer with the Gurkhas was increasingly unlikely to advance his career prospects. 'If you've spent your younger years in the jungle, without modern weapons systems, you can't expect to command a Brigade which has spent all its time on the North German plain.' The Gurkhas were increasingly seen as out of the mainstream of the British army, and it became a career disadvantage to be in the Brigade, especially if one had ambitions to earn promotion to higher ranks. 'If you went to the Gurkhas you might not get the right tickets, for instance service in Germany. And if you didn't have service in Germany you didn't exist. I'd never served in Germany, and that is true of my generation of British officers. There I was a Lieutenant-Colonel and had never been to Germany! The hierarchy would look at me and say "He's uneducated, what to do with him?"'.

The end of the 1960s, then, is seen as the point at which the officer's career, if he was to have one, began to take precedence over the interests of the regiment. Serving with Gurkhas came to be regarded as only one stage in a professional vocation. This meant attending courses, and leaving the Gurkhas for transfers to other parts of the army, possibly never to return. This came to be seen as a typical pattern.

Of course, there had always been officers who spent only brief periods of time in one Gurkha regiment in the course of a long military life. For one thing, promotion was usually only possible by moving to a different regiment. For another, if there was a war somewhere, officers would frequently try to wangle a transfer to a unit engaged in the action. And in the last analysis the high command always exercised the right to move people where they were needed. The upshot of all this was a substantial proportion of officers who moved between regiments rather than remaining in the same one. One late-nineteeth-century example was a senior officer with the 5GR who first joined his county regiment, and later volunteered for the Indian army. He was posted to the Bombay Infantry for a time, then to the Punjab Frontier Force with the 1st Sikhs. At the regimental hill depot they shared a mess with the 5GR, and he asked for a transfer to that regiment. But even while he was attached to the Gurkhas, he periodically arranged for temporary transfers to other units, because they were engaged in what he regarded as challenging actions or posted to interesting stations.

The point, then, is that although a significant minority of officers served for long periods in their regiments, the great majority did not. The 2GR's *Register of Officers* suggests that over seventy per cent for whom information is available had spent *under* five years in the regiment. Many of these served only during wartime or in the immediate post-war period of national service. However, about one-tenth of those with brief service in the 2GR had either come from or gone on to different Gurkha regiments or other units of the army in the course of pursuing a career.

For many Gurkha-philes the rise of the career officer meant the virtual demise of the regimental officer. The latter are pictured as having immersed themselves totally in the regimental way of life, which meant selfless devotion to brother officers, on the one hand, and to their Gurkhas, on the other (see Chapter 4). The quintessential regimental officer remained a bachelor (in spirit if not in flesh), and declared himself married to the regiment. The figure of the regimental officer was, needless to say, not unique to the Gurkha Brigade, nor to the Indian army. Baynes suggests that he could be 'obdurately defensive of the existing order, and so parochially-minded [as to be] blind to the interests of the army as a whole' (1991:118).

It was no doubt common for officers to assume that the preceding generation had been more committed to the regiment than the current one. But the dramatic transformations in the size and role of the Brigade of Gurkhas in the late 1960s contributed to the perception of a watershed, of a line separating the era of total regimental commitment from the modern period in which personal careers began to take precedence. Around this time, too, officers who had been educated in state schools—and were thereby not committed to public school ideologies—were beginning to enter the regiments, further encouraging a mood of professionalism.[42] Those who have produced the literature on Gurkhas by and large emerge from the tradition of the regimental officer. Most belong to the generations which served in the Gurkhas during and between the world wars or during the immediate post-World War II period, when the Brigade was at its highest numerical and regimental strength. They mostly spent long years in the Brigade. And they were part of a culture which disdained careerism, laughed at staff-college products and enjoyed the panache of an elite corps which had a clear and vital role to play in the Indian, and later British, armies. With the end of the military campaigns in South East Asia, and the transfer of the Brigade to Hong Kong, that culture effectively ceased to exist.

Conclusion

Some years ago a brief correspondence in the *Journal of the Society of Army Historical Research* (Vol 1, 1922, p.126) debated whether the notion of 'officer' was synonymous with that of 'gentleman'. The question was apparently answered in the affirmative when one correspondent quoted the passage in Shakespeare's *Henry V* (IV.1) where Pistol inquires of a suspected intruder: '[A]rt thou officer? or art thou base, common and popular?' and receives from the King the answer: 'I am a gentleman of a company'.

This image of the officer as gentleman underwent a significant transformation in the latter part of the nineteenth century, as the notion of chivalry was adapted to accommodate the expanding middle and professional classes, and take account of their crucial role in the governance of Britain's empire. In the same period the ethos of the public schools—which increasingly were relied upon to provide the officer corps—changed from one which fostered independence and individuality of mind to one which sought—mainly through the medium of games—to mold disparate elements of the ruling classes into this new kind of gentleman. Both developments were occasioned to serve imperial ends (Girouard 1981:260; Chandos 1984:340). At the same time, the image of imperial manliness was transformed as the stress on morality receded to be replaced by a cult of muscularity. It moved, as Vance has phrased it, 'from the chapel to the changing-room' (1975:124). The regimental system was an outgrowth of the Victorian and Edwardian public schools, so that British officers were raised on a uniform diet of games, an ideology of chivalry, and imperial triumphalism. But the idea of a single, undifferentiated British discourse is unhelpful. For despite the bonds created by a shared tradition and outlook, officers nonetheless had to contend with the realities of social differentiation within the military, and in India this was based on the historic division between the Royal and Indian armies. Gurkha regiments were therefore compelled to carve for themselves a place in the military pecking order, and by and large succeeded in establishing a discrete identity and reputation as an elite corps. Each regiment evolved a sense of its own history along with a repertoire of ritual and custom, whose symbolism, while incorporating Gurkhas, was addressed primarily to and meaningful only for its British officers. Regiments thus created distinctive cultures to which, ideally, their own officers were fervently committed.

Latterly, however, these regiments have been engaged in a struggle for survival in a rapidly contracting British army, having to compete for a place in this smaller force against older, more prestigious, influential and technologically sophisticated units. They have also had to contend with advancing professionalism in the form of the military career which requires incremental qualifications and ready mobility, thereby threatening the very idea of the regimental officer. These specific historical, political and socio-military developments provide both the context within which the British officers have produced their representations of Gurkhas, and the background against which these narratives must be read.

Notes to Chapter 3

1. In Otley's view, the purchase system was designed to ensure that the British army was closely tied to the propertied class (see 1970:214–15).

2. Bryant suggests that in the course of time, an increasing number of Company officers came from 'better' families (1978:205).

3. This apocryphal story is repeated by a number of writers on the Gurkhas, and certainly underlines the uneasy relationship between the two sets of officers. But to be fair, many former British officers with the Gurkhas recall the time spent with a British unit before joining their regiment in the most favourable of terms.

4. *Regimental Register of British Officers 2nd K.E.VII's own Goorkhas, 24 April, 1815—24 April, 1965.* The *Register* was compiled by Lt.-Col. J.S. Holy-Hasted and Col. D.R. Wood. Although some 900 names of officers are listed in the Register, there is information about fathers' occupations relating to only about 110 of these, which makes any numerical analysis pointless. Moreover, since details about army background were probably more readily available

to the compilers than other kinds of occupational data, the likelihood of a military 'bias' becomes obvious. Undoubtedly, many of the officers who obtained Emergency Commissions during war-time, or National Service Commissions during the immediate post-World War II period would have come from very much more mixed (middle class) occupational backgrounds. The *Register* has been painstakingly compiled over many years and I am extremely grateful to Col. D.R. Wood who allowed me to invade the privacy of his home to examine it.

5. Greenhut reports that in 1876, an Indian army lieutenant earned over 60 per cent more than someone of the same rank in the Royal army (1984:15).

6. See bibliography for a list of the unpublished diaries, letters and memoirs consulted.

7. This is extremely modest by comparison with the scale of domestic service to which officers in the Indian army at the beginning of the nineteenth century were apparently entitled: roughly ten to a subaltern, twenty to a captain, thirty to a field officer, and so on (Turner 1956:112). Moreover, 'they expected to live as luxuriously in the field as in cantonments, with china, plate, table linen, condiments and wine' (Pemble 1971:101).

8. Otley remarks that by the 1870s the bond between the military and the public schools was so firmly established that the army 'had nothing to fear' from the abolition of the purchase system and the introduction of open competitive entry to its military academies (1970:216).

9. I have been told by several officers who served in other regiments that the 2GR probably had more officers from the 'better schools' than any other Gurkha unit. I have no way of verifying this claim.

10. According to Chandos, before this change of direction the public schools had become foci of 'intemperate license and wild escapades in a world of increasing orderliness and standardized public propriety' (1984:320–1).

11. One well-known example of this jingoist outpouring was, of course, Sir Henry Newbolt's *Vitaï Lampada*, which sums up the empire's public school code of behaviour, and features the school boy who 'rallies the ranks' with the famous cry 'play up, play up, and play the game!' (see Richards 1983; Macdonald 1988). Newbolt was for a time the poet of Clifton College (Green 1980:222), and the Poet Laureate (Mangan 1988:145).

12. In one letter home, an officer serving with the 3GR between the wars, thanks his mother for 'the three Kiplings' she sent him.

13. In Girouard's view, the 'whole vast fabric of contemporary sport derives ... from the small percentage of Victorian Englishmen who went to the public schools' (1981:232).

14. In the early nineteenth century, Ensign John Shipp advised young men about to embark for India not to indulge in 'violent sports and exercises' since 'they encourage an inclination for drink' (Shipp 1829/1:275).

15. According to the author of *Hunting in the Himalaya* (1860): 'Anglo-Saxons are the only true sportsmen in the world: and in the case of English gentlemen, there is no doubt but that instinct and habit ... do much in producing that activity, and energy of mind and body, that promptitude in danger, and passion for fair play which they carry with them wherever they wander' (quoted in Bennett 1984:77).

16. '... an honourable opponent and a good loser; he play[s] games for the pleasure of playing, not to win ...' (Girouard 1981:260).

17. Heathcote (1974:29) suggests that the Punjab Frontier Force regiments generally saw themselves as the Indian army's *corps d'élite*, but this is probably true of other regiments as well, including the Gurkhas.

18. According to one diarist, when he went out to India at the commencement of the First World War 'there were many wanting to get into Gurkhas and few vacancies'. Another, arriv-

ing in the country in the 1930s, noted that there was competition for most cavalry regiments, both Frontier Force regiments and all Gurkhas. In the same period, Masters records, Sikh regiments were also much in demand by British officers in the Indian army (1956:74).

19. According to Woodyatt, the Commanders-in-Chief in India for a time jealously guarded their patronage of appointments to Gurkhas, and both Lord Roberts and Lord Kitchener made all first appointments personally (1922:175).

20. Anthropologists will recognise a comparison here between such regimental families and Evans-Pritchard's description of Nuer *dil*, members of the dominant clan in a tribe, and regarded by the people in their heterogeneous settlements as the true aristocrats of the place (Evans-Pritchard 1940).

21. Some forty-nine Indian cadets enrolled at Sandhurst between 1919 and 1925, and of these twenty-nine were commissioned, while the rest either resigned, died, failed, were 'removed', or were deemed 'unsuitable'. There was only one Nepali on the register at Sandhurst in these years, the son of a subedar-major in the 4GR. But his English was weak and he did not complete the course. (L/MIL/9/319, Oriental and India Office Collections of the British Library).

22. The 'opt' is a sensitive issue in the history of the Brigade of Gurkhas (see Chapter 4).

23. There is much informal discussion about the wisdom of the Sandhurst Gurkha scheme. Some British officers think privately that it has been less than an unqualified success, while others find in it much to praise.

24. After India's Independence and the division of Gurkha regiments, a new category of Gurkha Commissioned Officers was introduced in the British Brigade of Gurkhas. They received the Queen's Commission, but without attending Sandhurst. This status was abolished and in the late 1950s Gurkhas became eligible for a full Sandhurst commission.

25. A Gurkha battalion of approximately 1,000 men was divided into four Rifle companies, with three or four platoons in each, and three or four sections in each platoon (James and Sheil-Small 1965:9).

26. There were also Gurkhas serving in other Indian army regiments (see Chapple 1985).

27. See *2nd King Edward VII's Own Goorkhas, Notes for Officers*.

28. See for example, *Orders of Dress, 1st Battalion, 7th Gurkha Rifles*, 1937.

29. One officer on posting to the 2GR wrote his family to note 'the correct way to spell my regiment. We are different from the other Gurkha Regiments'.

30. *Bugle and Kukri* Vol. 5, 1989, pp. 23, 25.

31. This custom was not peculiar to the Gurkhas. Baynes recalls that in his (Scottish) regiment, 'talking shop' was forbidden in the mess (1967:28).

32. See *British Officers' Mess, Queen's Gurkha Engineers, Rules of the Mess*.

33. Morris's description of a typical six-course meal eaten in his officers' mess, despite being served with extreme decorum on the most precious silver, suggests an appalling culinary banality. 'It began with *hors d'oeuvres*: either one sardine, one slice of tomato or half a hard-boiled egg arranged on a piece of soggy toast. The soup … tasted like, and generally was, a mixture of hot water and Worcester sauce … If we were lucky the fish also was tinned; otherwise it was … served floating in a pool of glutinous anchovy sauce. After this the usual joint … [then] a pudding (trifle or pink blanc mange) and finally a savoury. The composition of the last depended upon the *hors d'oeuvres*. If we had started with a slice of tomato we finished with a sardine and *vice versa*' (Morris 1960:86).

34. According to Masters (1956:103) 1GR were earnest; 2GR idle; 3GR illiterate; 5GR narrow minded; 6GR downtrodden; 7GR unshaven; 8GR exhibitionist; 9GR brahmanical; 10GR alcoholic. (He served in 4GR for which he provides no epithet.)

35. In the nineteenth century engineers and gunners were alone in not having to purchase their British army commissions. Their recruitment was different from the rest of the officer corps, and they were trained at Woolwich, while all other officers went to Sandhurst (Garnier 1977:89).

36. Among the miscellaneous items discovered in the Gurkha Museum was a Menu card for a Brigade dinner held at the Savoy Hotel in London in 1949, and attended by eighty-five officers belonging to all ten Gurkha regiments.

37. The 2GR's *Register of Officers* records that one officer who entered the regiment in the early part of this century had one brother in the 9GR, another in the 6GR and a third in the 10GR.

38. Macmillan reports a high incidence of intermarriage within the military generally (1984:105).

39. Farwell (1989:102) cites the 'rule of thumb': 'subalterns must not marry; captains may marry; majors should marry; and colonels must marry'.

40. As often as not, however, wives remained with husbands in India, and were separated for long periods from children sent to school in England. It was also thought necessary to separate children from the dangers of 'tropical lethargy and disease' to which they were deemed 'particularly susceptible' (Stoler 1989:149). In the unpublished autobiography of one officer with the 9GR he explains his decision to leave the army after a relatively brief service during and immediately following the First World War in terms of avoiding a prolonged separation from his young son. 'It was taken for granted', he writes, 'that if white children were kept in the Indian climate and "atmosphere" beyond 5 or 6 years they would deteriorate permanently in health, stamina and character'. This was a source of considerable worry and strain to officers' families, according to Macmillan (1984:98).

41. Brigadier N. Short, for a time Colonel of the 6GR, remarks in his Foreword to *Allanson of the 6th*, that 'Allanson's record dispels the myth, once prevalent in Gurkha regiments, that no one could be a capable staff performer as well as a good regimental officer' (1990:8). He thus acknowledges the tenacity of the belief while denying its validity.

42. According to Macdonald, the army now claims that over half the Sandhurst intake are educated in state schools, and that forty-five per cent are university graduates (1988:235; see also Otley 1973:205). One of the officers involved in current recruitment of British officers to the Gurkhas suggested in an interview that the school base is now much wider than it was even a few years ago, but that the public schools are still disproportionately represented among the officer intake. This tends to confirm Garnier's finding that despite a greater spread of school backgrounds among officer cadets at Sandhurst, there continues to be a close and parallel association between regimental and school hierarchies (1977:88).

....

CHAPTER 4

REPRESENTING GURKHAS

The Rhetoric of Martiality

The Gurkhas are above all a martial race.

Lieutenant D. Bolt *Gurkhas*, 1967.

Introduction

The British required a large army to defend their imperial possessions, much of it drawn from the indigenous population of India. Policies regarding the recruitment of this population varied as between the different components of the army, but following the sepoy Mutiny in the Bengal force, they relied increasingly on the notion of martial races—an idea which grew out of the scientific environment of the day—to provide a framework for and a guide to recruitment. While the British believed themselves to constitute a martial race, only certain ethnic groups within the native population earned such a designation, and after 1857 the Gurkhas were firmly incorporated in this select category. Military thinkers (including some authors of the Gurkha literature) elaborated a comprehensive classification of such groupings, as well as the detailed criteria for their identification and enlistment. This task was aided by the simultaneous categorisation and stigmatisation of a penumbra of non-martial races, whose only grace, it would seem, was to highlight the virtues of the chosen.

This chapter examines how the Gurkhas are represented, focusing especially on the theme of martiality, which in turn gives rise to the collateral notion of masculinity. As Seidler points out, this is seen to be ruled by reason, strength and will, and has been defined since the Enlightenment in opposition to nature, the passions and the emotions, all of which characterise 'femininity' (1989:14), and in the Indian context are associated with the non-martial. Representations of Gurkha loyalty, a quintessential aspect of their martiality, are then explored, alongside the alternative discourses of Nepalese intellectuals. Attention is also turned to the strong and enduring bonds which are presented as having developed between the British officers and their Gurkha soldiers, which are characterised by both dominance and affection. In this connection, British military writers seek to transcend what Burke (1969), and Empson (1935) before him, refer to as the 'mystery of courtship' between people of different social classes (and, in this instance, cultural backgrounds).

Martiality

The British military establishment in India did not originate the idea that some people make good soldiers and others do not. Even the *varna* system,[1] after all, which allocates military responsibilities to certain categories of Hindu society, can be and was sometimes interpreted as an embryonic martial theory. But while the British were certainly aware of such ideas, these were by no means systematically applied in their own recruitment policies. For a long time the Bengal army, which was the largest of the three components of the Indian army, actually enlisted many if not most of its ordinary soldiers (sepoys) and NCOs from among the Brahmans (the quintessential non-martial sector in Hindu society). As late as 1855 official policy was to exclude low castes (Kolff 1990:187). But when the Bengal army rebelled in 1857 the British felt the need to reconsider their thinking about the suitability of certain groups for a military career. There was a dramatic fall in the number of battalions recruited from traditional areas in the east and south between 1862 and the First World War, and a corresponding rise in the numbers recruited from the north (Omissi 1991:12). By the end of the war the proportion of troops enlisted from the north had reached eighty per cent (Goddard 1976:273). The men from Oudh, who had been the 'backbone' of the Bengal army, were 'recategorised as unsuited for soldiering' (Enloe 1980:36).

The intellectual justification for the revision of enlistment policy was provided by Field Marshall Lord Roberts (see Chapter 3). In his memoir, *Forty-One years in India*—which was apparently a best-seller in its day, and 'widely studied for information on Indian military questions' (Heathcote 1974:88)—Roberts notes how his aim had been to 'substitute men of the more warlike and hardy races for the Hindustani sepoys of Bengal ...'. But he had found it difficult to get his views accepted because of the 'erroneous belief that one Native was as good as another for purposes of war' (1897/2:441). While the 'military instinct [is] inherent in English, Scotch and Irish alike', he argued, the same could not be said for the diverse peoples of India (ibid.:442).[2] A few years later, in *The Armies of India* (published in 1911), which had a Foreword by Roberts, Major (later Lieutenant-General) G.F. MacMunn, an officer with the Royal Field Artillery (assisted by Major A.C. Lovett of the Gloucestershire Regiment who provided the paintings and sketches) outlined the martial theory succinctly:

> It is one of the essential differences between the East and the West, that in the East, with certain exceptions, only certain clans and classes can bear arms; others have not the physical courage necessary for the warrior. In Europe as we know every able-bodied man, given food and arms, is a fighting man of some sort ... in the east, or certainly in India, this is not so ... (1911:129-30)

It was thus through the efforts (and writings) of Roberts, MacMunn and others that the British 'formulated and codified the principle [of martiality] into a dogma' (Mason 1974:349).[3] The 'theory' had several strands, which were at first glance contradictory. One was based on the idea of natural qualities. It emphasised that martiality was an inherited trait and therefore an aspect of 'race'. In the view of Bingley and Nicholls, authors of a military handbook on Brahmans, 'fighting capacity is entirely dependent on race ...' (1918:47). In this conception, a martial race, to quote Enloe, flags an ethnic community as inherently inclined towards military occupations; it possesses some special characteristic embedded in its physical make-up, in its 'blood' (1980:39). In this period blood was widely regarded as the substance responsible for the transmission of hereditary features, so that all members of a particular race would be endowed with the same qualities. Martiality (along with many other characteristics) was thus deemed to be inherited in the blood. In this sense, martial theory did not emerge *sui generis* to meet specific military needs in the nineteenth-century Indian context. Rather, it has to be understood as but one manifestation of the wider European doctrine of biological determinism, which gained at least some of its currency from contemporary anthropological ideas about race, culture and evolution (see Fox 1985:150–53; also Street 1975:5; Green 1980:233).

A second strand in martial thinking introduced a climatic-environmental element. There was a great deal of theorising about which conditions produced the best soldiers. The argument put forward by Creagh was that we find warlike peoples in hilly, cooler places while in hot, flat regions races are timid, servile and unwarlike (see Creagh n.d.:233)[4] The flat plains of Bengal were thus thought too enervating to produce proper fighting men, and the hot climate of south India had a debilitating effect on military virtues. Heathcote points out that this hypothesis, viz. that 'hard countries breed hard men' goes back at least as far as Herodotus and was popular in the post-Mutiny Indian context because of its simplicity (1974:93). The problem, of course, was that not all populations who shared the same climatic-environmental conditions were regarded as martial.[5]

A third strand—comprising a ragbag of political, cultural and hygienic explanations—completed the theory of martiality. Thus, Roberts observes—while insisting on the primacy of hereditary factors—that failure to utilise their inborn military abilities can have a 'softening and deteriorating effect' on Asiatics (but apparently not on Europeans). So during long years of peace 'the ancient military spirit [dies] as it had died in the ordinary Hindustani of Bengal ...' (1897/2:383). Moreover, to both heredity and the climate-environment, MacMunn later added 'prolonged years of varying religions', early marriage, juvenile eroticism and one thousand years of malaria and hook-worm as explanations for the lack of martial aptitude among people of the plains (1932:2). Fox, denying that these components of martial theory were contradictory, suggests that while 'pseudo-scientific evolutionary monogenism' preached the inheritance of racial characteristics, such as martiality, it allowed that they could decline in certain environments, thus requiring 'better races' to be vigilant in perpetuating their superior qualities (1985:151).

The martial theory provided a rationalisation for the change in recruitment policy which, following the Mutiny, was concentrated on the Punjab and among Sikhs, Muslims and others labelled martial races. The preference for Muslims especially became widespread: Brigadier-General John Jacob insisted that the 'Mussulmans of Hindoostan are the very best men for our army ... there cannot be better Eastern soldiers than these men ...' (see Pelly 1858:133–4). This attitude was reflected in the literature of empire, for example in Kipling's writing (see Green 1980:289), and constrasted sharply with the earlier preference in the Bengal army for Hindus who were said to be 'more popular with their European officers than the truculent Muhammedans from the north ...' (Bingley and Nicholls 1918:8).

Martial Nepalis

Alongside the new bias towards north India, attention was increasingly focused on Nepal. The notion that some groups are more suited to miltary occupations than others predates, as I have already noted, the flowering of martial-race theory in nineteenth-century British India. Prithvi Narayan Shah, the ruler of Gorkha at the time of the invasion of Kathmandu Valley, and regarded as the 'father' of the Nepalese nation, is reported to have favoured the idea that only four *jat* ('castes' or 'tribes') should be enlisted in his army—namely, the Thakuris, Khas (Chetris), Gurungs and Magars—and that the priestly (Brahman) and lowest ('untouchable') groups should be excluded (Stiller 1989 [1968]:44).

The ethnic or caste composition of the Nepalese army at the time of his conquest of the Valley of Kathmandu is a matter of some uncertainty and much speculation. While there is widespread agreement that Chetris and other high-caste groups provided the officer class, opinions as to the identities of the other ranks are mixed. Bennett, for example, in her study of a rural area in central Nepal points out that the high castes ('Chetri-Bahuns') regard themselves as having formed the bulk of the conquering army of Prithvi Narayan when he invaded the Valley in the third quarter of the eighteenth century (1983:10). This reinforces Kirkpatrick's observation that in the latter part of the eighteenth century, Brahmans and Chetris 'compose[d] the army of the state' (1811:183). Others, like Shaha, insist that the Gorkha army included Magars and Gurungs as well as Chetris and Thakuris (1986:5). This view accords with that attributed to King Prithvi Narayan himself in *Dibya Upadesh*.[6]

A series of Nepalese government orders issued during the war of 1814–16 suggests that not all groups were expected or allowed to fight. While 'weapons-bearing castes' were instructed to report with their swords, shields, bows, arrows and muskets, members of the ('untouchable') Blacksmith caste (Kami) were required to make themselves available for metal work at munitions factories and forts; Newar traders were ordered to set up shops to supply the troops; Damais (musicians)—also 'untouchables'—were instructed to bring their musical instruments to accompany the troops; while Brahmans were ordered to recite scriptures and pray for victory.[7] Brahman prayers were evidently a matter of some concern to the Nepalese generals during the Anglo-Nepal war. A letter from the commander of one garrison near Kangra to the Nepalese king refers to the latter's failure to honour his promise to restore Brahman lands previously confiscated, and which had led to 'universal commotion as a result'. He suggests that the Brahmans should be assembled and a promise made to restore their property in the event of victory over the English. By these means, he suggests, 'many thousand respectable Brahmans will put up their prayers for your protection, and the enemy will be driven forth' (quoted in Fraser 1820:525).

Where irregular troops were concerned, Rathaur insists that many were in fact Kumaonis and Garhwalis and 'other such hill tribes' (1987:35). Indeed, since irregulars were recruited wherever the permanent garrisons were stationed, they would probably have formed an extremely heterogeneous body. Pahari makes the interesting observation that anyone who fought on the side of the regime became a 'Gorkhali', so that political allegiance and not race was the primary consideration in the making of a Gorkhali (1991:6).

Subsequently, most western (and especially military) authors insist on, though do not provide much evidence for, a preponderance of Magars and Gurungs in the Nepalese forces at the outbreak of the Anglo-Nepal war (see Vansittart 1894:213; Pemble 1971:26). This may simply be a case of reasoning *ipso post facto*, since following the war, at the insistence of Brian Hodgson, who was Assistant British Resident in Kathmandu, Magars and Gurungs were singled out as pre-eminently suited for military occupations and became the principal groups enlisted as recruits (see Chapter 2). One British Gurkha officer, writing about the war, argues: 'we may surmise that the Nepalese troops opposed to [the East India Company's Generals] Gillespie and Ochterlony were of the pick of their service and composed to a great extent of the classes (e.g. Magars) we value so much nowadays' (Shakespear 1913:379).

Probably the first European to refer to Nepal's 'martial tribes' was Hamilton (1819:19), and from the time of the East India Company's war with Nepal, during which the British 'discovered' the fighting qualities of their Nepalese opponents, certain ethnic groups were regularly labelled in this way. Like those in north India, they were believed to have something in their make-up, in their blood, which made them inherently inclined towards military occupations. Hodgson labelled particular groups as 'martial classes' (1833:220) and urged their recruitment. In the view of one historian, 'the more these turbulent martial people were drained away from Nepal, the brighter would become the prospect of Nepal being a weak and peaceful neighbour of British India' (Mojumdar 1973:160). This was, indeed, a principal reason for Nepal's initial opposition to British enlistment of its civilians (see Chapter 2). So Hodgson's classification had a very pragmatic political motive, but in time the underlying reason for his plea disappeared in the general rhetoric surrounding the development of martial race ideas in the Indian army.

The notion of Gurkhas as a martial race developed fully towards the end of the nineteenth century. British officers enthusiastically proclaimed the virtues of their soldiers. 'Their fighting qualities' wrote Vansittart (endorsing a previous comment by Oldfield), 'are *nulli secundus* amongst the troops we enrol in our ranks from the varied classes of our Indian Empire' (1894:249). They are, he later added in his revised handbook on the Gurkhas, 'natural fighters' and, moreover, the cool and bracing climate of the Nepalese hills produced a robust character, physically as well as morally superior to that of any Hindu of the plains or valleys (1915:10).

At first the Gurkha units were apparently not too discriminating in their recruitment policies. Garhwalis and Kumaonis were taken on, and there are even reports of 'fugitive criminals and outlaws', who later deserted, finding their way into the battalions (Mojumdar 1973:165). Chapple concludes that all four of the earliest Gurkha battalions included persons whose names would 'not now be recognized as either Nepali or Gurkha' and that there were, furthermore, 'a fair number' of low (i.e. 'untouchable') castes among them. He also provides an approximate breakdown of the *jat* designations of the Nasiri and Sirmoor battalions (later the 1GR and 2GR) for the year 1830: Brahmans were approximately nine per cent in both battalions, and 'untouchables' seven per cent in one and five per cent in the other (Chapple 1985:6–7).

Indeed, in the list of men belonging to the Sirmoor Battalion killed, wounded or decorated with the Order of Merit during the Bengal army mutineers' siege of Delhi, approximately one quarter have names readily recognisable as belonging to groups not regarded as martial, and at least half to groups subsequently not recruited by Gurkha regiments. This, despite the insistence by the British officer who commanded the battalion during the attack that he 'would never enlist any but *real* Goorkas, and none but the fighting castes'.[8] Rundall, referring to the recruitment during 1888–89 of a second battalion for the 3GR, observes not only that formerly 'our Goorkha regiments ... have enlisted Garhwalis from Lower Garhwal ...' but that the aim was to raise the new battalion as much as possible from Upper Garhwal (1889:46–47).

If the reality of recruitment did not quite live up to the rhetoric of martiality in the course of the century, by the end they more nearly coincided, as regiments were permitted to enlist only men from the martial tribes or classes, prescribed by headquarters. As India had been, Nepal was divided up into ethnic units and a particular set of characteristics was attributed to each on the basis of personal observations. This was especially extemporaneous in the case of Nepalese groups, since British recruiting officers were unable to visit the country (which was closed to all foreigners until after 1951), and so had no first hand knowledge of it.[9] Nonetheless, a few officers became avid ethnographers, producing handbooks in which ethnic differences were stressed and highlighted (see, for example, Vansittart 1915; Morris 1933; Gibbs 1947). According to Omissi, Indian army handbooks were part of 'the urge to measure, codify and classify the Indian population' so that 'India could be comprehended (and therefore controlled) ...' (1991:19).

The tendency was to attribute particular characteristics (like martiality) to whole groups, which, as we have already noted, were thought to be passed on from generation to generation.[10] Stereotyped ethnic identities were thus carefully cultivated over many years, and continually reiterated and reinforced both in the literature produced by military writers, and orally within the informal contexts of British officer interaction (such as the mess). This is what Enloe appears to mean by her comment that 'building militaries has been, in part, an ethnographic enterprise' (1980:28).

These strategies of division and classification have been seen as part of 'the instinctive defence mechanism of imperialism, an understandable tendency to seek out those groups who might be relied upon by the colonial power and exclude those who could not' (Omissi 1991:8; see also Enloe 1980:25). What has also drawn comment was the policy of emphasising the differences between selected martial classes. In Heathcote's view, the 'special virtues of each class, some real, others illusory, were developed and exploited to improve regimental *esprit de corps*' (1974:102). Some military historians, such as Saxena, have criticised the policy as an invitation to 'racial antagonism' between ethnic groups concentrated in particular regiments, thus enabling the colonial authorities 'to play off a regiment of one class against a regiment of another' (1974:263). Gurkha units, as we have seen, were encouraged to think of themselves as virtually a species apart from the rest of the Indian army (see Chapter 3; also Ragsdale 1989:49–50). But whatever the practical politico-military implications of these policies, it is important not to overlook or dismiss the content of the ideology itself which came, in time, to be regarded as a 'truth emergent from the nature of society itself' (Des Chene 1991:75).

For some years, Hodgson's identification of martial groups in Nepal formed a recruiting blueprint, and mainly (Tibeto-Burman) Magars and Gurungs were taken. Indeed, at one point the Nepalese Prime Minister is reported to have begged the Indian army not to insist so exclusively on enlisting only members of these two communities, since the areas of western Nepal in which they lived were becoming denuded of their young men (Husain 1970:246). Hodgson's other specified military class, the (higher caste) Khas (or Chetris)—which implied the Thakuris as well—whom he deemed to be somewhat less desirable because of their 'brahmanical prejudices' and devotion to the House of Gorkha (1833:220), were lightly recruited before the Mutiny, but hardly at all for several decades after it (Cardew 1891:136). In 1893 a special regiment was formed for Khas and other high caste groups.[11] But by the close of the nineteenth century the Gurkhas were still drawing their numbers predominantly from among the Magars and Gurungs whom Vansittart asserted were 'by common consent recognised as the *beau ideal* of what a Gurkha soldier should be' (1894:223).

The Newars who had, in the 1760s, resisted fiercely the attacks of the invading Gorkhali army on the Valley of Kathmandu, were nonetheless characterised as lacking the essence of martiality, as were members of both the lowest ('untouchable') castes, and the highest, judged too 'brahmanical'. Hence, the consensus grew among officers that the 'NBCs' (Newars, Brahmans and Chetris) were much like the non-martial Indians of the plains (see Chapter 3). Similarly, men of the Doti region ('Dotiwals'), in what is now far-western Nepal, who were recruited into the first Gurkha battalions in some numbers during and after the Anglo-Nepal war (see Chapple 1985:12) were gradually re-categorised as non-martial, and declared of 'not much military value' (Northey 1937:6).

Even some Tibeto-Burman groups, who shared a common middle-hill environment, as well as many aspects of history, language and culture with the Magars and Gurungs, were not initially labelled martial. Peoples of the eastern hills, like the Rais and Limbus, while acknowledged as good fighters, and taken into para-military units such as the Burma Military Police and the Assam Rifles, were deemed too headstrong and quarrelsome, and so too undisciplined to be labelled real martial classes.[12] These latter groups, however, were gradually re-classified. At first a number of these men were enlisted in 'western' regiments consisting mainly of Magars and Gurungs, but with the raising of the first 'eastern' regiment (the 10GR) in 1889, and another (the 7GR) in 1907, Limbu and Rai recruits were separated in their own units.[13]

Another Tibeto-Burman community, the Tamangs, who were even closer, both in terms of geographical propinquity and culture-history to the Gurungs and Magars (see Chapter 2) did not acquire a martial label until the middle of this century, when it was declared that the Tamang makes an 'excellent soldier' (Leonard 1965:113). While a few Tamangs from eastern Nepal were previously enlisted into the 7GR and 10GR, only those who were able to pass themselves off as Gurungs were accepted into western regiments (see Höfer 1978).[14] While early handbooks tended to blame 'orthodox' Gurkha officers who disapproved of Tamang dietary habits (certain clans ate beef) for the virtual ban on their enlistment, later handbooks pointed out that the principal region of Tamang settlement in central Nepal was closed to recruitment on the insistence of the Nepalese government (Gibbs 1947:21). The Gurkha handbook of 1933 informs recruiters that certain districts are 'reserved for recruiting by the Nepalese Army' (Morris 1933:147). Pahari, however, suggests that these areas were closed because they immediately surrounded the capital, and the country's political rulers exercised a virtual monopoly of Tamang labour which was in 'bondage to the state and Kathmandu elites'. Thus while they were relatively numerous in the Nepalese police and army, their number in foreign armies was 'disproportionately low' (1991:9; see also Tamang 1992; Campbell 1993).

The implication is that British recruiting policy and the theory of martiality took account of such circumstances. In similar fashion, they acquiesced in the tea-planters' request not to interfere with their labour pool for the tea gardens, and for a time recruitment was prohibited in Darjeeling, where many Tibeto-Burmans had migrated (Vansittart 1915:157).[15] By the commencement of the First World War Magars, Gurungs, Rais and Limbus were acknowledged as the principal 'Gurkha tribes', Thakuris and Khas (Chetris) were still being listed as such, and another Tibeto-Burman group, the Sunwars, had also been given the label (ibid.:47).

Thus, despite the notion that martiality was 'bred in the bone', and/or environmentally determined by the climate of the middle hills, the identity of Nepalese fighting groups—like those in India—did not remain static over time, and was subject to various external influences. Nonetheless, martiality was perceived to be the key ingredient in enlistment. On the basis of Vansittart's data, Ragsdale estimates that approximately sixty per cent of men entering Gurkha service between 1894 and 1913 were recruited as Magars and Gurungs, 27.5 per cent as Rais and Limbus, while all other ethnic communities (including Khas and Thakurs) contributed about 12.5 per cent of recruits (1990:13). Ragsdale notes, too, that military writers stressed only their martial traits, omitting the knowledge and skills many members of these groups possessed in other areas of life. He points out, for example, that the army stereotype of the Gurungs left no room for the 'sophisticated adaptability and cleverness of the long-distance trader [the] large-scale salt or tea merchant ...' (1989:48).

The Place of Martiality

British officers with the Gurkhas also stressed the importance of place in certifying groups and individuals as martial. Thus, a group which was normally deemed martial, could only be so in its own native territory. There was a belief that when, for example, Gurungs or Magars migrated to the east of the country from their original homes in western Nepal, as many of them did, they somehow ceased to retain the qualities which characterised them as martial in the first place. So military writers make statements such as 'Gurungs of eastern Nepal are practically not Gurungs at all' or 'the Magars of Eastern Nepal are ... very much inferior to those of Central Nepal ... in all respects' (Vansittart 1915:78,86), or again, Magars and Gurungs outside their native habitat are 'usually of inferior quality and are not normally enlisted' (Northey 1937:94).[16]

Such assertions were usually unaccompanied by any explanation, but where a reason was given it was that intermarriage had occurred—so the blood which carries the military qualities had been contaminated. Officers with the Gurkhas shared the general British abhorrence of miscegenation and insisted on recruiting unsullied members of the martial classes. Vansittart refers to the Magars' 'proper habitat' west of the Kathmandu Valley, where 'undoubtedly the best and purest Magars are found' (1915:82). But one section (the Gharti) was pronounced more mixed than other (pure) Magar sections, so those responsible for enlistment were warned to beware when confronted with members of the former group (1894:230). Similarly, recruiters were informed that whereas Thakurs were 'good material', the Hamal Thakur or progeny of a Thakur and Brahmin should not be enlisted by any regiment (1915:62).

Even within areas containing martially-eligible communities, there would be a league table of districts or regions which were thought to produce good recruits, and others which did not.[17] So, Gurungs in Palpa, Rais in Dhankuta and Limbus in Ilam (among others) were deemed 'not of good type', while Magars in one area west of the Kali river were pronounced 'of good type' but 'liable to be coarser' than those east of the river (Morris 1933:133–37). With the influx of Nepalese refugees fleeing the Japanese occupation of Burma in 1942, recruiters were exercised about their 'Gurkha character' and credentials (see Gibbs 1947:6).

British officers in the Gurkhas also believed in the idea that character could be fundamentally influenced by place. For years they debated the respective merits and traits of 'western' and 'eastern' Gurkhas. Men belonging to regiments recruited in western Nepal were thought to be more phlegmatic, but of better humour, while those enlisted from the eastern side of the country were comparatively dour and quicker to anger. While explanations for these attributes were seldom given, when pressed at interview officers might account for the differences in terms of settlement patterns or the productivity of land.

The significance of place also featured centrally in the long-standing debate about the martial quality of 'line boys', the sons and grandsons of soldiers who had been born in the family lines of the Gurkha battalions, had been to school, and had experienced the fleshpots of India before Independence, and later of Malaya, Brunei or Hong Kong, where the regiments subsequently were quartered. The view was widespread among British officers that contact with towns corrupted a Gurkha's purity and simplicity, and so his fighting ability, and elaborate precautions were taken by recruiters to enlist only young men from the more remote parts of the Nepalese hills.

The literature is replete with speculations about the extent of martial deterioration as a result of growing up in the lines. MacMunn reasoned that if such a boy had a Gurkha mother he would have 'sucked in' (sic) the regimental tradition with her milk, and kept most of the warlike traits of his father for at least one generation (1932:199). Similarly, early Gurkha handbooks reported that while their physique does not deteriorate much in a single generation, their morality does, so that 'they are often men of loose habits, and are not dependable, the chief characteristics of the Gurkha being almost entirely absent from their characters ... There is no doubt that the real Gurkha despises them ...' (Morris 1933:126; see also Vansittart 1915:92). Another military author concluded that by the second generation the line boys can hardly achieve the standard of the 'hill-bred article' as far as things like morals and dependability are concerned (Northey 1937:195).

This prejudice against line boys developed fully in the latter part of the nineteenth century alongside the general British preference for what were assumed to be simple villagers, and the distrust of literate or semi-literate urban dwellers. Parry quotes a comment by the Parliamentary Undersecretary of State for the Colonies when he was asked why the colonial administrators preferred unsophisticated natives. 'We frequently get on better with people different from us, and we appreciate the differences more than the points we have in common' (1972:50; see also Anderson 1983:21).

Yet, in the middle of last century, the Gurkhas actually seemed anxious to recruit line boys. In a letter to the Deputy Adjutant General of the Indian army, the Commander of the Sirmoor Battalion reported that he was 'encouraging men to bring their families with them, so as to have boys on the Lines. These lads ... I find just as good in the Field as the fresh Goorkah from Nepaul ... and far more intelligent ...'[18] But within a few decades— and especially following the Mutiny—any idea of favouring men raised in the lines or in towns had disappeared. It was the 'extra wild Goorkhalees' who were now regarded as the 'most trustworthy'.[19] Uneducated youths from the hills were definitely preferred to educated young men from the plains, i.e. towns. 'If we were to judge by the Gurkha soldier', wrote one senior British officer, 'then we would conclude that mankind is happiest and

most honest where ... civilising influences are least' (Tuker 1957:3). The
most severe deterioration in martial qualities was assumed to occur among
what one author called the 'flotsam and jetsam who have drifted into the big
cities' (Gibbs 1947:5). In Calcutta, we are informed, 'evil communications
corrupt good manners', and the Gurkha declines rapidly (Northey
1937:195–6; see also Morris 1933:126).[20]

In the jargon of contemporary British officers with whom I discussed the
matter, it was a choice between *pahar* (hill/village) or *bazaar* (town). In the
words of one who had spent many years as a recruiting officer: 'The "bazaar rat"
tended to be better educated, and had a more alert attitude to the outside
world. But he also had the vices—smoking, drinking, womanising, the soft,
easy life; he stood up for his rights, and all that sort of thing. In short, it was felt
that he had seen too much of us, and hadn't spent enough time in the hills.'

In fact, Gurkha regiments continued to enlist a proportion of their men
from among the 'bazaar rats', although I was told that town recruits, aware
of the prejudice against them, would often disguise the fact by giving an
address in the hills. Line boys were also recruited as clerks and bandsmen, or
into units like the Gurkha Engineers and Signals Corps which required a
better standard of education. Recently, as Gurkhas have become eligible for
Sandhurst commissions, it is principally the line boys who have dominated
the ranks of entrants. In evidence to a recent House of Commons Select
Committee on the future of the Gurkhas, the Brigadier of the Brigade noted
that the (small number of) Nepalese officers trained at Sandhurst tend to be
the sons of retired Gurkha officers who have been at British army schools,
i.e. from the lines (House of Commons 1989:26).

The Persistence of Martial Thinking

Although the martial-race theory was effectively suspended during both
world wars—in order to achieve the massive recruitment targets set by the
Indian army—the end of hostilities on both occasions saw its return as the
main basis of enlistment. Omissi shows that the post-World War I Indian
army 'returned to its pre-war ethnic mix' and that martial-race thinking was
not abandoned. If the theory was no longer the colonial strategy it had once
been, it had nonetheless become a 'habit of mind' (1991:21–22). If anything, it received a fillip with the publication in 1932 of MacMunn's volume
on *The Martial Races of India*, to which I have already referred.

Even the Second World War, in which over 200,000 Nepali men of every
description took part, appears not to have seriously shaken the confidence of
British military thinkers and authors in the soundness of the theory of mar-

tiality, since it persisted in providing the basis of recruitment to the Brigade of Gurkhas. The section of the population from which recruits are sought continues to comprise only a tiny proportion (some six per cent) of the total population of the country, and the area of the middle hills in which this population is found constitutes about one-third of the total area of Nepal (Edwards 1978:228).

Gibbs's manual on the Gurkhas, prepared in 1943 and published just after the Second World War, defines the 'true Gurkha' as 'a man of the martial clans of Nepal' (1947:6), and lists those ethnic groups which provide true Gurkhas. Similarly, Leonard's handbook of 1965—prepared for a postwar, post-Indian-Independence generation, and which is recommended to British officers joining the Gurkhas even today—has a table listing the districts in which ethnic groups who supply Gurkhas are to be found, with comments about their martial qualities. Thus, Gurungs in one administrative area are said to be available only in small numbers and 'are not of the best type', while Magars in another area are numerous and 'of good type'. Even particular clans are labelled: in Palpa there are 'excellent' Thapa Magars, but 'careful selection is necessary and the foothills must be avoided' (Leonard 1965:138–9).[21] These reproduce the kinds of assessments offered by Vansittart in his 1915 handbook (this clan 'needs careful enlisting' or that clan 'should not be enlisted').

Thus, on the basis of evaluating a few individuals at one point in time, entire groups inhabiting large tracts of territory continue to be stereotyped as fit or unfit for martial tasks. The latest handbook also indicates the persistence long after the end of the Second World War of ideas about the sigificance of place, with statements insisting that, for example, Thakurs in eastern Nepal must be cautiously selected because it is not their 'natural habitat' (ibid.:139). Finally, the underlying theory of martiality is reiterated and reinforced when the same author traces the origin of the martial spirit in Nepal to the 'infusion of north Indian blood into the brave, but unenterprising hill tribes' (ibid.:27).

Recent contributors to the literature on Gurkhas still refer to 'martial tribes' (see Bredin 1961; Davis 1970; Niven 1987) and express a traditional view on line boys. Thus, although the prejudice against the latter is said to have eased somewhat following the First World War (see Woodyatt 1922:194), Cross continues to insist that by being raised away from their villages, line boys are 'robbed of that recognizable but undefinable quality required in all Gurkhas wanting to be recruited' (1985:29); they simply do not possess the 'inherent chemistry engendered by an upbringing in the hills' which enables them to 'make good if they are enlisted', although he shares the widespread opinion that the education they receive in British army schools 'is useful when technicians and specialists are being recruited' (1986:133–4). Writers also continue to refer to the 'demanding environment' of the middle hills which form the 'hardy, stoical, self-disciplined but cheerful characteristics in the Gurkhas who join the British army' (Edwards 1979:222).

Young men seeking enlistment in the Gurkhas are by now well aware of these British predilections for rural recruits possessing the idealised characteristics of a martial people. So although many young Nepalis nowadays want to join the Gurkhas precisely to escape the village, and to have money to live well in what *they* regard as modern and civilised conditions (i.e. the towns), they feel obliged to present themselves to recruiters as rustics, and to stress their martial qualities, playing up to the British image of the ideal Gurkha (see Des Chene 1988). In other ways, too, the Gurkhas reproduce the rhetoric of martiality created by the British. While in Nepal in 1988, I was told by one former soldier that the governments of other countries regularly request Nepal to send quantities of Gurkha semen/seed (*biu*) so as to acquire their martial attributes. Like others labelled martial, then, Nepalis who were, are, or seek to become Gurkhas are, as Fox observes of the Sikhs, compelled 'to adapt to British beliefs about them' (1985:4).

Masculinity

An important element in the notion of martiality was that of masculinity, indeed the two terms were occasionally used interchangeably. MacMunn, for example, might refer to martial classes as 'manly' classes (1932:358). Martial races possessed obvious masculine qualities which the non-martial races lacked. The British, we are told, found the 'fighting races' more attractive than the 'passive, supine Hindus …' (Parry 1972:50). Said (1984:23) has pointed out that the Orient was routinely described as feminine, and Inden has recently reiterated that imperial India was widely imagined as a female presence, lacking western (masculine) rationality. Hinduism was seen to exemplify a mentality favouring the passions over reason and will, 'the two inevitable components of world-ordering rationality' (1990:85–89). Even the greater attention paid to female goddesses was attributed by reputable orientalists to a 'weaker, erratic, thoroughly feminine nature' (ibid.:85–89, 115).[22] In the novels of empire, too, the people of India were seen as 'volatile and passionate', quintessentially female qualities (Mannsaker 1983). Even male dress was described as graceful but essentially feminine (Tarlo in press). The widely held perception was therefore of European (masculine) reason dominant over an Indian (feminine) nature. Kakar has argued that this 'obsession with manliness' even led to an unseemly admiration for India's conquerors on the part of at least some early nationalist thinkers. Swami Vivekananda, for example, maintained that no race understood as the British did 'what should be the glory of a man' (1978:175). He and other sages sought to play down the androgynous themes in the old texts which they felt portrayed India as effeminate, and stressed instead the masculine side of the Vedic teachings (Gilmore 1990:184).

If western (and some Indian) intellectuals purveyed such views, it is no wonder that the military establishment—and the military authors who have created the discourse on Gurkhas—shared them. Moreover, many of these early officer-writers were brought up on the children's literature of the late-nineteenth and early-twentieth centuries, much of which, as already noted, focused attention on the empire and the frontier, and the virtues it taught were 'dash, pluck and lion-heartedness ...' (Green 1980:220–22). They would have been acquainted with at least some of the dozens of magazines devoted to 'manly adventure' for boys (Daniell 1983:119–20),[23] and would have read or known about the works of authors like Kingsley (*Westward Ho*) and Hughes (*Tom Brown's School Days*), which contributed to the development of 'muscular Christianity', favouring a 'healthy and manful Christianity, one which does not exalt the feminine virtues to the exclusion of the masculine' (Girouard 1981:142–43). They would also have been familiar with the adventure stories of Henty, who became a 'preacher of manliness' (Green 1980:221). And finally, as we have seen, the schools these officers (and military writers) attended played a vital role in shaping and furthering the idea of manliness. Public-school games, Chandos insists, were the 'guardian deities of all manly virtue' (1984:266; see Chapter 3).

Against such a background of education in masculinity, it is not surprising that these military authors discovered in non-martial India the very anthithesis of manhood. They found the merchants and town-dwellers lacking guts (MacMunn 1932:345), while the intelligentsia were dismissed as effeminate (ibid.:354). South Indians, Masters tells us, who inhabited the 'sloth belt', were all thought timid (1956:145).[24] But the Bengalis had the worst of it. They were castigated as 'soft' (Roberts 1897/2:383); 'languid and enervated' (Oldfield 1974 [1880]:262); and 'hopeless poltroons' (MacMunn and Lovett 1911:130). Bengali men especially were labelled 'baboos', which carried the implication of 'superficially cultivated, and effeminate', and they were the subject of endless ridicule (see Farwell 1989:187–88).[25] MacMunn referred to 'baboos' more generally as the 'clerkly-werkly' classes, and made it plain that the British had little regard for them, reserving their respect and affection for martial classes (1932:345). Indian army handbooks spoke with disdain of the large cities, like Calcutta, 'where the effeminate and feeble Babus vegetate' (see Mason 1974:165).[26] It was perhaps no coincidence that this ideological assault was aimed especially (though perhaps not exclusively) at that section of the Indian/Bengali population—high caste, increasingly educated and urbanised—which had provided the leadership during the Mutiny.

Masculine Nepal

Nepal came out rather well in the masculinity stakes. It benefited especially by contrast, since it bordered on what one military writer called the 'least masculine' of India's people—in Bihar and Bengal (Tuker 1950:626). The Gurkha—although not highly ranked in the Nepalese caste system—was deemed the very opposite of the low-ranked Sudra of India—who the same author described as a 'humble, rather cringing man' (1957:26–7). Nepalis also compared well against the 'effeminate races of the South' (Roberts 1897/2:442). The contrast between plains and hills, moreover, served almost as a metaphor for masculine-feminine distinctions. The hills bred robust and sturdy men, who looked down on men of the plains as soft and supine (Forbes 1967:54–55). One British officer wrote to his mother after his transfer from the regimental station in the hills of what is now Pakistan to the plains that 'all the locals seem half-dead after the Pathans ... the Pathan has his faults but is a man anyway'.

Nepal itself has, since the Anglo-Nepal war, been consistently portrayed by the British very much in masculine terms. Vansittart conveys the image by noting, for one thing, that the purity of Nepal's soil (as compared to that of India) had not been sullied by the 'foot of the Mohamedan conqueror'. (It is interesting that he does not consider India's soil as having been 'sullied' by the British conqueror). For another, that the Nepalis fought the Company 'in fair conflict like men'. Even Nepal's *lingua franca* (Khas-kura or Gurkhali, as the British writers called it) had a hard, masculine quality: 'terse, simple ... very characteristic of the unlettered but energetic race of soldiers and statesmen who made it what it is' (Vansittart 1915:10, 32, 67).[27]

Military writers also conveyed the manliness of the country in two main kinds of trope. In one, Nepal was seen as a military state in which a military outlook pervaded every section of society. So that the whole ethos of the Nepalese state was perceived to consist in militarism, a manner of thinking which Vagts defines as 'rank[ing] military institutions and ways above the ways of civilian life, carrying military mentality and modes of acting and decision into the civilian sphere' (1959:17). Hodgson wrote not only of the martial propensities and habits of the highland tribes, but more generally of the 'warlike enthusiasm of the people' (1833:205). He interpreted Nepal's system of a civilian reserve army as consitituting a 'hereditary force, whose sole career in life was military service' (Hunter 1896:106), and referred to the 'exclusive military and aggressive genius of the Gorkha institutions, habits and sentiments' (see Hasrat 1970:234). Campbell, the Assistant Surgeon at the British Residency in Kathmandu during much of Hodgson's tenure also detected a natural propensity for the masculine activity of warfare and the 'abhorrence of all the military tribes in Nepal to engaging in other pursuits than that of arms ...' (ibid.:226).

The Nepalese historian Ludwig Stiller regards as 'sheer nonsense' the British Residency's 'constant refrain' that Nepal was a nation of soldiers.

> The military accounted for a small percentage of the population, and even if we consider only the military castes (so called), we will find that the percentage of fighting men within those castes was still small. Nepal was then, as it is now, a nation of farmers. If the British residents formed the impression that Nepal was a nation of soldiers it was because the military dominated the government and no major decision could be taken without considering the effect it would have on the officer corps (1976: 205).

Another Nepalese historian suggests that it was only the dominant classes, those 'above the ordinary peasants working on the land' which thrived on military service and benefited from its successes, but he seems not to subscribe to the view that this added up to a military state (see Shaha 1987:28).[28]

But the tendency to present Nepal and the Nepalese as naturally warlike—and masculine—prevailed. Gurkhas were described as possessing the 'warlike qualities of their forefathers' who conquered Nepal and were thereby 'imbued with and cherish the true military spirit' (Temple 1887/2:233). And the theme was taken up by military writers. Bruce, who had served in both the 5GR and 6GR, writes (no doubt approvingly) of the Government of Nepal as being:

> ... run on purely militarist lines ... [it is the] purely militarist government of a purely military people [and the] whole attitude to life is a militarist one. All officials, or very nearly all of them, bear military titles ... The people seem intensely interested in everything to do with military matters ... Military tradition and military reputation is the one thing which interests all classes (Bruce 1928:xxiii–xxiv).

Northey later echoed this view of the state as run on purely militaristic lines (1937:14), and the theme of Nepal as having a masculine bearing was still a prominent feature of later British military writings. In his handbook on the Gurkhas for the British Ministry of Defence (1965:48), Leonard notes that 'Nepalese youth look down on a man without military experience' (see also Bredin 1961:72 for a similar remark), while recently Cross has insisted yet again that 'soldiering is seen as the one honourable profession open to the Gurkhas of Nepal ...' (1986:7).

In a second kind of trope, these authors stress the contrast between what they perceive as the pervasive obsequiousness of Indians—especially those who inhabit the plains—with the spirit of independence found among the martial people of Nepal. According to one author, the latter quality is found quintessentially among the Gurungs, described as nomadic pastoralists who, like the Pathans, were 'a tribe of warriors, preferring the spoils of war to the tedium of weaving blankets, tilling the fields and minding their flocks. Moving about amid the remotest Himalayan steeps and valleys ... [Even today] Perched on the heights, with their flocks ... the more solitary herdsman seldom comes into conversation with other folk' (Tuker 1957:33). Like many an anthropologist, these military writers see in this imagined pastoralism what Rosaldo refers to as the 'idealized characteristics of a certain masculine imagination—fierce pride, a warrior spirit, rugged individualism ...' (1986:96).[29] An alternative to the Gurkha as pastoralist free-spirit is the image of the soldier as 'yeoman'. The Gurkhas, writes one military author, 'were freehold yeoman farmers' who had 'bred in them a spirit of independence' (Forbes 1964:55). As Green has pointed out, the English also believed themselves to be a nation of yeoman soldiers (1980:34), and the label was frequently attached to the martial classes in the Indian, and especially the pre-Mutiny Bengal army (see Peers 1991:551). However misleading this application of a category delineating nineteenth-century British society to south Asian contexts, it was meant to imply, among other things, that these martial people came from the middle order of the agricultural classes, and thus shared the pride and self-esteem thought to characterise the small landowner. As one senior British officer who had served with the Gurkhas commented in an interview: 'We only recruited people with land, and not landless labourers, so we creamed off the best—the independent yeomen.'

It is not only the Gurkha as an individual or member of a martial group who possesses the qualities associated with autonomy and self-reliance, but the whole political ambiance in which he has lived for generations. These authors therefore contrast the colonial subjugation of India, on one side, with what they term Nepal's spirit of independence, on the other, which is thought symptomatic and generative of the kingdom's military strength, dignity and, by implication, masculinity. Nepal, wrote Woodyatt, 'enjoys complete independence' (1922:158), while according to Morris, it is a 'completely independent country and in no way subject to the orders of the Government of India ...' (1935:425). Northey, for his part, insists that in light of Nepal's independent status, the British Resident in Kathmandu occupies an 'entirely different position from that of a Resident in a native state in India' (1937:59). But the treaty which ended the Nepal-East India Company war of 1814–16 had imposed the Resident—the only representative of an outside power permanently stationed in the country—who kept an eye on Nepal's internal affairs, and severely restricted for over a century its right to conduct its own foreign policy. Nepal was forbidden to have direct communications with any external power except the Government of India, so that Nepal's independence 'was clearly limited to the extent allowed by the British' (Mojumdar 1973:234). It was not until 1923 that the treaty was abrogated and the independence of Nepal fully recognised by the British government in a new agreement.

Political historians continue to argue whether the new treaty, which compelled Kathmandu to consult the Government of India on its relations with the neighbouring states of Tibet, Sikkim, Bhutan and China, yet again compromised Nepal's independence (see Chhetry 1989). And even when in 1934 the British government agreed to the establishment of a Nepalese Legation in London, Britain's own envoy in Kathmandu continued to be drawn from the middle level of the Indian Political Service, which was interpreted by the *durbar* as tantamount to accrediting a political agent rather than a minister (Rose 1971:171–2). Whatever Nepal's legal status *vis à vis* the British, however, the Ranas' reliance on the latter for subventions—in the form of annual monetary payments, luxury goods, and honours—in return for the right to recruit was seen by the Government of India as a crucial means of securing the durbar's continued economic and political dependence.[30]

It is perhaps worth noting that these British constructs of Nepalese masculinity are not reflections of, nor replicated within, the cultures of the middle hills among people recruited into the Gurkhas. Hitchcock (1959) identifies an ethos of the 'martial Rajput' in north-western India, which encompasses such notions as physical prowess (implicit in the 'expressive gestures and mannerisms' of the men), a tendency to rely on force in relations with caste equals and inferiors, negative attitudes to physical work, seclusion of women, and insistence on ancestral links to medieval warrior kings. This idea of the martial Rajput, moreover, was fed by some of the epic literature as well as by more contemporary idealisations of the Rajputs in British writings about Rajasthan.

In his study of masculinity, Gilmore alludes to this Rajput stress on a 'rugged, courageous manliness of action', and suggests it is akin to that practised by 'their most famous exemplar, the fierce Gurkhas of Nepal' (1990:176). But Gilmore does not distinguish self-images from those assigned by outsiders. Tibeto-Burman groups in Nepal themselves evince no such cult of aggressive masculinity, nor any strong code of 'honour and shame' of the kind widely reported for parts of the Mediterranean, the Middle East and Latin America (see Goddard 1987; Herzfeld 1980; Lindisfarne 1993). Thus, while their officer-chroniclers see the Gurkhas as the progeny of a strongly masculine environment—natural, social and political—the cultures in which these soldiers are actually nourished appear not to have elaborated any ideology of 'machismo'.

In these representations of martiality and masculinity we may clearly identify what Enloe has called a 'Gurkha syndrome' (1980:26–7). This consists in labelling as martial a people who are usually remote from the centre both in the geographical and politico-economic senses. Moreover, the perfect martial race is an ethnic group that produces men who are both martial and *loyal*. This, says Enloe, is at the heart of the Gurkha syndrome. Let us turn now to the question of loyalty.

Loyalty

A derivative principle of the martial theory stipulates that the fighting abilities of martial classes actually render them a danger to themselves and everyone else unless they are controlled and led (MacMunn 1932:358). Brigadier-General John Jacob, in singing the praises of 'Hindoostanee Mussulmans', strongly recommended them as the 'best materials for our [Bengal army] soldiers *in proper hands*' (see Pelly 1858:214; my emphasis). Indeed, Indian army handbooks on martial groups frequently stressed that 'the hand that controls them must be firm' (Omissi 1991:17). So too with the Gurkhas. Without a strong hand, wrote Vansittart, 'they very soon deteriorate and become slovenly' (1915:59),[31] and the strong hand can only be provided by British officers. The literature on the Gurkhas abounds with comments on how these Nepalese soldiers could only ever realise their enormous martial potential under the tutelage, supervision and direction of British officers. I return to this theme below.

The Gurkhas needed a firm hand because they were, in effect, regarded as simpletons. A British Resident (Captain H. Ramsay) towards the end of last century, described them as an '... ignorant, stupid, roving race of men ... possessing very small aptitude for intellectual employments, which they invariably regard with the greatest dislike' (quoted in Husain 1970:237). This set the tone for many of the later military writings. In his handbook published in the early part of this century, Vansittart portrayed the Gurungs as 'unlettered, illiterate, [and] extremely simple minded' (1915:74). Virtually all groups comprising the Gurkhas were depicted as slow to learn. Candler informs his readers that the average 'Gurk' is 'not as a rule quick at the uptake ... [he] sees what he sees, and his visual range is his mental range' (1919:15). Masters, for his part, suggests that Gurkha skulls are round and 'thick', and relates a story about the mule who kicks a Gurkha and 'goes dead lame' (1956:92). Farwell retails another story of a British officer who is killed when a bullet ricochets off a Gurkha's head (1984:49).

Morris is one of the few military writers on the Gurkhas to protest at this portrayal, and attributes it to the refusal of British officers to learn Nepali properly (Morris 1935:438). Only the Thakuris, members of the caste to which the Nepalese royal family belongs, get somewhat better treatment from these authors. Northey describes them as 'very intelligent, smart in appearance, and endowed with the highest military qualities ... the beau-ideal of the Gurkha soldier' (1937:93).[32] But for the most part, and especially in respect of the Tibeto-Burman soldiers, the stereotype of the dull, plodding Gurkha persisted.[33] Even in a book published only a few years ago, we are told that the Gurkhas are 'unimaginative' and 'not able always to take the unexpected in their stride' (Niven 1987:83, 88).

This was part of a wider tendency to regard martial groups generally as lacking intelligence. Omissi notes that north Indian Jats and Sikhs were stereotypically characterised as 'stolid and unimaginative ...' (1991:17). It is no small irony that the British officers who represented the martial groups they commanded as lacking in intelligence, were themselves consistently portrayed as intellectually backward. Described as 'that queer animal in the matter of books' (Ellis 1981:152), the officer was reputed to 'place[...] far more emphasis on appearance, drill and sports than on intellectual attainment' (Greenhut 1984:15; see also Vagts 1959; Chapter 3).

In a sense, the characterisation of the Gurkha as simple is self-fulfilling since, as we have seen, policy all along has been to recruit from the 'backwoods'—from the villages and so from the most rustic and least sophisticated segment of the population. Undoubtedly, this policy stemmed in part from the widespread view, shared by military thinkers, that people and the lives they led were closer to nature and hence more virtuous the farther away they were from the towns and cities (see Street 1975:120). But implied in the description of Gurkhas—and other martial groups—as simple, uncomplicated warriors was the notion that they are apolitical and unquestioning in their allegiance. In addition to noting their simple-mindedness, Vansittart described the Gurkhas as 'intensely loyal' (1915:74), and Forbes remarked that 'uneducated youths from the hills were preferred ... for their qualities of steadfastness and loyalty ...' (1964:158).[34] This suggests, for one thing, that the Gurkhas endorsed the geo-political aims and goals of British colonial and neo-colonial policy, even if they did not always comprehend what these were.

So we are assured that although the Gurkha riflemen had understood little of the causes and implications of the numerous wars in which so many had fought and died, they were always ready to do battle with any enemy of Britain (Cross 1986:120). Those who died gave their lives for Queen Victoria and the British empire (see Bishop 1976:48, 81). Moreover, 'they are [still] happy to serve as trusty and loyal warriors of Her Majesty our Queen [Elisabeth]' (Lord Harding, Foreword to Bredin 1961).[35]

So, the Gurkhas have been used in virtually every one of Britain's military actions since becoming part of the Indian army, and from 1875, when they were first sent to Malaya, have also fought overseas. Regimental histories depict their every campaign: the Mahratta and Sikh wars; the sepoy Mutiny, where they stood loyal to the Company; the Afghan war and successive campaigns on the Frontiers; the Boxer Rebellion in China; in virtually every theatre of battle during both world wars (including Gallipoli, where forty per cent of the Gurkhas were killed); in the post-World War II insurgencies in South East Asia; and, most recently, in the Falklands and the Gulf (see House of Commons 1989:x). Gurkhas were also employed in curbing the nationalist uprisings of Indians in the latter part of the nineteenth and early twentieth centuries (Parmanand 1982:4; Des Chene 1991:3).

None of these military authors thinks to question the propriety of having used Gurkha troops in politically sensitive situations, and especially where Kathmandu itself may have been embarrassed. Thus, the Gurkhas' participation in the Mahratta war of 1817–19—which the Nepalese rulers hoped the Company's adversaries might win—is viewed not as British lack of concern for the *durbar*'s existing political alignments, but as a 'fair illustration of the hillmen's detachment from the policies of Kathmandu' (Bolt 1967:61).

Nepal has certainly been criticised by friendly governments (e.g. Indonesia) who have found themselves facing Nepalese troops in the employ of the British, the most recent instance being the Argentine protest over the use of

Gurkhas in the Falklands (see Muni 1973:174; Dixit 1991:10).[36] In the past the *durbar* could hardly protest at the manner in which Gurkha troops were utilised, but even since the recognition of Nepal's independent status (see above) and Britain's withdrawal from India the Nepalese government has seldom, if ever, made its views on the employment of Gurkhas known openly. This reticence has only encouraged speculation that economic reliance on Gurkha soldiering (and other forms of dependence) has rendered successive governments during the Rana regime and since unable to determine an autonomous foreign policy for the country.[37]

While sympathising with Nepal's attempts to remain neutral in external disputes and conflicts, even when Gurkha troops are involved, some Nepalese academics and intellectuals have urged their government to be more sensitive to interpretations placed on these activities by 'other parties' (Rana and Malla 1973:252).

The policy of providing Gurkhas for the Indian and British armies has, for at least forty years, been viewed by many Nepalis as an anomaly in the country's foreign policy, impinging on the country's professed non-aligned, anti-imperial and anti-colonial stance.[38] Opposition to the recruitment of Nepalese citizens into Britain's armed forces has from time to time surfaced as an issue in Nepal's internal political debates (see Chatterji 1967:115–16; Rose 1971:191). Most recently, according to Mishra, there was a 'significant divide' between the 1991 election results in eastern and western Nepal which 'may have been related to recruitment' (1991:17).

Antagonism to enlistment was expressed most forcefully in 1986 following an incident in Hawaii, when almost an entire company of Gurkhas (some 109 men) with the 7GR was sent back to Nepal and dismissed after apparently refusing to cooperate with an investigation by the Royal Military Police into an affray during which a British and a Gurkha officer were attacked and injured.[39] The official (i.e. government-controlled) Nepalese press (and radio) remained silent throughout the weeks following the announcement of their dismissal.[40]

The opposition press, however, used the occasion not only to castigate the *durbar* for its hesitancy in taking a public stand on this 'act of ingratitude' (*Saptahik Bimarsha* 15 Aug. 1986), and 'humiliation to all Gurkhas and all Nepalis' (*Naya Samaj* 13 Aug. 1986), but to comment more generally about the employment of Gurkhas outside Nepal. These troops, the papers argued, have been used in 'operations of imperialist military alliances' (*Nava Jagaram* 2 Sept. 1986), and in wars against 'Nepal's friends' (*Mulyankan* 3 Sept. 1986). Their recruitment has therefore 'exposed Nepal as a semi-colonial country' (*Jana Jagriti* 17 Aug. 1986), since Gurkha blood was used to 'safeguard Britain's interests and its colonies' (*Achel* 14 Aug. 1986). The enlistment of Gurkhas represents the 'last vestiges of slavery, kept alive for the benefit of imperialist ruling classes' (*Mulyankan* 3 Sept. 1986), and is a 'curse of history' which 'enlightened Nepalis' have for a long time been seeking to abolish (*Matribhumi* 26 Aug. 1986). So the Tripartite agreement should be reviewed forthwith (*Naya Samaj* 13 Aug. 1986). Finally, the British have themselves decided that the end of colonialism has made the Gurkhas unnecessary, so their disgrace and discharge is one way of resolving the problem of Britain's Gurkha regiments (*Chalphal* 7 Aug. 1986).[41]

In a recent seminar on the Gurkha question held in Kathmandu (see Chapter 2, Note 20) many of these same points were raised, although in relation to the Indian as well as British armies. However, a number of former soldiers (and others whose family members had been in the Gurkhas) were present at the discussions and reminded the critics of military service in foreign armies that for members of certain ethnic communities there were few alternatives to such occupations. This underlines Enloe's general observation that the relatively low incidence of politicised opposition among 'ethnic soldiers' is attributable largely to 'the determining force of the conditions that led recruiters to rely on them in the first place: their lack of alternative livelihoods' (1980:38).

Any criticism of Britain's use of Gurkhas in politically sensitive situations has generally been treated contemptuously by British military writers. In a rare admission of doubt regarding the employment of Gurkhas to do Britain's bidding, Smith recalls a letter he wrote while a young officer in which he had questioned the 'readiness to sacrifice Gurkha soldiers in difficult tasks rather than [employ] British troops'. But with the hindsight provided by a long career in the Brigade, he goes on to wonder where he could possibly have obtained such an impression 'that Great Britain was exploiting the Gurkhas of Nepal' (1978:124). The censorious remarks of others are presented as 'hostile propaganda' whose intent is mischievous (Cross 1986:136), and the writers save some of their sharpest barbs for politicised Nepalis, usually the most educated and articulate members of high-caste elites, who of course do not provide Gurkha recruits (see Chapter 2). There is little attempt at understanding the depth of feeling in these sections of Nepalese society against the enlistment of Nepalis in foreign armies,[42] and a woeful absence of dialogue between them and British officers who produce the literature on Gurkhas.

The Bond of Trust

In the view of most military writers, it was above all their British officers to whom the Gurkhas gave their loyalty, and were content to follow the latter 'to hell and back' (Carew 1954:140; see also Candler 1919:9; Tuker 1950:626–27; Slim 1957:94). British officers in the Indian army had long believed it their inherent right and duty to lead native troops. General Jacob (who was for a time Aide-de-Camp to the Queen and the Governor-General of India) proclaimed, in the wake of the Mutiny, that Britain could only rule India because the European officer was a 'superior being by nature to the Asiatic' (Pelly 1858:427), while a half-century later Field Marshal Roberts was still insisting that an 'army of Asiatics ... must never be allowed to lose faith in the prestige or supremacy of the governing race.' (1897/1:434–5).

In time, this kind of triumphalist rhetoric gave way to one stressing the natural, organic ties 'between loyal and obedient sepoys and their enlightened and courageous British officers' (Peers 1991:547). It was to be expected, we are told by Mason, for the young recruit—following 'a deep and ancient tradition'—to transfer the allegiance he might have given to his village superior to a sympathetic British officer (1974:350). So that in 'memoir, poetry, and novel' the latter came to assume the responsibility for leading his 'gallant, trusting, if somewhat childlike Indian soldiers ...' (Greenhut 1984:15). The 'most remarkable feature' of the Indian army, according to one former Indian army officer, 'was surely the affinity between officers and men' (Goddard 1976:275).

Indeed, Saxena, in his history of the Indian army, insists that its success was assured as long as the officer-soldier tie was close and warm. He even suggests that the deterioration of the Bengal army prior to 1857 was largely due to the estrangement between officers and men. The relationship had grown to depend mainly on the 'cold authority of rules and regulations' rather than on 'mutual confidence and respect' (1974:16). One 'native officer', who served for 48 years (1812–1860) in the Bengal army, regretted that towards the end of his career, 'there were great changes in the *sahibs'* attitude towards us'. He thought that British chaplains were largely responsible for the deterioration in relations, although the Mutiny was obviously a contributory factor (see Lunt 1970:24–5).

The relationship between the Gurkha and his British officer receives continuous emphasis in the literature. Although Morris suggests that it is their 'innate laziness' which is 'partly responsible for the fact that most Gurkhas are content and in fact anxious to be led rather than to be leaders' (1935:437), this is very much a minority view. For the great majority of military writers the officer-rifleman tie is portrayed as a natural, even mystic bond (Niven 1987:70). According to Northey, 'the devotion and loyalty of the Gurkhas to their British officers are too well known to need enlarging on' (1937:98). We are told by one author that when the 'little highlanders' met the Company's British officers, that 'mutual respect and admiration was sparked off which was to burn as a steady flame for the next 150 years' (Bolt 1967:59). Another comments: 'It is no insignificant thing that the relations between the British [officer] and the Gurkha … have from the beginning exhibited the natural devotion of the men of both races for each other' (Tuker 1957:3). 'Both wholly benefit from their partnership in arms' (Adshead and Cross 1970:xvi).

Whatever the state of the relationship between the East India Company, later the Crown, and the Nepalese *durbar*, intense camaraderie is seen to have characterised the relationship between the Gurkhas and their British officers. In its recent report on the future of the Gurkhas, the British House of Commons Defence Committee refers to the 'unique bond of loyalty and friendship between Gurkhas and their British officers' (1989:x). Indeed, so natural was the link believed to be that its apparent absence could not fail to draw comment. Introducing the diaries of one officer who served with the 2GR, the editors feel compelled to remark that '[p]erhaps the most surprising thing to come through from the diaries is the comparative lack of rapport which he seems to have with his own soldiers, and the scant regard he sometimes displays for their welfare' (Chapple and Wood 1981:207).

To be members of a martial race, according to Enloe, entailed being dependant on ethnic outsiders for their officers (1980:29). The need for ethnic outsiders to command Gurkha troops was—according to British military writers—a consequence of the deficiency in Nepalese leadership qualities. This was evident during the Anglo-Nepal war of 1814–16. While the British were unstinting in their praise for the performance of the enemy in battle, military writers tended to lavish admiration differentially. It is conferred only upon the ordinary Nepalese soldiers. In their accounts of the war, they compare the Nepalese soldiers with native troops in the Indian army and find the former infinitely superior.[43] Moreover, admiration for the Nepalis is not unreciprocated: the *mutual* recognition of fighting qualities is noted again and again. The British, goes one frequently repeated comment by an (anonymous) Nepalese soldier, 'are very brave. Nearly as brave as us'. The Nepalis, we are told, 'obviously recognised a kindred spirit among the British officers' (James and Sheil-Small 1965:16; see also Bolt 1967:58). In a word, British officers and Gurkha soldiers are portrayed as having fallen instantly in love.

The Nepalese army's weak points, these writers claim, were its officers (see Vansittart 1915:42; Northey and Morris 1928:89). There may indeed have been valid grounds for judging Nepalese officers of the time as less able than some contemporary Indian army generals or even the military leaders of other armies on the sub-continent; Captain Cavenaugh (1851:13) of the Bengal Native Infantry, for example, rated Nepalese officers as inferior tacticians to those of the Sikh army. Still, such criticism of the Nepalese military leaders seems especially inappropriate considering the striking weakness of the British officer cadre in the initial phases of the war.

During the first several months of the campaign the Company met with reverses on every front, and Shaha attributes this as much to the incompetence of the British generals as to Nepalese courage (1983:3). Even Vansittart, regarded by many as the doyen of military authors on the Gurkhas, acknowledges that the war was 'very discreditable to the military abilities of our Generals' (1915:31). Pemble accounts for the Bengal army's poor performance partly in terms of the 'fatal deficiency' of its promotion system—by seniority and not by merit—which resulted in an aged and cumbersome senior-officer cadre (1971:353).

In their assessments of the Nepalese army's leadership, writers on the Gurkhas employ not so much military criteria, as those based on natural qualities. This is in keeping with a conviction that was widespread in India by the early nineteenth century, which held that only members of certain races were capable of command. Lord Roberts of Kandahar articulated this view very succinctly:

> ... history and experience teach us that eastern races (fortunately for us), however brave and accustomed to war, do not possess the qualities that go to make leaders of men, and Native officers in this respect can never take the place of British officers ... I have never known [a native] ... who would not have looked to the youngest British officer for support in time of difficulty and danger (Roberts 1897/2:444).

The Nepalis, therefore, would only realise their enormous potential under the tutelage, supervision and leadership of British officers. Shortly after the Anglo-Nepal war, the Nepalese government actually offered to place units of its own army—with its own officers—at the disposal of the Company, but the British refused, and insisted on recruiting only ordinary riflemen who would be commanded by British officers. The need for British officers was, moreover, apparent not only to the British, but (in the view of these military writers) to the ordinary troops in the Nepalese army from the very beginning. This is expressed clearly in what can be regarded as the founding myth of the British officer-Gurkha soldier bond.

The central event takes place during the Anglo-Nepal war. It focuses on a British officer, Lieutenant (later General) Frederick Young, who subsequently came to be regarded as the 'father' of the Brigade of Gurkhas. Lieutenant Young, at the head of a column of some 2,000 native Indian troops, is sent to intercept a force of Nepalese soldiers on their way to relieve the besieged Nepalese fort at Jythuk. Although there are only two hundred of them, the Nepalis attack and disperse the larger group under the British. Young and several of his officer colleagues find themselves alone, their own native troops having fled in disarray. They look up and see the Nepalese soldiers surrounding them. The Nepalis ask Young: 'Why did you not run away too?' Young looks at them with his 'fearless Irish eyes', and answers: 'I have not come so far in order to run away. I come to stop.' And he sits down. This wins the hearts of these 'merry men of the Nepalese hills', who reply: 'Ah, you are brave men. We could serve *under* men like you' (my emphasis). Lieutenant Young is then taken captive, and the Nepalis 'treat him well and teach him their language'. Thus, what begins as mutual recognition of fighting abilities is very soon transformed into an acknowledgement of hierarchy: the British to lead and the Nepalis to be led. The story is retold almost verbatim in numerous books about the Gurkhas (see, for example, Tuker 1957:86; Bredin 1961:21; Bolt 1967:60; Bishop 1976:26–7; Chant 1985:22).[44]

A recurrent theme is the warmth of feeling on the part of officers for their soldiers. The ideal chivalrous officer 'saw that his men were looked after before thinking of himself' (Girouard 1981:260). For officers who served with Gurkhas the relationship was thought to have a special significance because 'our soldiers were much more different to ourselves than other soldiers in the British army were to their officers', as one ex-officer put it. It is a frequently expressed belief that regimental officers got to know their men intimately. They spent so much time with their *mukhs* (faces/chaps) that 'they became half-Gurkhas themselves, fluent in their language .... often sharing the same curry ... they had become an integral part of the happy band of brothers' (Bolt 1967:114–15).

On a typical day, I was told by one officer who joined the 7GR in the mid-1960s, 'you would lead them in P.T., then some instruction, then later play volleyball, football or basketball with them. New officers were encouraged to spend time off duty with their men. After a game you sat down and had a beer with them. This is the time you learned about their culture, songs or dances. I had a lot of that'. Another officer who joined the same regiment at around the same time was told that he was expected not to marry until his second leave (six or seven years after joining). 'As it happens I didn't get married until I was in my thirties, probably typical of my generation. It meant that in the evening we came home from work, got into our sports kit, had a cup of tea, and then back down to the company to join in a game with the men. Then afterwards a few drinks'.

In battle situations, the attention of all officers, whether married or not, was focused exclusively on their men. 'On operations in the jungle, when we weren't doing anything in particular we would chat about a lot of things, and get to know them as individuals. All these forms of contact were beneficial to the relationship between officer and soldier'. Some regimental officers became avid 'collectors' of the customs, folklore, religious views, festivals and histories of their men. Without access to the country itself, they relied entirely on their own observations and the data gathered from soldiers under their command for their ethnographic knowledge.[45]

The rise of the career officer is seen to have altered the quality of the bond, since he is too busy going on courses and secondment in pursuit of his ambition to bother unduly about his relationship with the men. During an interview one serving officer mused that some of his colleagues decide to leave the army because the opportunities for getting to know the men are 'fewer nowadays than in the past when they would have spent weeks in a jungle ambush together'. Ultimately, of course, the hierarchical chasm—military, political, social and cultural—between officer and Gurkha could not be denied. Mason notes that between people so different there could be courtesy, kindliness and liking, but no dealing on equal terms. The relationship was paternal, and accepted as such on both sides. There was no thought of equality (quoted in Parry 1972:51).[46]

Despite their insistence on the *mutual* respect obtaining between Briton and Nepali, the Gurkhas are portrayed as admiring quite different qualities in their officers than do the latter in their Gurkhas. 'How does a Gurkha see his British Officer?' asks one military author. As a 'fair-minded, professional soldier' with 'breadth of vision' who 'can be implicitly trusted in all matters … Gurkhas marvel at their officers' compassion and their sincerity' (Cross 1985:31). The few comments I heard from former soldiers about their British officers mainly concerned the latters' height, colour, diet and education. For these ex-Gurkhas the officer seemed to be an icon, distanced by rank, mess life, wealth and cultural background, and therefore without individual foibles and character.

A constant refrain in these writings is the unwillingness of the Gurkha sol-dier to be commanded by other than British officers. 'The idea of military service under Indians [was] unacceptable to these men ...' (Tuker 1950:626). British officers, writes one Indian military historian, 'were firmly of the opin-ion that only they could successfully officer Gurkha regiments; that Gurkhas would never serve under Indian officers' (Proudfoot 1984:26).[47] The division of Gurkha regiments between the armies of Britain and newly-independent India in 1947 may therefore be seen as a test of this assumption.

Defiant Gurkhas

A referendum was held after the Independence of India, among the men belonging to the four regiments assigned to the British army to determine if they wished to remain with their regiments (and British officers), to trans-fer to another regiment assigned to the Indian army (with Indian officers), or go on discharge. The outcome was that a significant majority of the men in these regiments opted to transfer to the Indian army, although the pro-portions varied in each battalion. Farwell states that in one battalion of the 7GR only fifty-seven men elected to stay (1984:262). According to an Indian military historian all but a handful of men in the 1/6GR elected to remain in India (Praval 1987:129), while another insists that as many as ninety per cent of those who had the option chose to 'serve India' (Proud-foot 1984:27).

On the basis of (incomplete) official figures Des Chene calculates that only about one-third of Gurkhas eligible to vote decided to stay with the British army (1991:206, fn 61). I have seen no precise figures on the out-come of the 'opt' in the British military literature. Smith comments that in one or two battalions 'the number of men who opted for service with HMG was surprisingly low ...' (1973:146), while Tuker calls the result 'dismal' (1950:639). These authors have explained the result of the referendum in various ways: that (a) British authorities were slow to formulate their con-ditions of service whereas the Indian army made their terms clear early on; (b) there was a great deal of propaganda and disinformation from the new Indian political leadership; (c) pressure was exerted on the men by Gurkha officers (VCOs) who had decided to join the Indian army; (d) where a bat-talion was stationed, or what its military role was at the time of the opt influenced the vote; (e) the prospect of having to move to Malaya was a dis-incentive; and so on. Whatever the reasons, Proudfoot (1984:27) is no doubt right in saying that the result of the vote came as a 'rude shock' to the

British military authorities, and to the long-held conviction that Gurkhas would only ever agree to be led by British officers. He is echoed by Praval: '[The British officers] had come to believe in the myth, largely of their own creation, that the Gorkhas were in the Indian Army only on account of them' (1987:128).

The Hawaii incident some forty years later (see above) would also appear at first glance to throw doubt on the much vaunted link between the Gurkha and his British officer. Indeed, the official reason given for the dismissal of almost an entire company was that as a result of the assault on an officer and the men's refusal to cooperate with the inquiry there had been 'a total breakdown in trust between these Gurkhas and their officers. The bond of trust is broken, they have to go'.[48]

In the view of the majority of officers with whom I discussed the 'Hawaii affair' there could not have been a great deal of trust existing in the first place, since the British officer at the centre of events was not a 'real Gurkha'. He had only been on temporary secondment to the regiment and therefore (obviously) could not possibly have established the necessary rapport with the men. The general consensus among the British officers I spoke to was that the problem, as one expressed it, 'stemmed from the fact that he came from a British regiment, did not speak the language, and did not understand that we do things differently in the Brigade of Gurkhas.' It is essential, I was told, that if an officer is seconded to a Gurkha regiment, he is counselled to take the advice of his senior Gurkha officer, and carefully supervised by regular regimental officers to make sure he is not doing things the men do not like. This clearly had not happened in Hawaii. Thus, for these officers the principal issue at stake was the specific competence required to relate properly to Gurkhas, which gift only someone nurtured in a Gurkha regiment could hope to acquire. If the tie had broken down, the fault lay with the officer who was *in* but not *of* the Gurkhas.

Several Indreni residents—serving (on leave) and ex-soldiers, though none of them personally involved—with whom I raised the matter during my visit to Ilam in 1988, some eighteen months after these events had taken place, stressed two quite different themes. One was that the Nepalis had been humiliated by the British officer concerned. No one seemed to know, and certainly no one mentioned, that he was on secondment to the regiment. For these soldiers it was enough that he was a British officer. He 'used swear words' against the Gurkhas, I was told, and 'put them *down*' (the English word was used). '"You are beggars, you come here because you have not got enough to eat", he said. The boys were not happy about it, and spoke back in anger, and made trouble. They beat him. Whoever is put down will be angry. If you come here and I put you down will you be angry or not?'

The second was the severity of the punishment—discharge—for what they regarded as a not very serious offence, and the consequent loss of income and benefits. While no attempt was made to excuse the attack on military superiors, the consensus was that the army did wrong to send the men back. 'It should have been settled internally (i.e. within the regiment) and some punishment given, but not to send them back like that, so that they lost everything'. Discharge in such circumstances was not regarded as a humiliation, but was viewed as a tragedy for those concerned since they were made to forfeit a secure future. Parenthetically, I would add that the majority were dismissed because they chose—or possibly were cajoled—to close ranks and not inform on one another. They thereby followed a code which most British officers themselves would have recognised and upheld.

Morris acknowledged that even by the time he came to serve in the Gurkhas (just after the First World War) this assumed loyalty of men to their British officers no longer survived, and all that remained was a 'pathetic tendency to believe in a loyalty that did not exist' (1960:125). Another officer who joined the Gurkhas on an emergency commission during the Second World War had similar doubts about the tie which, he surmised, 'did not go so deep as many of us liked to think' (Davis 1970:106). But these were rare admissions, not shared by the great majority of British officers. It is clear from the literature, as from the above comments by contemporary and recently retired British officers that belief in the 'bond of trust' endures, although the evidence suggests that Gurkhas themselves understand the relationship in quite different terms.

Conclusion

The application of martial theory to people inhabiting the middle hills of Nepal presented military authors with certain difficulties. The area was settled by ethnically and linguistically-diverse populations, occupying different locations in a national caste hierarchy, and distinguished internally in terms of numerous economic and cultural criteria. There was the potential problem, therefore, of assuming that these various groups and classes constituted a single social category. But the problem remained at the analytical level, and was more apparent than real. On the whole, most military authors disregarded this heterogeneity in their assumptions about the uniformity of Gurkha customs and traditions, and of course in their stereotypes of Gurkha character traits.

Most significantly, differences were rendered insignificant by the premise of a common 'biology' which transmitted the collective martial inheritance.

There was an alternative predilection on the part of some military authors to postulate rigid (and biologically given) 'tribal' divisions, each with distinctive traditions, beliefs and practices, where in fact historical realities suggested permeable boundaries, both physical and socio-cultural (see Chapter 2). But what disparities were deemed to exist were ultimately mitigated by Indian army policies which integrated several such units into a single battalion, created strong regimental cultures (along British military lines), and fostered the use of a single *lingua franca* ('Gurkhali' as they referred to Nepali) throughout the Brigade.

The rhetoric of martiality embraces an idealised notion of manliness. Dawson has drawn attention to the durability of the image within western cultural traditions of the soldier as paragon of masculinity. In the Indian context this ideal 'became intimately bound up with … the imagining of imperial identity, in which the Englishman enjoyed a natural, racial superiority over the … peoples who had been subordinated to British imperial power' (1991:119). The representation of Gurkhas by their British chroniclers in strongly masculine terms may be seen therefore as a recognition in the Gurkhas of those very qualities which enabled the British to fashion an empire. The Gurkhas' manly qualities—robust, sturdy figures, and proud, independent natures—are consistently emphasised, moreover, by contrast to the supine, dependent, and ultimately 'feminine' Indians of the plains. Roland, following Nandy, has argued that this heightened stress on Indian 'femininitiy' may have been a way of 'projecting the rejected parts of British male personality onto those Indians who had most challenged the raj' (1988:19).

In their portrayal of the 'mystic bond' between British officers and their Gurkhas, the military authors endeavour to preserve the memory of a relationship which no longer exists, if indeed it ever did. In the context of the inevitable advance of the army careerist, who has so little time for the ordinary soldier, they inscribe an image of the ideal regimental officer, who knew his men personally and cared passionately about them. In these writings, a recurrent theme is the warmth of feeling between Briton and Gurkha. Indeed, it is precisely the social and cultural gulf between officer and soldier which this rhetoric attempts symbolically to bridge. It is one way of dealing with what Burke calls the 'mystery of courtship' between persons of widely different stations (1969 [1950]:208; see also Empson 1935). And following Burke, Rosaldo refers to this way of representing subordinates as the 'pastoral mode', which conveys a 'peculiar civility' and 'tender courtesy' in relationships that cross social boundaries (1986:97).

The military authors appear to transcend the hierarchical gulf separating officers from men, Britons from Nepalis, but in the end, the pastoral mode 'reveals inequalities and domination' (ibid.). But the domination of European officers is mitigated through affection—'the flow of warmth and protective love from the superior to the inferior'—and this blend of dominance and affection produces the characteristic attitude towards the pet (see Tuan 1984:162–3). Seen as gestures of affection bestowed by superiors on inferiors, these representations therefore fostered and reinforced the view that it was part of the natural order for the British to rule, provided that the rule was benevolent, and equally natural for colonial peoples (including Nepalis) to be ruled (ibid.:174).

Alternative discourses on Gurkhas emanate both from sections of Nepalese society historically excluded from the Gurkha project and from the Gurkhas themselves. As for the former, hitherto muted by the circumstances of their position both within a pseudo-colonial polity ruled by an autocratic and conservative regime, Nepalese intellectuals have recently focused on the Gurkhas as a symbol of neo-colonial and dependent status in respect of both Britain (and the West in general) and India. Their discourses defy the monopoly of knowledge about Gurkhas held for so long by the British, but these exist, as does Nepal itself, only in the political margins. Regarding the Gurkhas themselves, their challenges to the dominant military knowledge system have, for obvious reasons, surfaced into public awareness only sporadically, and reveal concerns and priorities at odds with what we have come to expect. The 'opt' and the Hawaii incident—as non-discursive modes of defiance—suggest that the Gurkhas themselves experience and understand their military worlds somewhat differently than their British chroniclers (and the Nepalese intellectuals) often assert on their behalf.

Notes to Chapter 4

1. This four-fold ideal hierarchy of functions comprises the Brahman (Priests), Kshatriya (Warriors), Vaishya (Merchants) and Sudra (Menials).

2. Mason suggests that nine out of ten British officers—and 'perhaps more'—thought as Roberts did (1974:348).

3. In a later publication, MacMunn asserted that the martial people of the north, if left alone, would devour the non-martial South, so he concluded that Britain had 'just as much right to rule in India as any other of the conquering races that form the martial classes' (1932:353).

4. General Sir O'Moore Creagh was Commander-in-Chief of the Indian army from 1909–1914. His book, *Indian Studies* was published shortly after the end of the First World War.

5. Date, in his study of warfare in ancient India, utilises a similar climatic hypothesis. He argues that one of the causes of India's 'military disasters' was the 'uninvigorating climate' which made the people 'indolent', so that invaders from the cold regions of central Asia 'put down the slow-moving warriors of the sunny plains of India' (1929:84).

6. According to *Dibya Upadesh*, Prithvi Narayan at first planned to include Brahmans among the warriors for his attack on the Valley, but his uncle advised him that if he did so, there would be 'sin everywhere' (Stiller 1989 [1968]:40). Thereafter, Brahmans were not included in his fighting *jat*.

7. See *Regmi Research Series*, Vol. 16, 1984, pp11–12. Chakravarti argues that Brahmans served as soldiers and commanders of armies in ancient India and were frequently represented as such in the epic literature (1941:78–9). Bingley and Nicholls show (1918:8–10) that the Bengal army had all along included many Brahmans, a fact of which the Nepalis would certainly have been aware. It is of course possible that while Brahmans were not compelled to bear arms in Nepal, many in fact did so.

8. Major C. Reid to Captain Norman, Deputy Adjutant-General of the Army, 5 August 1857 (*Letter Books*).

9. Several military authors did manage to visit Nepal at the invitation of the Rana Prime Ministers, but they were mainly restricted to the Kathmandu Valley.

10. This assignment of stereotypes was not only a military preoccupation. Colonial writers of fiction, like Henty, purveyed similar views of 'Easterners' and 'natives' (Green 1980:221).

11. Vansittart (1894) is somewhat contradictory in his discussion of recruitment policy. On the one hand, he identifies Khas, Thakuris, Magars and Gurungs as the 'military tribes ... from which the fighting element in our army is almost exclusively drawn' (p.215), but he then notes that 'none of our Gurkha regiments enlist Khas now ...' (p.220). In his revised 'Notes on Recruiting' Thakurs and Khas are again labelled as 'classes enlisted' (Vansittart 1915).

12. The Gujars of north India were apparently also deemed 'somewhat quarrelsome' (see Omissi 1991:17).

13. 'Western' regiments, in which Magars and Gurungs predominated, were the 1GR, 2GR, 3GR, 4GR, 5GR, 6GR and 8GR. Khas (Chetris) and Thakuris from various parts of the middle hills were recruited into the 9GR.

14. The problem of 'passing' occupied the attention of British officers for many years. In June, 1858 the commander of the Sirmoor Battalion complained to the Deputy Adjutant-General of the Army that some of his officers 'from want of knowledge' had enlisted many men 'who call themselves 'Goorkahs', but who are nothing of the kind ...' (*Letter Books*). Half a century later, Vansittart cautioned recruiters to exercise care in the selection of Thapas (a Magar sub-division) as 'a very large number of men adopt the title of Thapa, although they have no right to the same' (1915:86). Similarly, Morris warned that (non-martial) Thakalis try to pass as (martial) Magars or Gurungs (1933:76).

15. Nicolay later advised British recruiters not to take this prohibition 'too seriously' (Vansittart 1915:172).

16. This attitude, however, gradually changed and the latest handbook announces that settlements of Gurungs and Magars in eastern Nepal 'produce some excellent recruits' (Leonard 1965:140).

17. This was a common feature of Indian army handbooks. That on the Sikhs graded areas for the purpose of recruiting as Very Good, Good, Fair, Poor, Bad, and Very Bad (Mason 1974:354).

18. Major C. Reid to Major Norman, 25 January, 1858 (*Letter Books*).

19. Lieutenant-Colonel D. Macintyre, CO 2GR to Adjutant-General, 1 February, 1878 (*Letter Books*).

20. The same prejudice applied to Muslims in north India, who would not be recruited if they lived in towns. Omissi points to the irony of declaring such men to make poor soldiers when they could not be enlisted in the first place (1991:10).

21. Cohen suggests that the theory of martiality is still 'widespread' in independent India (1971:47). Though officially discredited, it appears to survive in how its soldiers are organised and portrayed. Not only are they still grouped in ethnic regiments, but military authors continue to list the special qualities of each, using terms made familiar by the British (see, for example, Das 1984).

22. The portrayal of many Hindu deities as androgynous or female is also a theme in the writings of modern Indologists—indigenous and foreign—although without the pejorative emphasis of earlier writers. Kakar has recently described Hindu cosmology as 'feminine to an extent rarely found in other major civilizations' and advances the argument that the Hindu male has a strong identification with his mother and so a 'maternal-feminine' stance towards the world (1978:109–10).

23. Daniell informs us that between 1890 and 1900 over half the more than 100 magazines founded offered boys' adventure tales (1983:119–20).

24. Kabbani (1986:9) quotes Richard Burton, who served for a time in the Indian army, on the Sindhis: '[They are] notoriously cowardly in times of danger …'.

25. The Frontispiece of Woodyatt's (1922) book on the Gurkhas contains a photograph of a British Gurkha General dressed (presumably for a costume party) as a 'Native Clerk', with *dhoti* and *kurta*, waistcoat, turban and umbrella. The resident British community of the period would immediately have recognised the stereotype, and no doubt found it immensely amusing.

26. For Kipling, they were akin to monkeys, who are neither hunters nor carnivores, the true marks of an imperial species. In a fascinating observation on his animal stories, MacKenzie suggests that, when describing monkeys, 'Kipling was thinking of the Bengalee Baboo, imitative educated Indians, but still vegetarian Hindus, whom he so disliked …' (1989:169).

27. In his study of masculinity, Seidler points out that masculine language is seen as 'deeply instrumental' (1989:63).

28. This contrasts with the British historian Landon's acceptance of the Residency's perspective on the masculine nature of Nepal and the Nepalese. 'The special merits of the Gurkha as a soldier consist in the unextinguishable devotion to the art of fighting for its own sake, the readiness with which discipline and hardship are accepted … War is the only sport as well as the only work worthy of a man's attention …' (1928/1:193).

29. 'The Nuer is a product of hard and egalitarian upbringing, is deeply democratic and is easily roused to violence. His turbulent spirit finds any restraint irksome, and no man recognises a superior' (Evans-Pritchard 1940:181). With only slight modifications, the foregoing passage about these East African pastoralists might have been written by a military author about the Nepalis enlisted as Gurkhas.

30. Des Chene cites some of the correspondence between Delhi, London and Kathmandu during this century which makes clear Britain's determination to retain Nepal's compliance with her policies (1991:153–58).

31. The same remark appears in *Notes for Officers* (p.11A–1) currently used to familiarise new officers in the 2GR with their Gurkha soldiers.

32. This is the very expression Vansittart had earlier used to describe the Gurungs and Magars.

33. British officers with whom I discussed the stereotype of the 'thick' Gurkha were quick to deny it. One pointed out that in his time Gurkhas had to take their exams in Urdu, 'which was more than we officers could do'. Another suggested that while he had met a few 'thick' Gurkhas during his years of service, he could tell 'as many tales that show them clever and cunning, in the old English sense of the word'. A third suggested that the officers were themselves responsible for embellishing the portrait, but 'no harm done, and there were some jolly good jokes to be told'.

34. Making the point more generally, Cohen (1971:51) observes that 'Ideological considerations rarely interfered, as the groups recruited into the [Indian army] were from the politically most backward regions of India—another reason why they were desirable to the British'.

35. The officers commanding Indian Gorkha regiments have, since Independence, tended to employ a similar rhetoric in written comments on their soldiers. Gorkhas are 'simple souls' and there is 'tremendous patriotism and love for India in every Gorkha breast' (Singh 1952:16).

36. Since Independence, the Indian government has, of course, utilised its own Gorkhas in both internal and international conflicts. Both Pakistan and China have expressed their displeasure to Nepal over the use of these troops in their wars against India (see Muni 1973:123, 173).

37. The British insist that the latest Nepal-India-Britain Tripartite agreement allowing recruitment does not 'impose any significant restriction on the employment of Gurkhas in the British Army' (House of Commons 1989:XX).

38. In the view of some critics, allowing Gurkhas to be recruited into the British army contributes nothing to Nepal's own defence, whereas independent India, which now also recruits soldiers from Nepal, has undertaken to meet Nepal's military needs regarding defence production, army transport planes, civil supplies and training facilities (Muni 1973:20).

39. The incident occurred at the end of May, 1986 but was only reported in the British and Nepalese press in August when the decision to discharge the men was announced. See *Daily Telegraph* 5 Aug., 6 Aug., 18 Aug. 1986; *The Times* 5 Aug., 6 Aug., 12 Aug., 13 Aug., 15 Aug. 1986; *Guardian Weekly* 10 Aug., 17 Aug., 24 Aug. 1986. The discharge of twelve men was apparently rescinded (see House of Commons 1989:xxxvi).

40. The official government of Nepal view, it seems, was that this was a 'matter of internal discipline for the British army' (*The Times* 12 Aug. 1986).

41. A digest of press comments appears in *Nepal Press Digest*, August-September, 1986.

42. A recent musical play produced in Kathmandu is said to have 'evoked strong responses from the audience for its emotionally charged messages against recruitment into foreign armies' (Pahari 1991:12).

43. Peers draws attention to the British military accounts of the Anglo-Burma war a decade later, which went on much longer than originally anticipated, due, it was claimed, to the failings of the Bengal army sepoys who were accused of being frightened of the Burmese soldiers opposing them (1991:559).

44. The origins of the story appear to be relatively recent. Prinsep (1825), in his history of the war, recounts the defeat of the Indian army at Jythuk and Young's participation in the battle, but there is no mention of the episode featured in this story. It is not recorded in Shakespear's and Stevens's (1912) history of the 2GR, nor is it reported in Vansittart's handbook of 1915, a key source for so much of the later writing, although he too mentions the defeat of Young's irregulars by a small Nepalese contingent (1915:31). As far as I can make out,

it appears for the first time in print in a biography of Young by his daughter, published over a century following the war (Jenkins 1923).

45. It was not until the 1950s that Nepal was opened to the outside world, and British officers, like other foreigners, allowed to visit those parts of the country from which their soldiers originated.

46. One additional reflection of this hierarchy was the absence of social contact between British and Nepalese wives (Morris 1960:100).

47. The Commander-in-Chief of the Indian army prior to the First World War was of the opinion that even Indian soldiers would much prefer serving under British than Indian officers on the grounds that a person of 'one Indian race' would or even could not 'deal out even-handed justice' to the member of another (Creagh n.d.:274).

48. *The Times* 5 Aug. 1986.

················

CHAPTER 5

COURAGEOUS GURKHAS
The Making of Warrior Gentlemen

Bravest of the brave, most generous of the generous,
never had country more faithful friends than you.

Professor Sir Ralph Turner *Nepali Dictionary*, 1931.

Introduction

That the Gurkhas constitute a martial race is above all demonstrated by their bravery in battle. For many people, Gaborieau points out, the Nepalis *are* 'les féroces Gurkhas' (1978:7). While the soldier as hero has become part of the West's most salient image of masculinity, the Gurkha may be said to represent its exemplar of instinctive courage. Unburdened by intelligence or education, which conduce only to cowardice in non-western peoples—and especially in Hindus inhabiting the plains of India—the Gurkhas possess those ingredients of character which, in the view of their officers and chroniclers, produce the consummate hero. But, while all martial peoples are brave, by definition, Gurkhas have certain additional qualities which are quintessentially those of their officers, and thus constitute them not simply as warriors, but as men of breeding and refinement as well. This chapter first examines the manner in which Gurkha bravery is represented in the military literature, then turns to those depictions which imagine them as gentlemen.

Before indicating how Gurkha courage is portrayed, it might be useful to consider briefly the notion of 'courage' in western thought generally, and western military thought in particular.

The Concept of Courage

Western philosophy seems to have identified two principal types of courage. The first, following Aristotle, sees it as an outcome of reflection and quiet acts of high principle. In Aristotle's ethical theory (concerned with qualities of noble character or personal excellence) courage, like all virtues, is defined as a mean or moderation between extremes of conduct, between excessive fear and excessive confidence, and its exercise earns personal merit (Walton 1986:9–11). Aristotle, Aquinas and some more recent philosophers also stress a good end, a noble purpose, for an act to be regarded as courageous. Facing danger for a worthless cause is not regarded as either virtuous or courageous (ibid.:52). So in the Aristotelian view, the mercenary soldier who fights with skill but for no noble purpose is not acting with courage (ibid.:62).[1]

Aristotle's insistence on thoughtful, practical deliberation as a distinguishing feature of the truly courageous, excludes the act of a person who is driven by passion. Yet the popular view of courage is that it is a bold and passionate response to danger rather than the outcome of calculated reflection. This passionate model of courage found its exponents in Carlyle and Nietzsche who adopted a 'heroic vitalism constructed around a courageous hero of lightning and frenzy, a man of bold actions …' (ibid.:34). So whereas the former view emphasised moderation, caution, reflection and temperate practical judgement, these nineteenth-century philosophers equated courageous action with intuition and stressed speed and boldness. Walton calls this the 'barbaric view of courage', which is typified by violent acts of bloodshed perpetrated in rage or revenge (ibid.:40). On this basis he suggests a distinction between actions which are *courageous* in the Aristotelian sense and those which, following Carlyle and Nietzsche, are *brave* (ibid.:99).[2]

Walton also suggests that Kantian philosophy seems to find courage a difficult concept. Where what matters is doing one's duty, courage, which consists in going beyond one's duty—performing a supererogatory act—constitutes morally indifferent behaviour. Hence a preoccupation with the requirements of duty has eclipsed such acts as a subject of importance to some western moral philosophers. They are seen as matters of personal rather than public standards (ibid.:15–16, 21, 41).

This contrasts with certain traditional Indian ideas about courage, which recognise it not only as a virtue, but as a natural duty (*dharma*) attaching to the status of the Kshatriya, or Warrior 'caste', and most especially to that of the king. Ancient texts, says Chakravarti, stress 'times without number' that fighting constitutes one of the essential functions of the king. The warrior who gains victory attains fame and glory in earthly life, while defeat and death in battle result in transportation 'straightaway to heaven' (1941:181–84). According to the Sukraniti, a noble death is earned by the Kshatriya who has met enemies on the battlefield and is 'well pierced with arms and missiles' (Oppert 1880:125). Nothing is deemed more worthy than heroism: 'The hero protects all, in a hero all is fixed' (ibid.:126–7). In one of the most famous scenes in the Mahabharata, when the epic battle is about to begin, Arjuna the great warrior discovers that he must kill members of his family and others close to him, and refuses to fight. Krishna seeks to persuade him of his duty:

> Happy the warriors indeed
> Who become involved in war …
> But, if thou wilt not wage this war
> Prescribed by thy duty
> Then, by casting off both honour and duty
> Thou wilt bring evil on thyself …
> [D]ishonour in a man well-trained to honour
> [Is an ill] surpassing death.
> (Zaehner 1966:257).

Krishna thus shows Arjuna not only that he cannot escape his duty, but by performing it achieves salvation (Biardeau 1989:115).

Military Perspectives on Courage

Tillich reminds us that both the Greek and Latin words for courage indicate its military origins in western thought, and that it was only when the aristocratic tradition disintegrated that courage came also to assume the wider connotation of 'wisdom', distinct from the soldier's courage (1984 [1952]:17). For military authors terms like courage and bravery are very much martial concepts, but despite their prolific employment, are seldom explored. Thus, although his biography of General Rollo Gillespie (who was killed during the Anglo-Nepal War) is entitled *The Bravest Soldier*, Wakeham nowhere explicitly considers how his subject might earn such an appellation. At times it would appear to refer to Gillespie's skills as a commander and tactician, at other times to his abilities as a swordsman (on one occasion Gillespie is reported to have killed six intruders at his house), his confrontation with a tiger, even his success with the opposite sex (Wakeham 1937). This is not too surprising since soldiers regard themselves as men of action and readily admit that they are not prone to 'intellectual inquisitiveness' (Baynes 1967:131). Nor is it fair to expect military men to ponder the topic of courage when neither philosophers nor psychologists have given it much attention.

Baynes is one of the few modern military writers to touch on the subject. In his study of 'morale', he argues that prior to the First World War patriotism flourished, and goes on to link feelings of patriotism and the cult of sport and bodily fitness among officers (1967:220; see also Chapter 3). Baynes then stresses the link between the latter and courage. Indeed, the two concepts are frequently perceived as two aspects of a single quality. He writes that 'there is a national admiration for physical stamina and physical courage' (ibid.:119), and again that officers have 'admiration for physical strength and courage' and are almost all 'brave and fit' (ibid.:131). Still, the notion of bravery itself is not scrutinised.

Recent research based on (US) Medal of Honor citations over the past century has identified a number of pragmatic dimensions of heroism. This has encouraged Anderson, a psychologist and officer in the US Army, to argue that the hero has 'certain measurable characteristics that distinguish him from common humanity' (1986:604). These include devotion to duty, personal example, accepting danger, overcoming injury, etc. Another study utilising the same data attempts to relate unit cohesion and altruistic ('heroic') suicide in battle, and provides support for an organisational as opposed to an individual approach to the topic (Blake 1987). Both studies aim for an 'operational' definition, omitting ideological and moral aspects which underlie most philosophical discussions.

British officers with the Gurkhas find the views of Field Marshall Sir William Slim more to their taste. Slim served with the Gurkhas and later commanded British forces in Burma during the Second World War, in which campaign several Gurkha regiments took part. In a radio broadcast, which was later published, he set out to examine the idea of courage based on his experiences during the war (1957). For Slim, courage is not merely one virtue among many; it is *the* virtue, the *most prized* virtue of a man. He distinguishes two kinds of courage: one, moral courage, which he does not explictly define, is regarded as a 'higher and rarer' virtue (ibid.:6). This cannot be taught, but is learned from parents, homes, schools, universities, religion. It is a 'long-term' virtue, and not all 'races' possess it: only 'certain lands' where nature is neither too easy nor too cruel breed courage as a 'national tradition'. The British certainly have it; the Japanese apparently do not (remember, he was speaking/writing just after the end of the Second World War). Moreover, this courage arises from a high moral purpose, a 'belief that we worked or fought for the things that mattered ...' (ibid.:12).

We have here two key aspects of martial theory discussed in Chapter 4: firstly, the idea that this kind of courage is a 'racial' and not an individual matter, and therefore is inherited in the blood; and secondly, like martiality, it can only flourish in particular climatic or environmental conditions. Moreover, although Slim does not specifically say so, moral courage tends towards the Aristotelian, and it is what the British officer would appear to possess in abundance; indeed, it is part of what defines him. Baynes also suggests that the officers' whole background and upbringing might have been designed to instill courage in them. The 'traditions of their class, the training in their homes and at their schools, and the conventions of their Regimental life all subscribed to make [them] brave ... to ensure that they never let the side down; these were their most cherished desires. Though the odd one might fail the test of battle, most were ideally conditioned to pass it with credit' (1967:197). Indeed, courage is deemed to be so natural a part of the officer's persona that at first the idea of introducing medals for gallantry was opposed, since it was considered inappropriate to award men for displaying the very quality they were expected to possess by virtue of their rank (Heathcote 1974:153). Ultimately, then, moral courage is the patrimony of a particular class.

Keegan's discussion of the British officer at the beginning of the nineteenth century conveys something of the meaning of this kind of courage. Officers were most of all concerned with the 'figure they cut' in their brother officers' eyes, and a prodigious accumulation of wounds often demonstrated courage. Courage bestowed honour, and when an officer, knowing full well that to obey an order meant 'going upon his death' still did so, he displayed the epitome of honourable conduct. It was 'by establishing one's honourableness with one's fellows that leadership was exerted indirectly over the common soldiers' (1976:191–2). This idea of martial self-sacrifice persisted throughout the Victorian and Edwardian periods. According to Mangan, the foremost image of the public school boy fostered by imperial propagandists (who included many school headmasters) was the 'warrior-patriot'. His purpose was 'noble and sacrificial—to fight and die for England's greatness overseas' (1986:122).

Another, less noble, kind of courage is physical courage, which Slim describes as an 'emotional state'. Such a view would appear to accord with the Carlyle-Nietzsche conception: the unthinking man's bravery. Thus, while it requires the appropriate upbringing to acquire moral courage, anyone (including officers)—given the appropriate conditions—can be brave. General Rollo Gillespie, who was killed at Kalunga during the Anglo-Nepal War of 1814–16, apparently made a not dissimilar distinction between 'cool and deliberate valour' and 'wild and precipitate courage', with the former much preferred to the latter (Wakeham 1937:256). For Slim, those who perform individual acts of the highest physical courage are either those with 'quick intelligence and vivid imagination', or are 'without imagination and with minds fixed on the practical business of living' (1957:7). It is interesting that Slim's principal example of the latter is a Gurkha who received the Victoria Cross (VC) for destroying an enemy tank from close range while suffering from multiple wounds. The Gurkha is said to have explained that he had been trained not to fire the weapon until he was certain of scoring a hit and so approached to within a few yards of the enemy tank. In the Gurkha, then, intrepid obedience to commands always outweighs a sense of danger, and numerous facetious stories are told (and re-told) in the military literature about the Gurkhas' inadvertent bravery in the course of carrying out orders or following instructions.

In the literature on Gurkhas, it is overwhelmingly the conception of courage as an act of passion which prevails. Most descriptions of Gurkha courage in combat conform to the model of the soldier who attacks in a violent frenzy, risking almost certain death to rush forward and kill the enemy. Walton notes how citations of heroism are usually filled with claims to 'derring-do … reminiscent of the best juvenile comic-book language'. For Walton, this demeans courage as a moral quality (1986:39).

The representation of physical courage raises questions concerning the status of fear as an ingredient of such action. Keegan (1976:70) quotes a mid-nineteenth century French infantry officer (du Picq) who suggested that men fight from fear; firstly, of the consequences of not fighting (i.e. punishment) and secondly of not fighting well (death). Among most modern military writers on the subject, physical courage is still widely believed to consist of the overcoming of fear, or in action to rid oneself of fear by eliminating its source (Baynes 1967:64–5; Kellett 1982). One retired officer quotes with approval Montaigne's observation that 'the thing in the world I am most afraid of is fear' (Goddard 1976:266). A text well-known and frequently cited by British military writers who have considered the topic is Lord Moran's *Anatomy of Courage* (1945), in which he argues for a view of courage as a triumph of willpower over fear. In an interview with one former senior British officer who served with Gurkhas and occasionally lectures to officer trainees on the topic, he admitted to following Moran in seeing courage as a limited asset, akin to a bank balance. 'No one can try to be courageous all the time, since the deposit would just disappear.' The line between courage and fear, moreover, is very narrow, and the former consists in conquering the latter. The question must then be posed: if courage is the mastering of fear, does this mean that the greater the fear the more courageous the person or the act? (Walton 1986:65).

Rachman (1978), in a review of psychological approaches to fear, which seem to have informed most studies of military courage, attributes the ability to conquer or cope with fear to factors such as proper motivation, strong leadership, and the need to avoid the disapproval of other group members. He argues that the increasing experience of overcoming fear ('habituation')—which is courageous behaviour—leads ultimately to a 'state of fearlessness'. Courage therefore leads to fearlessness, so that the latter no longer implies the former (ibid.:249).

Warrior Gurkhas

It is often suggested in the literature that Gurkhas know no fear. (In Rachman's terms, they would therefore not be courageous.) To an extent, this arises from the widespread view during Victorian times—and persisting into the present—of non-westerners as being unable to experience emotion in quite the same way as westerners do. The Gurkha, Candler tells us, 'has not a very high estimate of the value of life' (1919:16–17), and Slim offers the hypothesis that the 'Asian soldier' is 'usually more careless, less encumbered by mental doubts or humanitarian sentiment, not so moved by slaughter and mutilation …' (Quoted in Bishop 1976:129–30). His further assertion that courageous action can be the result of a lack of imagination, by which we may read among other things an absence of fear (as in the case of the VC winner) only provides the 'theoretical' background to the oft-stated idea that these soldiers are unable to experience fear. Farwell makes such a statement (1984:59), but this is countered by Cross who insists that Gurkhas do know what fear is, but are more frightened of showing their fear than of fear itself (1985:172). The assertion of Gurkha fearlessness tends, of course, to deny the humanity of these soldiers, as Dixit suggests (1990:10).

The indomitable bravery of Gurkhas, which is celebrated by British officer-authors in the literature on these soldiers, was first recognised during the Anglo-Nepal war. The memoirs of Ensign John Shipp of the Bengal Army record his impressions of the Nepalis at the battle of Muckwanpore:

> The enemy maintained their ground, and fought manfully. I hate a runaway foe; you have no credit for beating them. Those we were now dealing with were no flinchers; but, on the contrary, I never saw more steadiness or bravery exhibited by any set of men in my life. Run they would not, and of death they seemed to have no fear, though their comrades were falling thick

around them, for we were so near that every shot told
(1829/2:102).

This passage is quoted in several recent works on the Gurkhas (see, for
example, Tuker 1957:90). The high opinion the British formed of their
fighting qualities was only reinforced when Nepalis entered the Company's
army. The commander of the British forces during the Sikh war of 1845
noted their 'hardihood and bravery', and 'indomitable spirit', and compared
their 'ardent courage in the charge' to the 'Grenadiers of our own nation'.[3]

Their bravery in battle, moreover, was contrasted most favourably with
that of the Indian sepoys in the Company's armies, who were thought by
many officers to lack courage (see Carnaticus 1821:429). An anonymous
military observer of the Anglo-Nepal war concluded that since Indian sepoys
'live in a different stage of civilisation and intellectual development ... their
only courage is apathy, and their valour consists in animal ferocity ... A
native soldier, of whatever rank, has no heroism, and he is ignorant of honour in every acceptation of the word' (Anon 1822:x).[4]

This disdain for the Indian sepoy did not abate with time; it was, if anything, heightened by the Mutiny of the Bengal army. In 1861, someone who
claimed to have 'served with natives' suggested 'it was a well-known and
accepted axiom that the Asiatic soldier has not, as a body, the same pluck or
moral courage as the European ... he lacks the moral courage to face danger as a duty, unless drugged and maddened by opiates beforehand ... Individual bravery is to be found in every nation and under every clime; but I
am writing of races, not of individuals'.[5] Clearly, Gurkhas were in this regard
not 'Asiatics', a theme which recurs in British military writings (see below).

There is no printed work on the Gurkhas which does not refer to their
tenacity, strength and courage. The toughness of the Gurkha 'race' is universally acknowledged. One author admits that the 'stories, legends almost,
of Gurkha daring are too numerous' for inclusion in a single volume (Bolt
1971:95), but goes on to contribute his fair share to the making of what Des
Chene (1991) calls 'Gurkha tales'.[6] Their motto is said to be 'Better to die
than be a coward', and this, we are told, is quoted by 'many old soldiers to
their young sons as they set out to enlist in the British army' (Smith
1973:175). Their strength is legion. When, during an action against
Afghanistan in 1878, bullocks heaving a forty-pounder gun break down in
exhaustion, they are replaced by Gurkhas (Bishop 1976:51). They perform
miraculous feats of daring. One Gurkha is reported to disappear 'into a
milling mass of flailing arms and fists to reappear surrounded by twelve
German bodies' (ibid.:115). They fear no one, while their opponents are ter-

rified of them. 'Everywhere out of the night the little men closed upon the defenders ... for hand-to-hand fighting in which they have no peers' (Mullaly 1950:17). When they hear the war-cry *Ayo Gurkhali* ('the Gurkhas are coming') the Japanese and Germans freeze with fear (Bishop 1976:112). Their presence is said to have played a 'significant part' in the decision of the Argentinians to surrender during the Falklands war (Cross 1986:179).[7]

When others use rifles and more sophisticated weapons, the Gurkhas seem to draw only their *khukuris*—the short curved knife—which is a general utility instrument in the Nepalese countryside, but is represented in the discourse as the national weapon.[8] 'A l'armée,' Sagant comments, 'les colonels britanniques nous avaient dépeint le soldat gurkha le *khukuri* (sabre) à la main, un diable, un héros ...' (1978:156). And so it is. Carew, who admits to having given little thought to the Indian army when first contemplating military service tells us that his fancy had finally been captured (and his mind made up) by the thought of serving with 'those little hillmen who swooped on their enemies with their curved knives ...' (1954:140). 'The Gurkhas rose as one man and charged with the kukri', writes one (Bolt 1967:99). 'Head on the Gurkhas charged, kukris held high into a hail of machine-gun fire' insists another (Bishop 1976:112). The same author tells us that Gurkhas are known to 'stake the left hand in a wager and cut it off with a kukri when they lose' (ibid.:19). We read in Carew's account of a battle in Burma how a Gurkha 'decapitated the Jap with a single stroke of his kukri and the position was retaken' (1954:182).

In one fictionalised biography of a Gurkha soldier, the climax comes when the hero, fighting in Malaya during the Emergency, meets the leader of a gang of 'Communist Terrorists' (CT's, as they are referred to), a one-eyed Chinese, in hand-to-hand combat—the *khukuri* against the luger pistol (Marks 1971). The dust jackets of numerous books on Gurkhas highlight the *khukuri*. One contains an engraving which portrays three Gurkhas charging over a hill, *khukuris* held high in the right hand, rifles behind in the left (Bolt 1967). Another features a single Gurkha with *khukuri* ready to strike (Smith 1978; see also Chapter 1). Picture books on Gurkhas also invariably stress its deadly sharpness. A photo in one such volume shows two soldiers examining a *khukuri*, and the caption has one saying to the other: 'If you want to take a head off cleanly you must aim to strike about here!' (see Niven 1987:89). Indeed one of the 'humorous' stories which features in many books has a Gurkha meeting an enemy in hand-to-hand combat. He swings his *khukuri*, but the other responds with the taunt: 'you missed!' 'Try shaking your head', replies the Gurkha.[9] Even their enemies were apparently persuaded by these Gurkha tales. Hickey refers to a captured Japanese document which listed the qualities of Indian regiments. It noted that Gurkhas were 'extremely brave' and '[did] not hesitate to draw their knives and kill even in quarrels among themselves ...' (Hickey 1992:32).

Now by any standard Gurkhas have performed remarkably well in battle, and if the Victoria Cross is a measure, then it has to be noted that they have been awarded thirteen such medals since they became eligible during the First World War—a disproportionately high number.[10] During the Second World War alone Gurkhas won over 2,700 decorations for bravery, mentions in despatches, or gallantry certificates (House of Commons 1989:x). But that is not really the point. What is noteworthy is that the Gurkhas are made to appear larger than life.

Gurkha units, no less than most, have suffered defeat in battle, been taken prisoner by the enemy, and even retreated without orders (see Greenhut 1984:17). One military author recognises as much when, recounting his experiences during the Second World War, he acknowledges that Gurkhas are 'not supermen' (Smith 1978:73), and that the motto 'Better to die than be a coward' is an ideal which is 'rarely attained' (ibid.:144). Similar admissions appear from time to time in officers' private writings. An officer in the 3GR during the First World War confides in his war diary that his men (like himself) were 'very frightened' on first hearing high explosive shells. In conversation British officers are also likely to admit that Gurkhas 'are not all paragons of courage', as one phrased it. According to another: 'These stories [of Gurkhas' unthinking courage] are myths and fables institutionalised in the officers' mess'.

However, such admissions are uncommon. The overwhelming tendency is to represent them as invincible, the 'bravest of the brave', a phrase which appears in the Preface of Turner's splendid *Nepali Dictionary* (1931), and is quoted in many subsequent writings. (Turner was for a time an officer in the Gurkhas.) The romance becomes reality through repetition and publication, verbal and textual knowledge reinforcing one another to produce a coherent, integrated narrative about the officer-authors' experience of Gurkhas (Des Chene 1991:90). The latter, of course, are aware of the 'hype' and not above playing on their reputation for ferocity. They are now stationed in several parts of Britain and, I was told by a serving officer, are sometimes challenged in pubs: 'They'll say "push off, we're the famous Gurkhas". And it usually works. They have a good giggle about it. So [their reputation] has its own momentum.'

Gurkha Perspectives on Courage

How do Nepalis who have served in the Gurkhas conceive of courage? This is a difficult subject to interrogate, firstly, because the roots of the concept go back a long way in western thought and it would be folly to assume that such a contested notion can somehow be applied with impunity to a wholly different tradition. Secondly, even though honour and courage have a place in the epic literature of Hinduism, they are addressed indirectly, in the context of wider concerns about the significance of duty. Moreover, while Nepalis who serve or have served in the Gurkhas are often familiar with the classical stories (especially the Mahabharata and Ramayana), they cannot be expected to engage with their philosophical meanings. Finally, in the specific British military context to which Gurkhas were and are assimilated, ideas of courage, as we have seen, are embedded in a complex set of assumptions and values (e.g. patriotism) subscribed to by members of the class from which officers have been drawn, and which are for various reasons not shared by Gurkhas themselves. It is by no means inevitable that people who perform heroic deeds themselves value heroes (Colson 1971:24).

Perhaps the most appropriate way to begin, then, is by examining how the Gurkhas do use terms we gloss as 'courage'. There are several such terms in Nepali: *bir* (connotes brave [adj.] or hero [n.]); *birta* (bravery); *sahasi* (implies boldness, one who ventures); *sahi* (suggests enthusiasm and keenness); *antilo* (daring, resolved); *himat* (courage); etc. But the term which has the widest currency is *bahadur/bahaduri*, and it is this word which is almost universally employed in the Gurkha context, although one cynical ex-Gurkha in Ilam insisted that it was a term introduced to Nepalis by the British. *Bahaduri* is rendered in Turner (1931) as 'greatness, pre-eminence, brave act, courage'.

We should note that both *Bir* and *Bahadur* are common names for boys in Nepal, generally following the personal name and preceding the family, clan, or caste title (thus, a Limbu might be called Chandra Bahadur Nembang or Suk Bir Nogu). This practice is followed by virtually all sections of Nepalese hill society save the highest castes, whether or not they have a tradition of serving in the Gurkhas.

Turning now to how the Limbus I knew in Ilam who had served in the Gurkhas spoke about courage, I should point out that my notebooks contain hardly any unsolicited references to the topic. Although people in the course of numerous conversations narrated diverse experiences of their time in the army, including actions in which they had been involved, it was only at my prompting and as a result of my interest, that they offered views on Gurkha courage (*bahaduri*, and less frequently *antilo kam*).

In these comments several pertinent themes emerged. The first is that these ex-Gurkhas do not relate *bahaduri* or *antilo kam* to a high moral purpose—defeating an evil enemy, upholding a fundamental principle, achieving social justice, or the like. Nor, indeed, do they explicitly align themselves with the political projects of the British government (a kind of adopted patriotism), as many writings on the Gurkhas seem to imply they do. The British military texts, as we saw earlier—are replete with comments suggesting that whomsoever became the adversary of Britain—be they Mahrattas, Sikhs, Bengal army mutineers, Boxers in China, Afghans, Turks, Germans, Japanese, 'communist terrorists' in Malaya, Argentinians, or what have you—incurred the wrath of the Gurkhas. But if, as Des Chene points out, they have contributed to furthering Britain's politico-military goals, it should not be presumed that they have thereby supported them (1991:11).

Gurkha accounts of bravery focused on the quotidian aspects of the military campaigns in which they participated; they spoke of the places they visited, nights spent in the jungle, the food they ate, the skill of their opponents, the destruction of enemy tanks and guns, as well as of their own losses. They were seldom aware (and were frequently uninformed) of the precise political circumstances giving rise to these engagements.

The second theme emerging from Gurkha comments is that fear (*dar*) is regarded as a normal part of being a soldier, but in time is thought to be controllable (see Parkin 1986). One man who had fought in Burma during the Second World War put it like this:

> At first I was afraid for my life. But later I wasn't frightened. After getting used to war we no longer fear.

Another, who had seen action during the Malayan Emergency, commented:

> The first time they told us we had to go to fight I was very afraid. The second time too. Thereafter I knew how bullets came and where to look, how to avoid them. So then I wasn't afraid.

A third, who had been in the same campaign, admitted to 'shaking with fear', but found the emotion invigorating:

> A lot of excitement comes when you go to kill someone, but you know if you don't kill him, you're finished. When you go to war someone has to die.

Death in battle is not regarded as a 'bad death', and thus to result in a dissatisfied ghost (*bhut*), liable to attack the living—a common source of fear in Nepalese villages. 'A man killed by a bullet will not leave a *bhut*', I was told repeatedly. According to one former Gurkha:

> In a war I know in advance I may die. So my death is
> my responsibility (*iccha*). Those who die in war do not
> leave ghosts.

Several attributed their ability to cope with fear to their training and
weapons, others to the wider south Asian notion of serving unquestioningly
the one whose 'salt' you have eaten.[11] Among the older ex-Gurkhas, who
entered service before the advent of schools in Nepal, education is thought
to increase men's fear. One former subedar (Gurkha Officer) put it like this:

> Before, in our fathers' time, and in ours, they were told
> to go and do something and they did it. Now they don't.
> Why? Before they were not educated, now they are a lit-
> tle educated and an educated man is afraid. 'A bullet will
> get me', he thinks. That's my opinion.

While a few noted that uncontrolled fear would inhibit courageous
action, none of these ex-soldiers suggested that courage consists essentially
in managing fear. I was told that Gurkhas are regarded as brave because they
are always obedient and therefore ready to follow whatever orders they
receive, which is not something soldiers in other armies are thought to do.
Several older men noted that of late even Gurkhas had begun to disobey
orders, again the reason being because they are now better educated.
Another, who had retired on a private's pension, laughed at the suggestion
that Gurkhas are invariably brave.

> Only stupid (*lato*) ones are brave. 'Foolish, foolish', they
> say about us. 'They never care, just go to fight'. In my
> view, the clever (*bato*) ones are afraid.[12]

The theme of Gurkhas as obedient as a result of lacking intellect recurs
in these ex-Gurkhas' explanations of their reputation as courageous.

> We are the strongest; it's good to be strong, but we have
> no *dimag* (brain). If we are told to kill, we go and do so,
> and come back. That's why the British trust us. We obey
> orders.

But in numerous contexts these men made it abundantly clear that obedience, along with the acceptance of hardship and danger, are explicable in
terms of obligations towards kin and family: the compelling need to provide
support for the household. Ultimately, these are the paramount values for
which they are willing, albeit reluctantly, to sacrifice everything.

A third theme, which in part explains the dissociation of fear and courage,
is that for virtually all the ex-Gurkhas I spoke to, courage (*bahaduri*) is not

seen as an abstract property of action, or even a distinctive and definable form of behaviour, but a judgement of individual action arrived at retrospectively by others. In other words, the act or person can only be *bahaduri* if it is so recognised by military superiors, in the form of an appropriate decoration. One ex-Gurkha, who saw action in the Falklands, remarked:

> Whoever kills the enemy in war, and the British get some benefit, that one is given a medal, and called *bahaduri*.

Another, who served in Burma during the Second World War, suggested that to be regarded as brave, you had to kill a lot of the enemy (*dusman*), and destroy or capture their weapons. But he insisted that such actions did not constitute bravery unless they were officially recognised:

> I wanted to bring a medal, but the Havildar [Gurkha NCO] was wounded and he couldn't give my name. Only when you get your medal everyone knows about your *bahaduri*.

Bravery awards, moreover, have a monetary value, so that the recipient receives a monthly payment for life. Awards and the degree of bravery they imply are occasionally referred to and assessed in terms of their rupee value. ('For the MM we get Rs25, for the DSM Rs28, then the MC ...'). Most Gurkhas I talked to attributed the award of a medal to *bhagya* (fate, fortune, 'luck').

> To be *bahaduri* you need *bhagya*. You have to kill a lot of people, and then [the officers] recommend you.

These observations of course reflect Gurkha perceptions that the award of military honours could be extremely fortuitous, and this is attested by officers themselves. Davis recalls how after hearing reports of a particular encounter in Burma he had wanted to recommend one Gurkha for a VC. But he had not been near the battle, and neither he nor any other British officer had personally witnessed it. Moreover, he was still too junior for his advocacy to count for much, and a senior officer who might have succeeded was ill in hospital at the time. 'Perhaps I ought to have been more insistent', he muses, 'but I had little influence' (1970:234).

Some ex-soldiers suggested that it has all been pre-ordained in any case:

> I didn't do any brave act (*antilo kam*); it was not written [on the forehead] that I should do so.[13]

Thus, in the matter of courage, agency appears to lie elsewhere: either with the superior officer whose decision it is to label a particular act as 'brave' and recommend it as such, or with the deity who prescribes the individual's life course soon after birth. Above all, for these ex-Gurkhas, the notion of courage is not separable from the public recognition implied in the award of a medal. This contrasts, on the one hand, with the conception held by British officers for whom it is, above all, part of an unwritten code of honour acquired through the institutions of their class, and, on the other, with the officers' representation of Gurkha bravery as unthinking and instinctual, a lower virtue, but nonetheless a matter of pride and celebration.

Gentlemen Gurkhas

If, in these military writings, Gurkha bravery does not embrace the Aristotelian ideal of thoughtful deliberation, nor yet live up to Slim's notion of moral courage—a virtue attainable, it would appear, only by the officer class—it is distinguished nonetheless by its almost western civility. Their officer-chroniclers depict the Gurkhas as brave in an honourable, gentlemanly sort of way.

Fraser set the tone in his description of a wounded Nepalese soldier who in the midst of battle during the Anglo-Nepal war sought medical assistance from the British (graciously provided, of course), and after treatment returned to his side to resume his part in the battle. For Fraser, this indicated a 'strong sense of the value of generosity and courtesy in warfare, and also of his duty to his country', merits which British officers could readily applaud (1820:29–30). This theme—indeed, this very incident—is reiterated in later military writings. Northey, for example, refers to the Nepalis' confidence in their opponents' sense of fair play and sportsmanship by 'sending [whenever possible] their wounded into English camp hospitals for treatment' (1937:58).

Yet other contemporary assessments tended, if anything, to stress the unchivalrous side of Nepalese behaviour. Thus, Ensign Shipp, whose favourable comments on Nepalese courage were quoted earlier, also had some very unflattering things to say, which are not reproduced in the military literature:

> ... in this paradise of beauty [dwells] a cruel and barbarous people, proverbial for their bloody deeds, whose hearts [are] ... callous ... They are more savage in their nature than the hungry tiger ... cruel as the vulture; cold-hearted as their snowy mountains; subtle and cunning as the fiend of night ... (1829/2:82).

In a later passage Shipp remarks that 'they fight under the banner of gloomy superstition; cruelty is their creed; and murder of their foes the zenith of their glory' (ibid.:113); and in a final flourish he offers the view that Goorkah is 'a bastard Tartar, a race pre-eminently blood-thirsty and cruel ...' (ibid.:131).

They are said to have earned or lived up to this image in the course of Gorkhali rule in both Garhwal and Kumaon. The former was under direct Nepalese control for twelve years and the latter for twenty-five years, and in both the term Gurkha is purported to have become virtually synonymous with cruelty and injustice. Local families of rank were apparently banished or killed, villages burned, people forced to supply provisions for the army, and sold as slaves for failure to pay taxes (see Pant 1978; Dabaral 1987; Omissi 1991:20).[14] At the commencement of the Anglo-Nepal war, the British were keen to compare what they insisted was the tyranny of the Nepalese government's rule in these places with their own liberality, and thus to incite the people against the occupation. One leaflet addressed to the inhabitants of Kumaon noted that the British government had long been receiving 'distressing reports about the tyranny and atrocities of the Gorkhalis' in their land, and (after explaining that it could not do or say anything about this while relations were friendly between the British and Gorkhali governments) now proposed to come to their rescue. The Company had therefore despatched troops to drive out the Gorkhalis, and 'liberate the people of Kumaon from the hands of tyrants' (see Pant 1978:155).

Some reports of the Anglo-Nepal war, moreover, paint a picture of Gorkhalis as anything but generous to their enemies. Lord Hastings is reported to have complained that the Gorkhalis had recourse 'to the infamous and detestable act of endeavouring to destroy our troops ... by poisoning the water of wells and tanks' (Hasrat 1970:269). One contemporary 'observer' wrote that the 'Goorkas showed their barbarity by mutilating the dead' (Anon 1822:11), a charge repeated by the historian Pemble in his study of the war (1971:151; 234). The Gorkhalis had already earned an unsavoury reputation by their treatment of the vanquished Newar defenders of Kirtipur, the last of the towns in the Valley of Kathmandu to submit to the Gorkha invader. This, according to Oldfield, was the kind of 'savage barbarity with which they signalized all their triumphs' (1974 [1880]:275).

Of course, it may be that these reputed qualities of cruelty and brutality were precisely the attributes the British most admired in the Gurkhas, as Aitken has suggested, and which they came to call by the more dignified name of 'fighting spirit' (1991:13). But however that may be, such harsh assessments found no place in the discourse generated by the military authors on the Gurkhas. For them, the Gorkhalis were unfailingly civilised opponents. Thus Pearse, writing some eighty years after the Anglo-Nepal war remarked that 'England had found in the rugged highlanders of Nepaul the bravest and most *chivalrous* enemies encountered by her in the East' (1898:231, my emphasis). In like vein, the Gorkhali defence of one position during the war was so 'gallant' as to earn the defeated troops, according to Vansittart, the privilege of marching out 'with [their] arms, accoutrements, colours ... guns, and ... personal property' (1915:36).

Similar kinds of magnanimous terms were granted other Nepalis defeated by the British. Thus, the latter erected a monument below Kalunga Fort 'as a tribute of respect', in the words of the inscription, 'for our gallant adversary Bulbudder, Commander of the fort and his brave Goorkhas ...' (Wilkinson 1976:43). In another tribute to Nepalese valour, when an officer died leading his men in an attempt to regain a position previously lost, the British were so moved by his 'courage and sacrifice', that they had the corpse 'covered with a white sheet and returned with military rites and honours' (Shaha 1984:2–3). For Masters, it 'had been a good, clean war and each side seemed to have enjoyed the others' company' (1956:90), while for Bolt the war earned Gurkhas a reputation for 'good-humoured chivalry' (1967:56). Such willingness to concede to the enemy a noble character is part of what Vagts calls the 'internationale of the military', emanating from the 'feudal spirit' of the officer corps (1959:396).

This granting of the honours of war was also one aspect of the recognition and promotion of Gurkhas, not simply as brave warriors, but as honorary gentlemen. The British officers, themselves from a class 'obsessed with breeding, social precedence and heredity', as Mason observes (1974:360), insisted on recruiting—as we saw in Chapter 4—only from what they determined were genuine, unsullied martial communities. In their detailed ethnographic catalogues military authors labelled certain tribes, races, clans or sections as 'pure', or 'real', and thereby worthy of enlistment. They also identified what they regarded as the 'nobility' or the 'aristocracy' within especially the heavily recruited martial groups, interpreting indigenous status differences in western terms as hierarchies of pedigree and refinement. The assumption, of course, was that the higher and purer 'breeds' would provide the finest recruits (see Vansittart 1894; 1915; Morris 1933; Northey and Morris 1928; Leonard 1965). The Gurkhas could thus be represented as emanating from the best 'stock' (another favourite term), like the officers themselves.

Later, in creating such an image, it became vital to dissociate the Gurkhas from the negative idea of the mercenary. Pocock suggests that during the colonial period Gurkhas, along with their British officers, had sometimes been mocked as 'Mongolian mercenaries' by others in the British and Indian armies (1973:118), and more recently those who oppose Gurkha recruitment have frequently labelled these soldiers in this way. The military writers, however, abjure the term, and those who designate them as such are roundly criticised. They insist that the Gurkhas are full members of the regular forces of Britain (and India), as they were of the British Indian army, and do not 'rank as those whose loyalty is bought by pay' (Cross 1985–6:170–1).[15] What these writers find most 'offensive and even malicious' in the mercenary label is the suggestion that Gurkhas are 'amoral, bloodthirsty and entirely devoid of any feeling other than of hard cash' (ibid.). Like their British officers, the Gurkhas are part of the honourable profession of soldiering; they do not hire themselves out as soldiers of fortune to the highest bidder.[16]

In other ways, too, the Gurkhas are depicted as endowed with many of the qualities of the officers who command (and write about) them. Both are imbued with a 'martial spirit', and fight honourably and fairly. Both are 'honest and incorruptible' (Tuker 1957:122). The Gurkha, we are told, possesses the 'dogged characteristic of the Britisher ... taciturn by nature, brave and loyal to a degree' (Bolt 1967:91). He even holds his drink 'like the gentleman he is' (Bredin 1961:71) and, since he occasionally marries polygynously, is deemed 'a great man with the girls' (Leonard 1965:48). Both Gurkhas and their British officers have a 'cachet for smartness and turn-out' (MacMunn 1932:199). And both are fiercely self-reliant. This can be accounted for in the Gurkhas by the fact that they are 'freehold yeoman farmers', which, as we have already observed, is said to breed in them a 'spirit of independence' (Forbes 1964:55).

We noted in Chapter 3 the role of games and sports in the making of British gentleman-officers. Like the latter, the Gurkhas are depicted as having an abiding love of field sports of all kinds: they are said to 'delight in all manly sports—shooting, fishing, etc.' (Vansittart 1915:58), to have 'inborn hunting instincts' (Forbes 1964:130), and, like Jang Bahudur, their Rana Prime Minister in the third quarter of the nineteenth century, to be 'devoted to hunting [and] sport' (Bolt 1967:63). Thus, according to Tuker, the 'country bred Englishmen who came to soldier with [Gurkhas] found common ground ... in their love of field sports ... they and their Gurkhas were mighty hunters ... [The Gurkha] is very much a 'man of the rod and the gun' (1957:122).

In the West, of course, hunting is the traditional sport of kings and the nobility,[17] and in Nepal, according to Singh (1980:76), it was similarly confined to the ruling elite, from which of course the ordinary people of the middle hills were excluded. Yet the theme of Gurkhas as sportsmen recurs time and again in the writings and one author tells us that sport is 'universal' in Nepal, because from earliest childhood Nepalis are 'instructed in all [its] forms'; hence they are 'plucky and enterprising sportsmen'. Moreover, they recognise (and presumably share) the British 'sense of fair play and sportsmanship'. Finally, he admits to dwelling at length on sport in Nepal because it plays a 'large [part] in the development of the character of a people' (Northey 1937:58, 99, 102, 121). This is of course a familiar refrain, frequently applied to the character of the Victorian and Edwardian ruling class (see Chapter 3).

This emphasis is all the more interesting in light of Singh's statement that before the 1940s Nepal's most popular sport was wrestling, which is not mentioned in the military writings on Gurkhas. He also notes that modern games like football, badminton, hockey and cricket were 'practically nonexistent', and that with the exception of football, sports only developed in Kathmandu in the 1950s (Singh 1980:76). The anthropologist Nick Allen (1976:507–8) also reports that adults in Nepalese villages 'play no games or sports and have no call for a special concept of fitness', and I know of no ethnography of a Nepalese people which suggests otherwise. Nor can I recall ever seeing young people in the Indreni settlements, in which I lived for over a year, playing any team games.

Finally, Gurkhas, like their British officers, have a keen sense of humour. Vansittart found them a 'merry-hearted race' (1915:224), and since that time the Gurkhas' good humour comes in for a considerable amount of attention in the literature. It is 'proverbial' according to Nicholson (1974:3), while for Candler 'cheerfulness is most visible in the "Gurk"' (1919:4). According to Morris, it is the 'most striking element' in their character. 'Their sense of humour and especially of the ridiculous is highly developed, and no Gurkha can remain long without a joke, even though it be against himself' (1935:437). This unfailing cheerfulness is attributed by several authors to their Mongolian origin (see for example Northey 1937:97). In the most recent handbook there is the virtually obligatory reference to their humour and appreciation of sarcasm (Leonard 1965:47); indeed, no mention of Gurkhas seems complete without allusion to their ready smile or laughter (Bristow 1974:23).

In interviews with British officers this trait was highlighted again and again. 'They laugh at the same things we do' was one remark. 'It's a lovely trait, their banana-skin humour. They have a sense of fun, and enjoy life', was another. In literature meant to familiarise new officers with 'Gurkha character' the ability to 'laugh at his own faults' is stressed, as is his 'great humour for the best of life'.[18] The Gurkhas are, in short, 'happy warriors'.[19]

Their humour, we are told, more than any other single factor, distinguishes them markedly from the peoples of India proper, since this trait is not found in the 'austere races of Aryan descent' (Northey and Morris 1928:96–7; see also Morris 1935:437; Bredin 1961:71). The jocular, playful, even naughty Gurkha hillmen are frequently compared to the dour and humourless Indians of the plains, which category occasionally includes the high castes of Nepal itself, i.e. the Newars, Brahmans and Chetris ('NBCs').[20]

Thus, in virtually every respect the military authors differentiate the Gurkhas from the Indian/NBC 'others', who are made to appear their very antithesis. Hodgson's original and much-quoted observation on respective eating habits underlined the distance. The Company's Indian sepoys, he wrote, 'must bathe from head to foot' and 'make *puja* (pray) 'ere they begin to dress their dinner'; they eat 'nearly naked' (i.e. in a ritual *dhoti*) in the coldest weather, and thus take three hours over a meal. The Gurkhas, he noted, laugh (and presumably the British did too) at all this 'pharisaical rigour'. By contrast, they 'despatch their meal in half an hour' (Hodgson 1833:221; see also Smith 1852:136).

The passage is used by military authors to illustrate that Gurkhas, like their British officers, had rejected the shadow of their religion, retaining only its substance. They refused to be hampered by what were regarded as the 'bigotry and prejudices of Brahmanical law', i.e. the 'observances which were ... considered as essential by the more orthodox professors of that religion in the plains' (Vansittart 1915:10).[21] Thus, the Gurungs and Magars are Hindus, the same author suggested (reproducing Hodgson's very words), 'only because it is the fashion'; consequently their Hinduism is 'not very strict' (1894:224; Hodgson 1833:221). Later authors persisted in the view that because the ritual practices and beliefs of most Gurkhas did not replicate those of Brahmans, religion 'lies lightly' on them (Forbes 1964:198), or that the Gurkhas' 'idea of religion is still in a somewhat nebulous and unformed state ...' (Morris 1935:435). In fact, the readiness of the Sirmoor battalion to execute 'without a murmur' several Brahman rebels following the Mutiny is presented not simply as evidence of the Gurkhas' loyalty to the Company, but of their disregard for Hindu orthodoxies.[22]

The religious and other cultural predilections of Gurkhas came to symbolise for these writers not merely difference, but active hostility between these soldiers from Nepal and Indians (or more widely all non-martial groups). Hodgson (quoted in Vansittart 1915:56) was probably the first to assert that apart from their skill at arms, the Gorkhalis had an 'emphatic contempt of Madhesias' (people of the plains), a theme which was to recur in numerous subsequent writings. Vansittart himself simply repeats that 'the

vigorous hill races of Nepal speak [...] with contempt of the "Madhesia'"
while the latter regard the highlanders as 'unconverted barbarians'
(1915:10). This became the stereotyped rendering of the relations between
Gurkhas and Indians. In time, disdain for Indians was assimilated to the
idea that Gurkhas favour and have much in common with Europeans. Petre
reproduces a letter from one officer (dated 1855) in which he informs his
correspondent that Gurkhas 'get on capitally with Europeans and associate
with them but do not condescend to mix with N.I.'s [Native Infantrymen]'
(1925:47). Towards the end of the nineteenth century one senior British
officer with the Gurkhas (General Sale-Hill) was quoted as claiming that the
latter 'hate and despise Orientals of all other creeds and countries, and look
up to and fraternize with Europeans, whom they admire ...' (Temple
1887:232). Mason retails (without comment) the story that around the
time of the Mutiny Gurkhas asked to be allowed to pitch their tents with
British soldiers, not with 'the black folk'. They recognised in British soldiers,
he remarks, 'qualities they admired and wished to be reckoned with them
rather than with the high caste Hindus of the plains ...' (1974:309).

   In the course of cultivating this enmity, British officers insisted on certain
privileges for the Gurkhas which were not enjoyed by troops in other units.
Thus Gurkha regiments retained their own numbering system despite various
reorganisations of the Indian army, while Gurkhas became the only soldiers of
the Indian army allowed into British soldiers' canteens/messes. Gurkha disdain for Indians and their purported refusal to serve under Indian officers were
the reasons advanced for the exclusion of the Brigade from the Indianisation
programme in the early part of this century, which saw the inclusion of
Indians in the ranks of commissioned officers and their deployment in most
regiments of the Indian army (see Chapter 4; Gutteridge 1963).

   Nor has the rhetoric of enmity changed much in the course of time.
Despite the upheavals of two world wars and India's achievement of Independence, a military author (and former senior commander in the Brigade
of Gurkhas) insists that these soldiers 'despise the natives of India and look
up to and fraternise with Europeans' (Tuker 1957:93). This kind of view
persists, and certainly surfaced in the course of several interviews I had with
former or serving officers. The hillman, I was told by one, 'doesn't actually
like Indians, and distrusts ... the "NBC" [Newars, Brahmans and Chetris]'.

   Pahari is almost certainly right to suggest that the 'anti-desi air' in
Gurkha regiments was a 'social, racial and strategic distance' carefully cultivated by the battalions (and the officer-writers of the literature on
Gurkhas), rather than a reflection of the Gurkha soldiers' own dislike for
plainsmen (1991:10). Moreover, the tendency to claim for their soldiers an

aversion to Indians and a special relationship with Europeans was not only a feature of Gurkha regiments. Omissi quotes the Adjutant of the Royal Garhwal Rifles in the 1930s to the effect that Garhwalis do not regularly mix with other classes of Indians, preferring rather to mix with British troops. He also suggests that the cultivation of a separate identity through hostility to Indians was part of an attempt to ensure that martial groups like the Gurkhas or Sikhs 'would not ally themselves with Indian Hindus in political dissent' (1991:9).

Whatever the strategic aim of fostering such divisions, its rhetorical effect was to represent the Gurkhas as imbued with the very qualities of refinement of their European officers. Their courage, along with a sense of humour, good breeding, honesty, sportsmanship, courtesy and relaxed attitude to religious practice,[23] taken together, added up to a portrait of the Gurkha soldier as young gentleman. Indeed, in the way he is depicted the Gurkha conjures up an image of a late-nineteenth and early-twentieth century British public school boy. And this is explicitly recognized. The colonel of one of the Gurkha regiments at the beginning of this century wrote: 'the temperament of the Gurkha reminds us of our public school boy. The same light hearted cheerfulness, hatred of injustice, love of games, and veneration for superior ability or skill. There is the same mentality, with dogged affection (if well treated) and also, like the schoolboy, he works best and hardest with a firm controlling hand' (Woodyatt 1922:177; also quoted in Landon 1928/1:194). The public-school metaphor is called on by Candler, as well, when he compares the Gurkhas and their British officers to school boys and their masters (1919:8).

In this portrayal of the Gurkhas as reflections of their British officers, we have a device used by writers of Victorian colonial fiction, which was to acknowledge that even among those who are 'backward' or 'primitive', there could exist the qualities of an English gentleman—honour, dignity and courage (Street 1975:57).[24] But if an overriding concern of this discourse is to create the Gurkhas in their own image, distance and hierarchy are retained by disallowing their subjects the status of full adulthood. The Gurkhas remain forever boys, playful but simple, needing the firm hand of control and leadership. Indeed, the Gurkha needed the strong hand of the British officer precisely because he was at base something of an innocent, less than fully grown. British officers, we are told, regarded their soldiers 'with affection and admiration as we would our own children' (Sheil-Small 1982:183).[25] One officer with the 6GR, wrote home shortly after World War 1 that 'We have got some ...dear little baby-faced children whom one wants to pick up and kiss, or lay across one's knee and spank ...', and went on to refer to the riflemen under his command as 'simple souls, who are really children in most things' (McKeag 1921:25, 27). His outlook, another writes, is that of a 'healthy boy' (Candler 1919:7).

So Gurkhas are frequently described in diminutives, indicating immense affection and a patronising manner. They are tykes, little highlanders, little gurkhs, little blighters, doughty little Mongolian hillmen. Animal metaphors also abound: they are tigers, leopards, ferrets, mountain goats, and gambolling bull-pups. Candler even describes the fidelity and devotion shown by the Gurkha to his sahib as both 'human and dog-like at the same time' (ibid.:9). Part of the miniaturisation process was to draw attention (in words and pictures) to the contrast between the tall, thin British officer and his small, stocky Gurkhas, thus partly inverting what had been a widespread 'cult of grenadierism', which equated martial abilities with imposing height and physique (Farwell 1989:181; see also Omissi 1991:3).[26] Thus, through 'miniaturisation', as well as through a combination of dominance and affection (see Chapter 4), the Gurkhas are transformed into pets (Tuan 1984:100). As such, they can be little gentlemen—with the requisite qualities of courage and refinement—but remain forever juveniles and thereby subordinate.

Conclusion

In their portrayal of Gurkhas as the quintessential martial race, and as brave to a fault, British military writers single out for praise the very qualities of the officer class itself. But the identification is not total. Hierarchies of courage reflect social and cultural gradations. British officers possess moral courage, their concern is with honour, and they fight for a noble cause. Their courageous acts are subdued, deliberate—Aristotelian. Gurkhas display physical courage, based on emotion rather than the intellect. In Walton's terms, the Gurkhas are brave, their officers courageous.

If, for the British officers, courage remains an abstract concept, one element in an idealised, usually unspoken code of honour (Keegan 1976:194), Nepalis who have served in the Gurkhas offer a somewhat different perspective. For them, there could be no bravery (*bahaduri*) without concrete evidence. They are aware of the requisite behaviour, of the specific accomplishments expected (enemy killed, equipment destroyed), but in the end only a medal attests to the courageous act. Without it, there can have been no brave deed, and this recognition is the effect of *bhagya* (fate/fortune/'luck'). Gurkhas are therefore akin to

Homeric heroes whose successes had to be displayed in trophies, the 'indisputable measure of success' (Finley 1972:138–9, 143).

The Gurkhas are not merely brave warriors, they appear to have many other attributes of their officers—courtesy, a sense of fair play, good humour, skill in games and good sportsmanship, an appreciation of honour, etc. They are, in short, young gentlemen, and their comparison to British public school boys underlines precisely that point. Thus, while the Gurkhas are rendered exotic, there is no attempt in these portrayals to emphasise difference—as anthropologists are accused of doing in relation to the peoples and cultures they study. On the contrary, the military authors are anxious to depict their subjects as the very opposite of the enervated, effeminate and cowardly non-martial 'Hindus' of India (and Nepal), who in the eyes of British officers represent otherness. The Gurkhas are anything but stereotypical Orientals; they are rather honorary Europeans, miniature versions of the officers themselves. Distanciation is achieved and maintained through constraining the Gurkhas within the bounds of childhood and innocence.

The continued stress on Gurkha courage in an era when anti-heroism seems to be the dominant fashion in western culture generally and literature in particular invites comment. Rutherford (1989:4), quoting Fiedler, asks what meaning notions such as glory, honour and courage can have in the West where 'for the first time in a thousand years, it is possible to admit that no cause is worth dying for'? Mishra provides one kind of response: that a persistent emphasis on Gurkha bravery may be seen as part of a wider ideology glorifying war and war heroes, which serves the international bourgeoisie (1985–6:160–1). From a different perspective, we have to note the persistence of an ideology of courage even in an age when the technologies of warfare have supplanted individual effort and agency, and all but rendered the idea of the hero redundant. Dawson has argued, for example, that T.E. Lawrence was made into a hero in literature precisely at a time—the immediate aftermath of the First World War—when the actual circumstances of warfare (impersonal, mechanised, dehumanised) were inimical to adventure and heroism (1991:122–3). In this connection, Ellis points to the intense resistance on the part of the European officer corps to the introduction of the machine gun before the First World War. '[Their] conception of warfare was firmly rooted in … an age when the musket, bayonet and horse … had been the decisive weapons on the battlefield'. As gentlemen they viewed warfare as a matter of honour in which the individual pitted his abilities against others; he still counted for something. The machine gun, Ellis suggests, 'represented the very antithesis of this desperate faith in individual endeavour and courage' (1981:175).

There is something of this attitude in the literature on Gurkhas, in that it harks back to an imagined time when individual initiative and determination took precedence over machines—the *khukuri* over the tank—when men enjoyed primacy on the battlefield. Thus through their discourse on Gurkhas, British officer-writers articulate values which, in their own idiom, are 'time-expired'. The Gurkhas are made to stand for the integrity and nobility of an idealised British officer class which has all but ceased to exist. These author-officers therefore portray the Gurkhas as they would, but can no longer, portray themselves.

Notes to Chapter 5

1. British writers who have served with the Gurkhas insist that the latter are not mercenaries and tend to be abrupt with those who suggest that they are.

2. A third position should be noted, namely, that of recent ethical philosophers who are concerned with notions of equality and fairness, and seem not to allow for the moral value of virtues like courage. For them, courage is not a virtue but only a reminder of violence, war and domination. Courage, in this view, is a non-virtue (Walton 1986:18).

3. *Digest of Services*, p.17.

4. The anonymous 'observer' and author of *Military Sketches of the Goorkha War* (1822) is believed by Pemble (1971:287) to have been General David Ochterlony's son by a native wife.

5. 'Madoc' (pseud.), Letter to the Editor of *The Englishman*, 1861. (East India. Indian Army. India Papers, Oriental and India Office Collections of the British Library).

6. One recent publication relates a number of these tales (see James 1991).

7. Indian officers writing about Gorkhas in the post-Independence Indian army have adopted much of the same rhetoric. According to Singh '[h]is enemies have shuddered on hearing his battle cry and have quaked with fear on seeing his fearless and unbeatable charge' (1952:16).

8. During the 1814–16 war against the East India Company, the 'weapons-bearing' castes of Nepal were instructed by the *durbar* to report with their weapons: swords, shields, bows, arrows and muskets were specifically mentioned, but not *khukuri*s ('Jhara Services for the Nepal-Britain War', *Regmi Research Series*, 1984, Nos 11–12.)

9. The *khukuri* appears in the insignia of all Gurkha regiments.

10. Their British officers have won an equal number of VCs.

11. Parkin (1986) distinguishes between raw and controllable fear: the latter he terms 'respectful' fear and asociates it with unquestioning obedience.

12. Des Chene cited the Gurkha 'motto' ('It is better to die than be a coward') to a group of Gurung *lahures* (who had not heard it before). They responded: 'Perhaps it is better to be clever than dead' (1991:234).

13. These ex-Gurkhas believe, along with most Nepalis who inhabit the hills, that shortly after birth the deity inscribes a person's 'fate' on his/her forehead.

14. In this period the institution of forced labour and slavery also existed in Nepal.

15. During the negotiations over the Tripartite agreement, the Nepalese government was insistent that the Gurkhas not be regarded or treated as mercenaries in order that they would enjoy the same benefits as regular soldiers (see also Des Chene 1991:200).

16. Military writers refer to the Geneva Convention of 1949, which defines a 'mercenary' as, among other things, any person who 'is specially recruited ...to fight in an armed conflict', but 'is not a member of the armed forces of a Party to the conflict', and is motivated by private gain and the promise of 'material compensation substantially in excess of that paid to combatants of similar ranks and functions in the armed forces of that Party'. On these grounds alone British military authors argue that the Gurkhas are excluded from the definition (see House of Commons 1989:xxi).

17. Tuan points out that hunting is a 'martial art, the most highly organized and splendid of sports' (1984:95).

18. *Notes for Officers.*

19. This is the title of one book (Bredin 1961), and the reference is to Wordsworth's poem 'Character of the Happy Warrior', which Girouard remarks 'epitomized the pride and hero-worship which British victories evoked at home'. The phrase was to become 'popular and ... hackneyed' (1981:42). Baynes considers good humour one of the 'hall-marks' of high morale within an army (1967:108).

20. In his 'short notes ... on the characteristics of the principal classes' which make up today's Indian army, Das remarks in relation to numerous ethnic groups that they have a 'cheerful disposition', a 'keen sense of humour', or are 'good humoured' (1984:448–51).

21. This passage is taken from Oldfield (1974 [1880]:262) who was one of the 'principal authorities' consulted by Vansittart in preparing his handbook on Gurkhas.

22. *Digest of Services*, p.20.

23. British officers assumed that a lack of religious fervency was a sign of good breeding. The ideal public school boy, according to Mangan, was deemed to possess a 'foundation of true religion', but to 'do his best to conceal it' (1987:136). General John Jacob, who favoured north Indian Muslims as the best material for the Indian army, remarks that they have 'scarcely more prejudices of religion, &c, than Englishmen' and 'are, in fact, more like gentlemen than any other class of Indians' (Pelly 1858:134).

24. Mrozek reports that some US officers in the late-nineteenth century saw American Indians as 'sharing the same basic values which distinguished the manly civilised Victorian' (1987:221).

25. This attitude is not unique to British officers in the Gurkha Brigade. Baynes comments that many officers in the British army viewed their soldiers 'rather like children' (1967:170).

26. In his portrait of the ideal British officer, Baynes describes him as 'a tall man, about six foot, and lean. He has one of those aristocratic faces with a faintly Roman nose which epitomize the well-bred Englishman' (1967:123).

....

CHAPTER 6

CONCLUSION

Gurkha Fictions and Political Realities

> To the Gurkhas, who were not Indians but Nepalese, I
> took an immediate liking.
>
> Brigadier R.C.B. Bristow *Memories of the British Raj*, 1974.

Within anthropology there has lately been an increased awareness of the need to acknowledge the 'relativity of objectivity' (P. Caplan 1988:10)—what you see depends on who you are—and to include and scrutinise the self of the author within his or her text. This has resulted in a growing number of works which take the person of the ethnographer into account (see Okely and Callaway 1992). While welcoming this tendency to eschew the pretence of a spurious objectivity by acknowledging the participant-observer's presence, I agree with Kapferer that what is also pressing is to 'confront critically the ideological orders' from which the analyst comes (1988:95).[1] So, without denying the intrinsic interest of individual biographies of the military authors who represent the Gurkhas, I have supplemented my attempts to understand their writings by identifying the wider political and ideological frameworks within which they discovered, led, and imagined these soldiers. By attending to these contexts, I have suggested, we are better able to appreciate the character of the texts themselves.

Their first sight of Gurkhas occurred in the course of a war between two aggressive and advancing continental forces, the outcome of which called a halt to Nepal's expansionary tendencies, and confirmed the British as the ascendant power in South Asia. The officer class, from whose ranks the authors of these texts emerged, and whose views the latter both articulated and helped to mould, played a vital role in the maintenance of imperial India, and in its ideological constructions. Green suggests that in the 'theater of empire' that was India, the 'military caste provided the leading actors, and even quite displaced the merchants from public view' (1980:210). The officers were educated in the public schools, which from the mid-nineteenth century prepared young men from the rising middle and professional classes (including the sons of officers) alongside the gentry and aristocracy for the station of gentlemen. They were bonded by a code of chivalry which stressed, among other things, patriotism, manliness and courage, and subscribed to the widespread belief in their destiny as part of a governing race. These were the broad political and cultural orders within which the creators of the Gurkha texts were situated, but there were particular military contexts as well.

The Indian-Royal army dichotomy was a crucial divide, creating everyday rivalries of military precedence and ambition, and more subtle and insidious ones of status and position. Thus, each Gurkha regiment elaborated its own distinctive history and traditions, while the Brigade as a whole created an awareness of itself as a separate and elite force within the Indian (and later British) armies. Indeed, reading the literature on Gurkhas one comes to realise just how much energy the British officers, who controlled an awesome armoury to deploy against their enemies, actually expended in fierce battles with one another over the minutiae of regimental precedence, symbolic privileges, sacred trophies, and ultimately, individual and collective identities. This should caution us against assuming that members of the British imperial class all had the same agenda. To be sure, there were common interests and strong links among those who served the raj in India: merchants, soldiers, civilians, even writers of fiction. Mannsaker (1983) points out that many nineteenth-century novelists of the Indian empire were officers (or their wives). But there were distinctions and rivalries as well.

Of note, too, is that the codes of behaviour evolved in the Gurkha regiments by and large aped those of the Royal force. So while on the one hand the Indian army offered the opportunity for men from the rising middle and professional classes to challenge the monopoly of the military hitherto exercised by the nobility and gentry, on the other, Indian army officers (like those serving with Gurkhas) were totally shaped by, and in thrall to, the values and practices of the dominant groups. They preferred, as Anderson remarks, to 'play aristocrat' in the outposts of empire (1983:138). Moreover, while the regimental settings were tropical-imperial and the minor players in many of these activities Gurkhas, the cultures themselves were conceived in traditional British terms.

The discourse on Gurkhas was intimately bound up with the politico-military settings within which the European officer-chroniclers were situated, but there were other, taken-for-granted notions, based on nineteenth-century scientific (and anthropological) truths, which also influenced these military writings. The widespread acceptance of the belief that cultural characteristics could be inherited genetically was an important source of many contemporary representations of other peoples, and in India these ideas formed the basis of martial theory. After 1857 the theory was embellished to certify only certain groups as ideally suited for military pursuits, and to exclude others, like the groups from whose ranks the mutineers had originated. Certain Nepalis, already noted for their fighting qualities, were—along with Muslims and Sikhs from north India—especially targeted for recruitment.

The communities which by and large provided the soldiers were Tibeto-Burman speakers from the country's middle hills. With the migration into their homelands of technologically more advanced, literate, high-caste Hindu populations, these earlier settlers had become, by the end of the eighteenth century, economically reduced, and with the establishment of Gorkhali rule throughout the region, politically marginal as well. These groups were thus ideally suited to become, in Enloe's (1980) phrase, 'ethnic soldiers', although her model of the 'Gurkha syndrome' does not, paradoxically, wholly reflect the Gurkha situation itself. The Nepalis entered the service of an imperial power (and later of foreign powers), and not that of their own state elites. Indeed, the latter opposed and hindered their enlistment for many years. Moreover, even following their compliance and collusion with the recruitment of Nepalis, the *durbar* had virtually no control over how these soldiers were deployed.

Since India's Independence, Nepalese writers and intellectuals—by and large from the same sections of the population which provide its political elites—have seen their government's support for the employment of Gurkhas in foreign armies as a measure of the country's neo-colonial status. But any call for an end to recruitment has been resisted by the *durbar* as by members of Tibeto-Burman communities. Economically and politically subordinate, the latter have continued to regard military service as the principal means through which to effect an improvement in their lives.

The discourse also stressed the Gurkhas' martial abilities, along with the associated qualities of bravery, masculinity and loyalty. Those who possessed such positive virtues were consistently celebrated and their merits highlighted by comparing them to non-martial Indians and (by extension) high-caste Nepalis, who were found wanting on all these counts. The latter groups were portrayed as feminine, cowardly and untrustworthy, and seen to exemplify the very antithesis of the Gurkhas and their British officers.

All fighting groups in the Indian army shared at least some of the characteristics of their officers, who of course embodied the quintessence of the martial ideal. But the Gurkhas seemed to have an additional quality associated with those who led them: that special combination of traits (courtesy, humour, sportsmanship) which defines persons of breeding. They were, in short, not simply warriors, but gentlemen as well; hence their depiction as akin to public school boys. Their exoticism therefore lay not in their foreignness, but paradoxically in their very likeness to the officers who led them. Despite being 'Easterners', they possessed the most desirable qualities of western (European) civilised culture. The Gurkhas thus reflected back the officers' own image of themselves as men of honour and refinement. Such rhetorics belie the assumption that orientalist depictions are all of a kind—'othering' (Fabian 1990) their non-western subjects in both a moral and cultural sense. There was certainly no desire on the part of the military authors to represent the Gurkhas as the very antithesis of themselves (an image, as I have shown, reserved for non-martial Indians and Nepalis). These soldiers were, if anything, embraced as honorary Europeans.

However, this mimesis went only so far. Ultimately, hierarchy prevailed, and textual devices maintained distinctions between officer and soldier. So the literature made clear, for example, that like all martial peoples Gurkhas were invariably brave, though in an unthinking, instinctual, 'gung-ho' sort of way, as befitted their somewhat simple, unimaginative character. As such, they did not entirely replicate their officers whose courage was deliberate and directed to high moral purposes—in short, Aristotelian. Such courageous propensities, moreover, could only hope to be acquired in the cultural, social, and ideological ambiance of the institutions in which the officer was nurtured and in which his persona was formed. These attributes were therefore out of the reach even of Gurkhas, as of other martial races of India.

The Gurkhas were also distanced and subordinated by two other principal (and related) textual devices. The first combined affection and miniaturisation to produce the 'pet', ever loyal and obedient. The relationship between British officer and Gurkha soldier was depicted as a deep, indeed natural bond, but the actuality of this courtship could not allow of any dealing on equal terms, and the rhetoric confirmed the Gurkhas in their inevitable subalternity to their European Subalterns. The second trope turned these soldiers into Peter Pans, encapsulated in a permanent state of juvenility. Nandy has suggested that the colonies came to be seen as the abode of people childlike and innocent on the one hand, and devious, effeminate and passive-aggresssive on the other. The latter aspects of childlikeness were (as we have seen) associated with the non-martial (e.g. the

Bengalis), while the former, positive aspects were the attributes of the 'devoted, obedient martial races of India' (1983:38). Hence the insistence on Gurkhas needing a firm hand, as do all little gentlemen.

These textual modes were generated within and fostered by the colonial context, and the question must arise as to why they should continue to pervade post-colonial military writings. The discourse on martiality, for example, grounded in nineteenth-century biological determinism, has survived with some slight modifications into the period of post-Indian Independence and quite different scientific pre-suppositions, not to speak of greater sensitivity to issues of racism and First World-Third World relations. Although some scholars have from time to time declared the end of martial theory it endures in British writings about Gurkhas, although 'races' have become 'tribes' or 'classes', and the language of disdain for non-martial people has turned softer. Certainly, ethnological knowledge has grown as British officers have come into contact with a wider cross-section of Nepalese hill society, and personally gained access to many parts of the country previously closed, and this has been reflected in recent publications. Yet the portrait of 'Gurkha character' has remained remarkably consistent (see also Des Chene 1991:81). Despite the many changes in the home environments from which the soldiers originate, and in the role and nature of the Brigade itself, the Gurkhas appear caught in a time warp woven by their military chroniclers. While some officers informally contradict, even disclaim many of the stereotypes offered in the literature, latter-day texts continue to essentialise the Gurkhas in much the same way as they did in the past.

Why should this be so? One answer may simply be that images and perceptions of others tend to persist through time, despite the changing political and ideological environments in which they arose in the first place. This is especially so where those who represent others effectively control all aspects of their subjects' lives. The officers who perpetuate the discourse on Gurkhas are aware that their every judgement affects vitally the livelihoods of their soldiers and the households to which they are attached (as the Hawaii incident showed). Such omnipotence would encourage most authors to rest secure in the authenticity of their depictions.

Furthermore, tenacity is implied in the very notion of 'genre', which pre-supposes certain expectations on the part of the reader to which the author responds. There is, in other words, something of a conspiracy between writer and audience to preserve these Gurkha fictions, in the sense of their consistency over time.

But the perseverance of this discourse might also be understood against the background of political and military upheavals following the Second

World War: namely, fundamental changes in the size and role of the British army consequent on post-war economic and power realignments, and the rapid collapse of the empire. These developments had direct consequences for the Gurkhas, which were manifested in the traumatic division of regiments at the time of India's independence. The end of 'Confrontation' in South East Asia some twenty years later (in which the Gurkhas had played a vital part) had further repercussions for the Brigade. Sometimes described as the British army's last great colonial battle, it was followed not only by dramatic alterations in the size and dispositions of the Gurkha regiments, but by a felt transformation in the officers' attitudes towards their calling, encouraged in part by changes in the composition of the officer corps itself.

This period is perceived as heralding the rise of the career officer, for whom service with Gurkhas was only one of several possible stages in the course of professional advancement, and the corresponding demise of the regimental officer, devoted above all to his unit, his colleagues, and his soldiers. The great majority of officers who moulded the discourse and authored the literature on Gurkhas spent their formative years in this kind of colonial or neo-colonial setting, and regarded themselves as zealously attached to the regiment. Thus an important sub-text of post-colonial military narratives speaks of personal ambition displacing personal sacrifice, of bureaucratic efficiency superseding human intimacy, and of technology supplanting individual effort and agency. Regarding the latter, especially, machines were seen to have taken the place of heroism and the innate superiority of the Englishman. Thus, in the praises sung of Gurkha bravery, we can detect a harking back to an imagined time when individual gallantry stood for more than impersonal instruments, the *khukuri* for more than the machine gun and the tank.

Against the background of what appears to these officer-authors as retrogressive change, the continuity of Gurkha portraits might therefore be understood as an attempt to preserve an image of something which no longer obtains, but which they feel should be cherished. In this respect these Gurkha texts are like the pre-World War I travel books which sought to retain the illusion of bygone places which had long since passed out of existence (Fussell 1980:226). Through textualisation, a disappearing world can be preserved (Clifford 1986:112).

'If the Gurkhas depicted in the literature are a fiction, what are they really like?' This was a question invariably posed when I presented seminars on some of the issues raised in this essay, and it reflects of course the centrality in western thought of the relationship between language and its object. But we have to treat these texts as more than a problem in representation. I am not suggesting that the officer-authors have distorted or some-how neglected to depict the actuality of Gurkha life and death; in other words, that there has been a failure of representation. On the contrary, I am proposing that the Gurkha only exists in the context of the western military imagination. In this (Derridean) sense, these texts mourn the loss not simply of what is no more, but of what has never existed (Pinney 1991:231–2). Moreover, in offering this perspective on the Gurkha texts it does not follow that we have to insist on their autonomy, closure, or non-referability to events or objects outside themselves, as would seem to be the view of the more committed 'textualists'.

Throughout this essay I have attempted to understand these discursive constructs by reference to the wider circumstances in and against which they have been produced. It is not an argument for determinism, a matter of assigning priority to reality over the images of reality, an insistence that texts can only be 'explained' through contextualisation. Rather, through situating the depictions of these soldiers by their officer-chroniclers in the complex, changing historical and politico-military conditions of colonial India, semi-colonial Nepal, and post-imperial Britain—by examining the link between the word and the world, as Appadurai puts it (1991:196)—our under-standing of the Gurkha project is enhanced. My intention in this essay has been to demonstrate that the strategies of text and the strategies of power are integrally linked, and mutually implicated.

Notes to Chapter 6

1. Silverman has recently observed, for example, that while anthropologists on the 'periphery of an empire' might wish to focus attention on issues of power and exploitation, those from the metropolitan centre seem to find it 'sufficient and necessary' to be concerned with 'personal others' and intersubjectivity (1991:392).

······

REFERENCES

Authors marked * are or were officers serving with Gurkhas in the pre-Independence Indian and/or post-Independence British armies.

* Adshead, D.R. and J.P. Cross 1970. *Gurkha: the legendary soldier*, London: Leo Cooper.

Aitken, B. 1991. 'Pentax cameras and khukuris', *Himal* 4 (3):13.

Allen, N.J. 1976. Approaches to Illness in the Nepalese Hills. In *Social Anthropology and Medicine* (ed.) J.B. Loudon. London: Academic.

Anderson, B. 1983. *Imagined Communities: reflections on the origin and spread of nationalism*. London: Verso.

Anderson, J.W. 1986. 'Military heroism: an occupational definition', *Armed Forces and Society* 12:591–606.

Anon. 1822. *Military Sketches of the Gorkha War, in India, in the years 1814, 1815, 1816*. London: R. Hunter.

Anon. 1849. *On the deficiency of European officers in the Army of India. By one of themselves*. London: James Madden.

Appadurai, A. 1986. 'Theory in anthropology: center and periphery', *Comparative Studies in Society and History* 28:356–61.

———— 1991. Global ethnoscapes: notes and queries for a transnational anthropology. In *Recapturing Anthropology: working in the present* (ed.) R.G. Fox. Santa Fe: School of American Research Press.

Aryal, M. 1991. 'To marry a Lahuray', *Himal* 4 (3):18–19.

Asad, T. and J. Dixon 1985. Translating Europe's Others. In *Europe and its Others* (Vol.1) (eds) F. Barker et al. Colchester: Univ. of Essex.

Badenach, W. 1826. *Inquiry into the state of the Indian army, with suggestions for its improvement, and the establishment of a military police for India*. London: J. Murray.

Baxter, P. and R. Fardon (eds) 1991. *Voice, Genre, Text—anthropological essays in Africa and beyond,* Special issue, *Bulletin of the John Ryland's University Library of Manchester* 73 (3).

Baynes, J. 1967. *Morale: a study of men and courage.* London: Cassell.

————— 1991. *No Reward but Honour? the British soldier in the 1990s,* London: Brassey's.

Ben-Ari, E. 1987. 'On acknowledgements in ethnographies', *Journal of Anthropological Research* 43:63–84.

Bennett, L. 1983. *Dangerous Wives and Sacred Sisters,* New York: Columbia Univ. Press.

Bennett, S. 1984. 'Shikar and the Raj', *South Asia* 7:72–88.

Biardeau, M. 1989. *Hinduism: the anthropology of a civilization* (trans. by R. Nice), Delhi: OUP.

Bingley, A.H. and A. Nicholls 1918. *Caste Handbooks for the Indian Army: Brahmans,* Calcutta: Supt. Govt. Printing.

Bishop, E. 1976. *Better to Die: the story of the Gurkhas,* London: New English Library.

Bista, D.B. 1991. *Fatalism and Development: Nepal's struggle for modernization,* Calcutta: Orient Longman.

Blaikie, P., J. Cameron and D. Seddon 1980. *Nepal in Crisis: growth and stagnation at the periphery.* Oxford: Clarendon.

Blake, J. A. 1987. 'Military heroism: an occupational definition', *Armed Forces and Society* 14:149–153.

* Bolt, D. 1967. *Gurkhas,* London: Weidenfeld and Nicolson.

* Bredin, A.E.C. 1961. *The Happy Warriors: the Gurkha soldier in the British army,* Gillingham, Dorset: Blackmore.

* Bristow, R.C.B. 1974. *Memories of the British Raj: a soldier in India.* London: Johnson.

* Bruce, C.G. 1928. Foreword to Northey, W.B. and C.J. Morris *The Gurkhas: their manners, customs and country.* London: John Lane, The Bodley Head.

Bryant, G. 1978. 'Officers of the East India Company's Army in the days of Clive and Hastings', *Journal of Imperial and Commonwealth History* 6:203–27.

Burghart, R. 1984. 'The formation of the concept of the nation-state in Nepal', *Journal of Asian Studies* 44:101–25.

Burke, K. 1969 [1950]. *A Rhetoric of Motives,* Berkeley: Univ. of Calif. Press.

Burroughs, P. 1986. 'Imperial Defence and the Victorian Army: review article', *Journal of Imperial and Commonwealth History* 15:55–72.

Campbell, B.R.G. 1993. 'The Dynamics of Cooperation: households and economy in a Tamang community of Nepal', unpublished PhD thesis, School of Development Studies, University of East Anglia.

* Candler, E. 1919. *The Sepoy.* London: John Murray.

Caplan, A.P. 1972. *Priests and Cobblers: a study of social change in a Hindu village in western Nepal,* London: Intertext.

————— 1988. 'Engendering knowledge: the politics of ethnography', *Anthropology Today* 4 (5 & 6):8–12, 14–17.

Caplan, L. 1970. *Land and Social Change in East Nepal: a study of Hindu-tribal relations*, London: Routledge.

———— 1991. 'From tribe to peasant? the Limbus and the Nepalese state', *The Journal of Peasant Studies* 18:305–21.

Cardew, F.G. 1891. 'Our recruiting grounds of the future for the Indian army', *The Journal of the United Service Institution of India* 20 (86):131–56.

* Carew, T. 1954. *All This and a Medal Too*, London: Constable.

Carnaticus (pseud) 1821. 'General view of our Indian army', *The Asiatic Journal and Monthly Register* 11 (65):429–39.

Cavenaugh, O. 1851. *Rough Notes on the State of Nepal, its government, army and resources*. Calcutta: W. Palmer, Military Orphan Press.

Chakravarti, P.C. 1941. *The Art of War in Ancient India*, Dacca: Univ. Press.

Chandos, J. 1984. *Boys together: the English public schools*, London: Hutchinson.

* Chant, C. 1985. *Gurkha: the illustrated history of an élite fighting force*. Poole: Blandford.

* Chapple, J.L. 1980. *Bibliography of Gurkha regiments and Related Subjects*. Gurkha Museum Publication No. 4.

———— 1985 [1978, 1982]. 'The Lineages and Composition of Gurkha Regiments in British Service'. Unpublished.

———— and D.R. Wood 1981. 'Kabul to Kandahar, 1880: extracts from the diary of Lieutenant E.A. Travers, 2nd P.W.O. Goorkhas' (pt 1) *Journal of the Society for Army Historical Research* 59:207–28.

Chatterji, B. 1967. *A Study of Recent Nepalese Politics*, Calcutta: The World Press.

Chaudhuri, K.C. 1960. *Anglo-Nepalese Relations: from the earliest times of the British rule in India till the Gurkha war*, Calcutta: Modern Book Agency.

Chhetry, D.B. 1989. 'The treaty of friendship between Great Britain and Nepal and its achievement', *Rolamba* 9 (3):3–8.

Clifford, J. 1980. Review of E. Said's *Orientalism*, *History and Theory* 19:204–23.

———— 1986. Introduction: partial truths. In *Writing Culture: the poetics and politics of ethnography* (eds) J. Clifford and G.E. Marcus. Berkeley: Univ. of Calif. Press.

Cohen, S.P. 1971. *The Indian Army: its contribution to the development of a nation*, Berkeley: Univ. of Calif. Press.

Collier, P. and H. Geyer-Ryan (eds) 1990. *Literary Theory Today*, Cambridge: Polity.

Colson, E. 1971. Heroism, martyrdom, and courage: an essay on Tonga ethics. In *The Translation of Culture* (ed.) T.O. Beidelman. London: Tavistock.

Crapanzano, V. 1980. *Tuhami: portrait of a Moroccan*, Chicago: Univ. Press.

Creagh, M.O. n.d. *Indian Studies*, London: Hutchinson.

* Cross, J.P. 1985. Review of B. Farwell *The Gurkhas*, *Strategic Studies* 3:168–75.

———— 1985–6. 'The Gurkhas: as I see it', *Strategic Studies* 6/7:168–76.

———— 1986. *In Gurkha Company: the British Army Gurkhas, 1948 to the present*, London: Arms and Armour Press.

Dabaral, S.P. 1987. 'Gorkhali rule in Garhwal', *Regmi Research Series* 7/8:115–20; 9/10:143–50.

Dahal, D.R. 1985. *An Ethnographic Study of Social Change among the Athpahariya Rais of Dhankuta*, Kathmandu: Centre for Nepal and Asian Studies.

Dandekar, C. 1989. *Military Related Social Research: an international review*. Papers presented at the 1988 Munich Interim Conference of the Research Committee of the 01/ISA Armed Forces and Conflict Resolution (ed.) Jurgen Kuhlmann, Munchen.

Daniell, D. 1983. Buchan and the popular literature of imperialism. In *Literature and Imperialism* (ed.) B. Moore-Gilbert. Roehampton: English Department of the Roehampton Institute of Higher Education.

Das, C.N. 1984. *Traditions and Customs of the Indian Armed Forces*, Delhi: Vision Books.

Dasgupta, J. 1930. 'Nepal's relations with the outer world', *The Calcutta Review* 35:370–88.

Date, G.T. 1929. *The Art of War in Ancient India*, London: Humphrey Milford.

* Davis, P. 1970. *A Child at Arms*, London: Hutchinson.

Dawson, G. 1991. The Blond Bedouin: Lawrence of Arabia, imperial adventure and the imagining of English-British masculinity. In *Manful Assertions: masculinities in Britain since 1800* (eds) M. Roper and J. Tosh. London: Routledge.

Dawson, H.D. 1917. 'Who are the Gurkhas?', *Empire Annual for Boys*, pp.119–21.

Des Chene, M. 1988. 'In service to colonialism: the emergence of national identity among the Gurkhas'. Paper delivered at American Anthropological Association Conference.

———— 1991. 'Relics of Empire: a cultural history of the Gurkhas, 1815–1987', unpublished PhD Thesis, Stanford University.

Dixit, K.M. 1990. 'Ayo Gorkhali!', *Himal* 3 (1):10.

Donaldson, E. 1900. *Lepchaland*, London: Sampson Low, Marston.

* Edwards, J.H. 1979. 'Nepal and the Brigade of Gurkhas', *Royal Engineers Journal* 5:220–30.

Ellis, J. 1981. *The Social History of the Machine Gun*, New York: Arno.

Empson, W. 1935. *Some Versions of Pastoral*, London: Chatto and Windus.

Enloe, C.H. 1980. *Ethnic Soldiers: state security in divided societies*, Harmondsworth: Penguin.

Evans-Pritchard, E.E. 1940. *The Nuer*, Oxford: Clarendon.

Fabian, J. 1990. 'Presence and Representation: the other and anthropological writing', *Critical Inquiry* 16:753–72.

Fardon, R. 1990. Localizing Strategies: the regionalization of ethnographic accounts. General Introduction. In *Localizing Strategies: regional traditions of ethnographic writing* (ed.) R. Fardon. Edinburgh: Scottish Academic Press.

Farwell, B. 1984. *The Gurkhas*, London: Allen Lane.

———— 1989. *Armies of the Raj: from the Mutiny to Independence, 1858–1947*, London: Viking.

Finley, M.I. 1972 [1954]. *The World of Odysseus*, Harmondsworth: Penguin.

Fisher, J.F. 1986. *Trans-Himalayan Traders: economy, society and culture in northwest Nepal*, Berkeley: Univ. of Calif. Press.

* Forbes, D. 1964. *Johnny Gurkha*, London: Robert Hale.

* Forteath, G.M. 1991. *Pipes, Kukris and Nips*, Edinburgh: Pentland Press.

Foucault, M. 1979. 'What is an author?' In *Textual Strategies* (ed.) J. Harari. London: Methuen.

Fox, R.G. 1985. *Lions of the Punjab: culture in the making*, Berkeley: Univ. of Calif. Press.

Fraser, J.B. 1820. *Journal of a Tour through part of the Snowy Range of the Himala Mountains and to the sources of the Rivers Jumna and Ganges*, London: Rodwell and Martin.

Fussell, P. 1980. *Abroad: British literary traveling between the wars*, New York: OUP.

Gaborieau, M. 1978. *Le Népal et ses populations*, Bruxelles: Editions Complexe.

Gaige, F.H. 1975. *Regionalism and National Unity in Nepal*, Berkeley: Univ. of Calif. Press.

Garnier, M. 1977. Technology, organizational culture, and recruitment in the British military academy. *In World Perspectives in the Sociology of the Military* (eds) G.A. Kourvetaris and B.A. Dobratz. New Brunswick, N.J.: Transaction Books.

Geertz, C. 1989. *Works and Lives: the anthropologist as author*, Cambridge: Polity.

* Gibbs, H.R.K. 1947. *The Gurkha Soldier*, Calcutta: Thacker, Spink & Co.

Gilmore, D.D. 1990. *Manhood in the Making: cultural concepts of masculinity*, New Haven: Yale Univ. Press.

Girouard, M. 1981. *The Return to Camelot: chivalry and the English gentleman*, New Haven: Yale Univ. Press.

Gluckman, M. 1950. Kinship and marriage among the Lozi of Northern Rhodesia and the Zulu of Natal. In *African Systems of Kinship and Marriage* (eds) A.R. Radcliffe-Brown and M. Fortes. London: OUP.

Goddard, E. 1976. 'The Indian Army–Company and Raj', *Asian Affairs* 63:263–76.

Green, M. 1980. *Dreams of Adventure, Deeds of Empire*, London: Routledge.

Greenhut, J. 1984. 'Sahib and sepoy: an inquiry into the relationship between the British officers and native soldiers of the British Indian army', *Military Affairs* 48:15–18.

Gregory, C.A. 1982. *Gifts and Commodities*, London: Academic Press.

Gurung, H.B. 1991. 'The Gurkha Guide', *Himal* 4 (3):20.

Gutteridge, W. 1963. 'The Indianisation of the Indian army 1918–45', *Race* 4:39–48.

Hamilton, F. 1819. *An Account of the Kingdom of Nepal and of the Territories Annexed to this Dominion by the House of Gorkha*, Edinburgh: Constable.

Hart, K. 1982. On commoditization. In *From Craft to Industry* (ed.) E. Goody. Cambridge: Univ. Press.

Hasrat, B.J. 1970. *History of Nepal: as told by its own and contemporary chroniclers.* Hoshiarpur, Punjab: the Editor.

Haycock, R. 1988. British arms in India. In *British Military History: a supplement to Robin Higham's Guide to the Sources* (ed.) G. Jordan. New York: Garland.

Heathcote, T.A. 1974. *The Indian Army: the garrison of British Imperial India, 1822–1922,* Vancouver: David and Charles.

Herzfeld, M. 1980. 'Honour and shame: problems in the comparative analysis of moral systems', *Man* 15:339–51.

Hickey, M. 1992. *The Unforgettable Army: Slim's XIVth Army in Burma,* Tunbridge Wells: Spellmount.

Hitchcock, J.T. 1959. The idea of the martial Rajput. In *Traditional India: structure and change* (ed.) M. Singer. Philadelphia: The American Folklore Society.

———— 1961. 'A Nepalese hill village and Indian employment', *Asian Survey* 1:15–19.

———— 1963. 'Some effects of recent change in rural Nepal', *Human Organization* 22:75–82.

———— 1966. *The Magars of Banyan Hill,* New York: Holt, Rinehart and Winston.

———— 1970. Fieldwork in Gurkha Country. *In Being an Anthropologist* (ed.) G. Spindler. New York: Holt Rinehart and Winston.

Hodgson, B.H. 1833. 'Origin and classification of the military tribes of Nepal', *Journal of the Asiatic Society* 17:217–24.

Höfer, A. 1978. A new rural elite in Central Nepal. In *Himalayan Anthropology: the Indo-Tibetan interface* (ed.) J.F. Fisher. The Hague: Mouton.

———— 1979. *The Caste Hierarchy and the State in Nepal: a study of the Muluki Ain of 1854,* Innsbruck: Universitätsverlag Wagner.

Holy, L. and M. Stuchlik 1983. *Actions, norms and representations: foundations of anthropological inquiry,* Cambridge: Univ. Press.

* Holy-Hasted, J.S. and D.R. Wood (compilers) 1965. 'Regimental register of British officers, 2nd King Edward VII's Own Goorkhas, 24 April, 1815—24 April, 1965'. Unpublished.

House of Commons, Defence Committee 1989. *First Report: the Future of the Brigade of Gurkhas,* London: Her Majesty's Stationery Office.

Hunter, W.W. 1896. *Life of Brian Houghton Hodgson: British Resident at the Court of Nepal,* London: John Murray.

Husain, A. 1970. *British India's Relations with the Kingdom of Nepal 1857–1947,* London: George Allen and Unwin.

Hutt, M. 1989. 'A hero or a traitor? representations of the Gurkha soldier in modern Nepali literature', *South Asia Research* 9:21–32.

Inden, R. 1986. 'Orientalist constructions of India', *Modern Asian Studies* 20:401–46.

———— 1990. *Imagining India,* Oxford: Basil Blackwell.

* James, H. 1991. *Tales of the Gurkhas,* Lewes: The Book Guild.

———— and D. Sheil-Small 1965. *The Gurkhas.* London: Macdonald.

_____ 1975. *A Pride of Gurkhas: the 2nd King Edward VII's Own Goorkhas (The Sirmoor Rifles) 1948–1971.* London: Leo Cooper.

Jenkins, L. H. 1923. *General Frederick Young*, London: George Routledge and Sons.

Jones, R.L. and S.K. Jones 1976. *The Himalayan Woman: a study of Limbu women in marriage and divorce*, Palo Alto: Mayfield.

Kabbani, R. 1986. *Europe's Myths of Orient*, Bloomington: Indiana Univ. Press.

Kakar, S. 1978. *The Inner World: a psycho-analytic study of childhood and society in India*, Delhi:OUP.

Kapferer, B. 1988 'The anthropologist as hero: three exponents of post-modernist anthropology' (review article), *Critique of Anthropology* 8:77–104.

Keegan, J. 1976. *The Face of Battle*, Harmondsworth, Penguin.

Keesing, R.M. 1989. 'Exotic readings of cultural texts', *Current Anthropology* 30:459–79.

Kellett, A. 1982. *Combat Motivation; the behavior of soldiers in battle*, Boston: Kluwer Nijhoff Publishing.

Kirkpatrick, W. 1811. *An Account of the Kingdom of Nepaul*, London: William Miller.

Kolff, D.H.A. 1990. *Naukar, Rajput and Sepoy: the ethnohistory of the military labour market in Hindustan, 1450–1850*, Cambridge: Univ. Press.

Landon, P. 1928. *Nepal* (2 vols), London: Constable.

Laver, J. 1968. *The Book of Public School Old Boys, University, Navy, Army, Air Force and Club Ties*, London: Seeley Service & Co.

Leach, E.R. 1961. Aspects of bridewealth and marriage stability among the Kachin and Lakher. In *Rethinking Anthropology*, London: Athlone.

* Leonard, R.G. 1965 (for the Ministry of Defence). *Nepal and the Gurkhas*, London: Her Majesty's Stationery Office.

Lindisfarne, N. 1993. Variant masculinities, variant virginities: rethinking 'honour and shame'. In *Dislocating Masculinity: comparative ethnographies* (eds) A. Cornwall and N. Lindisfarne. London: Routledge.

Lunt, J. (ed.) 1970 [1873]. *From Sepoy to Subedar: being the life and adventures of Subedar Sita Ram, a Native Officer of the Bengal Army written and related by himself*, London: Routledge.

Macdonald, A.W. 1991. 'Language, literature and cultural identity of the Tamang'. Unpublished.

Macdonald, K.M. 1988. '"Vitai Lampada": preserving the elite', *Armed Forces and Society* 14:233–45.

Macfarlane, A. 1976. *Resources and Population: a study of the Gurungs of Nepal*, Cambridge: Univ. Press.

_____ 1990. 'Fatalism and development in Nepal', *Cambridge Anthropology* 14:13–36.

_____ 1991. 'Gurung Identity in a Period of rapid change'. Unpublished.

* Mackay, J.N. (compiler) 1952. *A History of the 4th Prince of Wales's Own Gurkha Rifles, Vol. III 1938–48*, Edinburgh and London: William Blackwood.

_____ 1962. *History of the 7th Duke of Edinburgh's Own Gurkha Rifles*, Edinburgh: Blackwood (for the Regimental Committee).

MacKenzie, J.M. 1987. The Imperial pioneer and hunter and the British masculine stereotype in late Victorian and Edwardian times. In *Manliness and Morality: middle-class masculinity in Britain and America, 1800–1940* (eds) J.A. Mangan and J. Walvin. Manchester: Univ. Press.

_____ 1989. Hunting and the natural world in juvenile literature. In *Imperialism and Juvenile Literature* (ed.) J. Richards. Manchester: Univ. Press.

Macmillan, M. 1984. Camp followers: a note on wives of the armed forces. In *The Incorporated Wife* (eds) H. Callan and S. Ardener. London: Croom Helm.

MacMunn, G. 1932. *The Martial Races of India*, London: Sampson Low, Marston.

_____ and A.C. Lovett 1911. *The Armies of India*, London: Adam and Charles Black.

* Mains, A.A. 1990. 'Further jottings on service in the army of India, 1934–39', *The Bulletin: Journal of the Military Historical Society* 41 (162):80–92.

Mangan, J.A. 1986. 'The grit of our forefathers': invented traditions, propaganda and imperialism. In *Imperialism and Popular Culture* (ed.) J.M. Mackenzie. Manchester: Univ. Press.

_____ 1987. Social Darwinism and upper-class education in late Victorian and Edwardian England. In *Manliness and Morality: middle-class masculinity in Britain and America, 1800–1940* (eds) J.A. Mangan and J. Walvin. Manchester: Univ. Press.

_____ 1988. Moralists, metaphysicians and mythologists: the 'signifiers' of a Victorian and Edwardian sub-culture. In *Coreobus Triumphs: the alliance of sport and the arts* (ed.) S.J. Bandy. San Diego: State Univ. Press.

Mani, L. 1986. 'Notes on colonial discourse', *Inscriptions* 2:3–4.

_____ and R. Frankenberg 1985. 'The challenge of Orientalism', *Economy and Society* 14:174–92.

Mannsaker, F. 1983. Early attitudes to empire. In *Literature and Imperialism* (ed.) B. Moore-Gilbert. Roehampton: English Department of the Roehampton Institute of Higher Education.

* Marks, J.M. 1971. *Ayo Gurkha!*, London: OUP.

Mascia-Lees, F.E., P. Sharpe and C. B. Cohen 1989. 'The postmodern turn in anthropology: cautions from a feminist perspective', *Signs* 15:7–33.

Mason, P. 1974. *A Matter of Honour: an account of the Indian army, its officers and men*, London: Jonathan Cape.

* Masters, J. 1956. *Bugles and a Tiger: a personal adventure*, London: Michael Joseph.

* Maxwell, R.M. 1986. *Desperate Encounters: stories of the 5th Royal Gurkha Rifles of the Punjab Frontier Force*, Edinburgh: The Pentland Press.

_____ 1990. *Villiers-Stuart Goes to War*, Edinburgh: The Pentland Press.

* McAlister, R.W.L. 1984. *Bugle and Kukri: the story of the 10th Princess Mary's Own Gurkha Rifles*, Vol. 2. Newport, Isle of Wight: The Regimental Trust, 10th P.M.O. GR.

McDougal, C. 1968. *Village and Household Economy in Far Western Nepal,* Kirtipur, Nepal: Tribhuvan University.

_____ 1979. *The Kulunge Rai: a study in kinship and marriage exchange,* Kathmandu: Ratna Pustak Bhandar.

* McKeag, H.T.A. 1921. *Letters from the East, being records of journeyings and sojourns in India, Mesopotamia and Persia.* Belfast: Printed & published by the author.

Messerschmidt, D.A. 1976. *The Gurungs of Nepal: conflict and change in a village society,* Warminster: Aris and Phillips.

Mikesell, S.L. and J. Shrestha 1985–6. 'The Gurkhas: a case study of the problem of mercenary recruitment in Barpak, Nepal', *Strategic Studies,* 6/7:146–54.

Mishra, C. 1985–6. 'The Gurkhas: its genesis', *Strategic Studies* 6/7:155–61.

_____ 1991. 'Three Gorkhali myths', *Himal* 4 (3):17.

Mojumdar, K. 1972. 'Recruitment of the Gurkhas in the Indian army, 1814–1877', *United Service Institution Journal,* 102:143–57.

_____ 1973. *Anglo-Nepalese Relations in the Nineteenth Century,* Calcutta: K.L. Mukhopadhyay.

Moore-Gilbert, B. (ed.) 1983. *Literature and Imperialism,* Roehampton: English Department of the Roehampton Institute of Higher Education.

Moran, Lord 1945. *The Anatomy of Courage,* London: Constable.

* Morris, C.J. (compiler) 1933. *Gurkhas: Handbooks for the Indian Army,* Delhi: Manager of Publications, Govt. of India.

_____ 1935. 'Some aspects of social life in Nepal', *Journal of the Royal Central Asian Society* 22:425–46.

_____ 1960. *Hired to Kill: some chapters of autobiography.* London: Rupert Hart-Davies, Cresset Press.

Mrozek, D.J. 1987. The habit of victory: the American military and the cult of manliness. In *Manliness and Morality: middle-class masculinity in Britain and America, 1800–1940* (eds) J.A. Mangan and J. Walvin. Manchester: Univ. Press.

* Mullaly, B.R. 1950. 'Scot and Gurkha: the continuation of a great tradition', *The Bugle and Kukri* 2 (1):16–18.

_____ 1957. *Bugle and Kukri: the story of the 10th Princess Mary's Own Gurkha Rifles,* Edinburgh: William Blackwood.

Muni, S.D. 1973. *Foreign Policy of Nepal,* Delhi: National Publishing House.

Nakane, C. 1966. A plural society in Sikkim. In *Caste and Kin in Nepal, India and Ceylon* (ed.) C. von Fürer-Haimendorf. Bombay: Asia.

Nandy, A. 1983. *The Intimate Enemy: loss and recovery of self under colonialism,* Delhi: OUP.

* Neild, E. n.d. *With Pegasus in India: the story of the 153 Gurkha Parachute Battalion,* Singapore: Jay Birch.

* Nicholson, J.B.R. 1974. *The Gurkha Rifles,* London: Osprey.

* Niven, B.M. 1987. *The Mountain Kingdom: portraits of Nepal and the Gurkhas,* Singapore: Imago Productions.

Norris, C. 1990. 'Limited think: how not to read Derrida', *Diacritics* 20:17–36.

* Northey, W.B. 1937. *The Land of the Gurkhas or the Himalayan Kingdom of Nepal*, London: Hefer and Sons.

———— and C.J. Morris 1928. *The Gurkhas: their manners, customs and country*, London: John Lane, The Bodley Head.

Nugent, S. 1988. 'The "peripheral situation"', *Annual Review of Anthropology* 17:79–98.

Okely, J. and H. Callaway (eds) 1992. *Anthropology and Autobiography*, London: Routledge.

Oldfield, H.A. 1974 [1880]. *Sketches from Nepal: historical and descriptive with an essay on Nepalese Buddhism and illustrations of religious monuments and architecture*, Delhi: Cosmo.

O'Malley, L.S.S. 1907. *Bengal District Gazetteers*, Darjeeling: The Bengal Secretariat Book Depot.

Omissi, D. 1991. '"Martial Races": ethnicity and security in colonial India 1858–1939', *War and Society* 9:1–27.

Oppert, G. 1880. *Of the Weapons, Army Organisation, and Political Maxims of the Ancient Hindus: with special reference to gunpowder and firearms*, Madras: Higginbotham.

Ortner, S.B. 1989. *High Religion: a cultural and political history of Sherpa Buddhism*, Princeton: Univ. Press.

Otley, C.B. 1970. 'The social origins of British army officers', *Sociological Review* 18:213–39.

———— 1973. 'The educational background of British army officers', *Sociology* 7:191–209.

———— 1978. 'Militarism and militarization in the public schools, 1900–1972', *British Journal of Sociology* 29:321–31.

Padel, F. 1988. 'Anthropologists of tribal India: merchants of knowledge'. Unpublished.

Pahari, A. 1991. 'Ties that Bind: Gurkhas in history', *Himal* 4 (3):6–12.

* Palit, A.N. 1954. 'With the 5th Gurkhas, 1910–11', *The Gorkha*, pp. 53–8.

Palsokar, R.D. 1984. 'On motivation', *United Service Institution Journal*, 114:164–70.

———— 1991. *History of the 5th Gorkha Rifles (Frontier Force). Vol. III, 1858 to 1991*, The Commandant, 5th GR.

Pant, M.R. 1978. 'Nepal's defeat in the Nepal-British war', *Regmi Research Series* 10: 150–9.

Parkin, D.J. 1986. Toward an apprehension of fear. In *Sociophobics: the anthropology of fear* (ed.) R. Scruton. London: Westview.

———— 1990. Eastern Africa: the view from the office and the voice from the field. In *Localizing Strategies: regional traditions of ethnographic writing* (ed.) R Fardon. Edinburgh: Scottish Academic Press.

Parmanand 1982. *The Nepali Congress since its inception: a critical assessment*, Delhi: B.R. Publishing Corp.

Parry, B. 1972. *Delusions and Discoveries: studies on India in the British imagination 1880–1930*, London: Allen Lane, Penguin.

* Pearse, H. 1898. 'The Goorkha soldier (as an enemy and as a friend)', *Macmillan's Magazine* 78:225–37.

Peers, D.M. 1991. ''The habitual nobility of being': British officers and the social construction of the Bengal Army in the early Nineteenth Century', *Modern Asian Studies* 25:545–69.

Pelly, L. (ed.) 1858. *The Views and Opinions of Brig.-Gen. John Jacob*, London: Smith Elder.

Pemble, J. 1971. *The Invasion of Nepal: John Company at War*, Oxford: Clarendon.

Perkins, R. 1989. *Regiments of the Empire: a bibliography of their published histories*, Newton Abbot (Devon): Privately Published.

* Petre, F.L. 1925. *The 1st King George's Own Gurkha Rifles: the Malaun Regiment (1815–1921)*, London: Royal United Service Institution.

* Pickford, S.C. 1989. *Destination Rangoon*, Denbigh: Gee and Son.

Pignède, B. 1966. *Les Gurungs: une population himalayenne du Népal*. Paris: Mouton.

Pinney, C. 1991. Ethnographies as Books: or, homage to the image. In *Voice, genre, text—anthropological essays in Africa and beyond* (eds) P. Baxter and R. Fardon. Special issue, *Bulletin of the John Ryland's University Library of Manchester* 73 (3).

Pocock, T. 1973. *Fighting General: the public and private campaigns of General Sir Walter Walker*, London: Collins.

* Poynder, F.S. 1937. *The Ninth Gurkha Rifles, 1817–1936*, London: Royal United Services Institution.

Praval, K.C. 1987. *Indian Army after Independence*, New Delhi: Lancer International.

Prinsep, H.T. 1825. *History of the Political and Military Transactions in India during the Administration of the Marquess of Hastings, 1813–1823*, London: Kingsbury, Porbury and Allen.

Proudfoot, C.L. 1984. *Flash of the Khukri: history of the 3rd Gorkha Rifles (1947 to 1980)*. New Delhi: Vision Books.

Rabinow, P. 1986. Representations are social facts: modernity and post-modernity in anthropology. In *Writing Culture: the poetics and politics of ethnography* (eds) J. Clifford and G. Marcus. Berkeley: Univ. of Calif. Press.

Rachman, S.J. 1978. *Fear and Courage*, San Francisco: Freeman.

Ragsdale, T.A. 1989. *Once a Hermit Kingdom: ethnicity, education and national integration in Nepal*, Delhi:Manohar.

——— 1990. 'Gurungs, Goorkhalis, Gurkhas: speculations on a Nepalese ethno-history', *Contributions to Nepalese Studies* 17:1–24.

Ramakant 1968. *Indo-Nepalese Relations: 1816 to 1877*, Delhi: S. Chand.

Rana, N.R.L. 1970. *The Anglo-Gorkha War (1814–1816)*, Kathmandu: the Author.

Rana, P.S.J.B. and K.P. Malla (eds) 1973. *Nepal in Perspective*, Kathmandu: Centre for Economic Development and Administration.

Rathaur, K.R.S. 1987. *The British and the Brave: a history of the Gurkha recruitment in the British Indian army*, Jaipur: Nirola.

Razzell, P.E. 1963. 'Social origins of officers in the Indian and British Home army 1758–1962', *British Journal of Sociology* 14:248–60.

Regmi, M.C. 1971. *A Study in Nepali Economic History 1768–1846*, New Delhi: Manjusri.

Richards, J. 1983. Films and the empire: Britain in the 1930s. In *Literature and Imperialism* (ed.) B. Moore-Gilbert. Roehampton: English Department of the Roehampton Institute of Higher Education.

———— (ed.) 1989. *Imperialism and Juvenile Literature*, Manchester: Univ. Press.

Ridley, H. 1983. *Images of Imperial Rule*, London: Croom Helm.

Roberts Lord 1897. *Forty-one Years in India: from Subaltern to Commander-in-Chief* (2 vols), London: Richard Bentley & Son.

Roland, A. 1988. *In Search of Self in India and Japan: toward a cross-cultural psychology*, Princeton: Univ. Press.

Rorty, R. 1982. Philosophy as a kind of writing: an essay on Derrida. In *Consequences of Pragmatism (essays:1972–1980)*, Brighton: Harvester.

Rosaldo, R. 1986. From the door of his tent: the fieldworker and the inquisitor. In *Writing Culture: the poetics and politics of ethnography* (eds) J. Clifford and G. Marcus. Berkeley: Univ. of Calif. Press.

Rose, L.E. 1961. China and the Anglo-Nepal war: 1814–1816. *Proceedings of the 24th Indian History Conference.*

———— 1971. *Nepal: strategy for survival*, Berkeley: Univ. of Calif. Press.

———— and M.W. Fisher 1970. *The Politics of Nepal: persistence and change in an Asian Monarchy*, Cornell: Univ. Press.

* Rundall, F.M. 1889. 'Raising a new Goorkha regiment in India', *Asiatic Quarterly Review* 7:46–73.

Russell, A. 1992. 'The Yakha: Culture, Environment and Development in East Nepal', unpublished D. Phil thesis, Oxford University.

Rutherford, A. 1989 [1978]. *The Literature of War: studies in heroic virtue*, London: Macmillan.

Sagant, P. 1970. 'Mariage "par enlèvement" chez les Limbu (Népal)', *Cahiers Internationaux de Sociologie* 48:71–98.

———— 1978. 'Quand le Gurkha revient de guerre...', *Ethnographie*, 120:155–84.

———— 1985. 'With head held high: the house, ritual and politics in east Nepal', *Kailash* 3 & 4: 161–221.

Said, E. 1978. *Orientalism*, London: Routledge.

———— 1985. Orientalism reconsidered. In *Europe and its Others* (Vol.1) (eds) F. Barker et al. Colchester: Univ. of Essex.

Sangren, P.S. 1988. 'Rhetoric and the authority of ethnography', *Current Anthropology* 29:405–35.

Sanwal, B.D. 1965. *Nepal and the East India Company*, Bombay: Asia.

Saxena, K.M.L. 1974. *The Military System of India (1850–1900)*, New Delhi: Sterling.

Scholte, R. 1987. 'The literary turn in contemporary anthropology' (review article), *Critique of Anthropology* 7:33–47.

Seidler, V.J. 1989. *Rediscovering Masculinity: reason, language and sexuality*, London: Routledge.

Sen, J. 1977. *Indo-Nepal Trade in the Nineteenth Century*, Calcutta: Firma KLM.

Shaha, R. 1983/1984. 'Historic battles in the Nepal-British war of 1814–16', *Rolamba* 3 (4):2–6; 4 (1):2–5.

_____ 1986/1987. 'The rise and fall of Bhimsen Thapa: the war of 1814–16 with British India and its aftermath', *Rolamba* 6 (1):2–7; 7 (2):22–31.

* Shakespear, L.W. 1913. 'The war with Nepal: operations in Sirmoor, 1814–1815', *Journal of the United Service Institute of India* 42:369–79.

_____ and G.R. Stevens 1912. *The History of the 2nd King Edward VII's Own Goorkha Rifles (The Sirmoor Rifles)*, London: Gale and Polden.

Sharma, G. 1988. *Path of Glory: exploits of 11 Gorkha Rifles*, Allied: Ahmedabad.

* Sheil-Small, D. 1982. *Green Shadows: a Gurkha story*, London: William Kimber.

Shipp, J. 1829. *Memoirs of the Extraordinary Military Career of John Shipp, late a lieutenant in His Majesty's 87th Regiment, written by himself* (3 vols), London: Hurst, Chance & Co.

* Short, N. 1990. Foreword to *Allanson of the 6th: an account of the life of Col. Cecil John Lyons Allanson CMG DSO, 6 Gurkha Rifles, compiled from his diaries, letters and personal papers* (compiler) H. Davies, Lowesmoor: Square One Publications.

Silverman, M. 1991. 'Dispatch 1. Amongst "our selves": a colonial encounter in Canadian academia', *Critique of Anthropology* 11:381–400.

Singh, H.L. 1980. *Principal Records of Nepal*, Kathmandu: Satish Singh.

Singh, K. 1962. *Ranjit Singh: Maharajah of the Punjab*, London: George Allen and Unwin.

Singh, T.N. 1952. 'The Gorkhas: an introduction by Lt.-Gen. Thakur Nathu Singh', *The Gorkha*, pp. 13–18.

Sinha, N.K. 1933. *Ranjit Singh*, Calcutta: Univ. of Calcutta.

* Slim, W. 1957. *Courage and other Broadcasts*, London: Cassell.

* Smith, E.D. 1973. *Britain's Brigade of Gurkhas*, London: Leo Cooper.

_____ 1976. *East of Kathmandu: the story of the 7th Duke of Edinburgh's Own Gurkha Rifles Vol. II, 1948–1973*, London: Leo Cooper.

_____ 1978. *Even the Brave Falter*, London: Robert Hale.

Smith, T. 1852. *Narrative of a Five Years' Residence at Nepaul* (2 vols), London: Colburn.

* Spaight, W.J.M. 1941. 'The name "Gurkha"', *Journal of the Royal Central Asian Society* 28:200–203.

Stiller, L.F. 1973. *The Rise of the House of Gorkha: a study in the unification of Nepal 1768–1816*, Kathmandu: Ratna Pustak Bhandar.

_____ 1976. *The Silent Cry: the people of Nepal 1816–1839*, Kathmandu: Sahayogi.

_____ 1989 [1968]. *Prithwinarayan Shah in the Light of Dibya Upadesh*, Kathmandu: Himalaya Book Centre.

Stoler, A.L. 1989. 'Rethinking colonial categories: European communities and the boundaries of rule', *Comparative Studies in Society and History* 31:134–161.

Street, B. 1975. *The Savage in Literature: representations of 'primitive' society in English fiction 1858–1920*, London: Routledge.

Subba, T.B. 1992. *Ethnicity, State and Development: a case study of the Gorkhaland movement in Darjeeling*, Delhi: Vikas.

Tamang, P. 1992. 'Tamangs under the shadow', *Himal* 5 (3):25–27.

Tarlo E. J. in press. *Dress and Undress in India: the problem of 'what to wear' in the late colonial and modern era*, London: C. Hurst.

Temple, R. 1887. *Journals Kept in Hyderabad, Kashmir, Sikkim, and Nepal* (2 vols.), London: WH Allen.

Tillich, P. 1984 [1952]. *The Courage to Be*, London: Collins.

Tuan, Y. 1984. *Dominance and Affection: the making of pets*, New Haven: Yale Univ. Press.

* Tuker, F. 1950. *While Memory Serves*, London: Cassell.

_____ 1957. *Gorkha: the story of the Gurkhas of Nepal*, London: Constable.

Turner, E.S. 1956. *Gallant Gentlemen: a portrait of the British officer, 1600–1956*, London: Michael Joseph.

* Turner, R.L. 1931. *Nepali Dictionary, Comparative and Etymological*, London: Routledge and Kegan Paul.

* Twiss, L.O. 1961. *Some of my Memories*, Privately published.

Vagts, A. 1959. *A History of Militarism: civilian and military*, London: Hollis and Carter.

Vance, N. 1975. The ideal of manliness. In *The Victorian Public School: studies in the development of an educational institution* (eds) B. Simon and I. Bradley. Dublin: Gill and Macmillan.

* Vansittart, E. 1894. 'The tribes, clans and castes of Nepal', *Journal of the Asiatic Society of Bengal* 63 (2):213–49.

_____ 1915. *Gurkhas: Handbooks for the Indian Army*, Calcutta: Government of India.

Wakeham, E. 1937. *The Bravest Soldier: Sir Rollo Gillespie, 1766–1814*, Edinburgh: William Blackwood.

Walker, A.R. 1991. 'The western romance with the Toda', *Sociological Bulletin* 40:21–46.

Walton, D.N. 1986. *Courage: a philosophical investigation*, Berkeley: Univ. of Calif. Press.

Wheeler, V. 1986. 'Travelers' tales: observations on the travel book and ethnography', *Anthropological Quarterly* 59:52–63.

Whelpton, J. 1983. *Jang Bahadur in Europe: the first Nepalese mission to the West*, Kathmandu: Sahayogi.

* Wilkinson, T. 1976. *Two Monsoons*, London: Duckworth.

Wilson, Lady 1984 [1911]. *Letters from India*, London: Century.

* Woodyatt, N. 1922. *Under Ten Viceroys: the reminiscences of a Gurkha*, London: Herbert Jenkins.

———— 1923. *My Sporting Memories: forty years with note-book and gun*, London: Herbert Jenkins.

Worthington, I. 1977. 'Antecedent education and officer recruitment: the origins and early development of the public school—army relationship', *Military Affairs* 41:183–89.

Zaehner, R.C. 1966. *The Bhagavad-Gita*, London: Dent.

Officers' Unpublished Diaries, Letters and Memoirs consulted

Gudgeon, Lieutenant D.G.F. (2GR), Imperial War Museum [Acc. 85/8/1]

Gray, Brigadier C. (3GR), Oriental and India Office Collections of the British Library [Acc. Eur D 1037]

Mains, Lieutenant-Colonel A.A. (9GR) Gurkha Museum [Acc. 9GR/309]

Moore, Lieutenant-Colonel D.J.R. (1GR) Oriental and India Office Collections [Acc. Photo. Eur. 226]

Villiers-Stuart, Brigadier-General W.D. (5GR) Gurkha Museum [Acc. 84/-1/-]

Fell, Colonel A.L.N. (2GR) Gurkha Museum [Acc. 90/12/05 Fl]

Bagot-Chester, Captain W.G. (3GR) National Army Museum [6012–337–1]

Judge, Major C.B. (2GR) National Army Museum [7207–47–1]

Penfold, Captain H.L. de (9GR) National Army Museum [7808–94–1]

Stewart, Major-General J.M. (5GR) Private Collection [Lieutenant-Colonel D.R. Wood]

......

INDEX

Author Index

Adshead, D.R. 7, 113
Aitken, B. 141
Allen, N.J. 44, 144
Anderson, B. 57, 98, 153
Anderson, J.W. 129
Appadurai, A. 7, 158
Aryal, M. 44
Asad, T. 26

Badenach, W. 27
Baxter, P. 9
Baynes, J. 58, 62, 65, 66, 78, 79, 81, 85, 128, 129, 131, 151
Ben-Ari, E. 9
Bennett, L. 91
Bennett, S. 65, 84
Biardeau, M. 128
Bingley, A.H. 89, 90, 122
Bishop, E. 6, 21, 109, 115, 132, 133, 134
Bista, D.B. 32
Blaikie, P. 32, 35, 40, 43
Blake, J. A. 129
Bolt, D. 36, 87, 109, 113, 115, 133, 134, 142, 143
Bredin, A.E.C. 100, 105, 109, 115, 143, 144, 151

Bristow, R.C.B. 64, 67, 69, 144, 152
Bruce, C.G. 1, 104
Bryant, G. 56, 83
Burghart, R. 14, 18
Burke, K. 3, 88, 120
Burroughs, P. 2, 8, 25, 65

Callaway, H. 152
Cameron, J. 32
Campbell, B.R.G. 96
Candler, E. 108, 112, 132, 144, 147, 148
Caplan, A.P. 35, 36, 46, 152
Caplan, L. 18, 30, 31, 35, 37, 38, 39, 40, 41, 46, 48
Cardew, F.G. 95
Carew, T. 112, 134
Carnaticus 133
Cavenaugh, O. 19, 114
Chakravarti, P.C. 122, 127
Chandos, J. 61, 62, 63, 79, 82, 84, 102
Chant, C. 115
Chapple, J.L. 11, 22, 25, 27, 72, 75, 85, 93, 95, 113
Chatterji, B. 110
Chaudhuri, K.C. 14, 16, 26
Chhetry, D.B. 106
Clifford, J. 1, 4, 10, 12, 157

Cohen, C.B. 26
Cohen, S.P. 56, 123, 124
Collier, P. 25
Colson, E. 136
Crapanzano, V. 12
Creagh, M.O. 90, 122, 125
Cross, J.P. 7, 26, 36, 50, 54, 100, 105, 109, 111, 113, 116, 132, 133, 143

Dabaral, S.P. 141
Dahal, D.R. 35
Dandekar, C. 26
Daniell, D. 102, 123
Das, C.N. 22, 27, 123, 151
Dasgupta, J. 13
Date, G.T. 122
Davis, P. 11, 67, 70, 100, 119, 139
Dawson, G. 120, 149
Dawson, H.D. 26
Des Chene, M. 8, 18, 38, 48, 51, 55, 70, 94, 101, 109, 117, 123, 133, 135, 137, 150, 151, 156
Dixit, K.M. 26, 110, 132
Dixon, J. 26
Donaldson, E. 32

Ellis, J. 59, 67, 108, 149
Empson, W. 88, 120
Enloe, C.H. 18, 27, 52, 88, 89, 94, 107, 111, 113, 154
Evans-Pritchard, E.E. 85, 123

Fabian, J. 3, 10, 12, 155
Fardon, R. 2, 7, 9
Farwell, B. 9, 26, 61, 64, 77, 78, 86, 102, 108, 117, 132, 148
Finley, M.I. 148
Fisher, J.F. 35
Fisher, M.W. 21, 36
Forbes, D. 12, 15, 16, 18, 28, 70, 103, 105, 109, 143
Forteath, G.M. 63
Foucault, M. 4

Fox, R.G. 26, 89, 90, 101
Frankenberg, R. 10, 12
Fraser, J.B. 15, 92, 140
Fussell, P. 157

Gaborieau, M. 126
Gaige, F.H. 32
Garnier, M. 66, 86
Geertz, C. 9
Geyer-Ryan, H. 25
Gibbs, H.R.K. 9, 94, 96, 97, 99, 100
Gilmore, D.D. 102, 107
Girouard, M. 61, 63, 82, 84, 102, 115, 151
Gluckman, M. 54
Goddard, E. 88, 107, 112, 131
Green, M. 6, 59, 62, 84, 89, 90, 102, 105, 122, 153
Greenhut, J. 61, 84, 108, 112, 135
Gregory, C.A. 30
Gurung, H.B. 26
Gutteridge, W. 68, 69

Hamilton, F. 92
Hart, K. 31
Hasrat, B.J. 18, 20, 34, 104, 141
Haycock, R. 1
Heathcote, T.A. 27, 54, 57, 65, 84, 89, 90, 94, 130
Herzfeld, M. 107
Hickey, M. 134
Hitchcock, J.T. 29, 31, 32, 36, 39, 46, 47, 54, 106
Hodgson, B.H. 19, 92, 94, 103, 104, 145
Höfer, A. 31, 32, 46, 47, 49, 95
Holy, L. 10
Holy-Hasted, J.S. 83
House of Commons 26, 36, 37, 38, 46, 69, 99, 109, 113, 124, 135, 151
Hunter, W.W. 19, 104
Husain, A. 21, 34, 94, 108
Hutt, M. 49

Inden, R. 9, 101

James, H. 19, 21, 80, 85, 113, 150
Jenkins, L. H. 125
Jones, R.L. 31, 36, 39, 41, 43, 44, 45
Jones, S.K. 31, 36, 39, 41, 43, 44, 45

Kabbani, R. 4, 8, 123
Kakar, S. 101 123
Kapferer, B. 4, 152
Keegan, J. 61, 66, 130, 131, 148
Keesing, R.M. 3
Kellett, A. 131
Kirkpatrick, W. 16, 17, 91
Kolff, D.H.A. 54

Landon, P. 19, 123
Laver, J. 71
Leach, E.R. 54
Leonard, R.G. 7, 15, 26, 95, 100,
    105, 122, 142, 143, 144
Lindisfarne, N. 107
Lovett, A.C. 89, 102
Lunt, J. 112

Macdonald, A.W. 29
Macdonald, K.M. 59, 84, 86
Macfarlane, A. 29, 30, 32, 35, 39,
    40, 41, 42, 43, 44, 50, 51, 54
Mackay, J.N. 22, 71, 72, 74
MacKenzie, J.M. 65, 123
Macmillan, M. 75, 86
MacMunn, G. 68, 74, 89, 90, 98, 99,
    101, 102, 107, 121, 143
Mains, A.A. 58, 64, 74
Malla, K.P. 110
Mangan, J.A. 61, 63, 84, 130, 151
Mani, L. 2, 10, 12
Mannsaker, F. 12, 101, 153
Marks, J.M. 134
Mascia-Lees, F.E. 26
Mason, P. 19, 61, 68, 89, 103, 112,
    116, 121, 123, 142, 146

Masters, J. 5, 21, 57, 58, 60, 63, 66,
    75, 77, 85, 102, 108, 142
Maxwell, R.M. 71, 79
McDougal, C. 36, 39, 44
McKeag, H.T.A. 147
Messerschmidt, D.A. 36, 39, 40
Mikesell, S.L. 44, 53
Mishra, C. 32, 110, 149
Mojumdar, K. 20, 21, 92, 93, 106
Moore-Gilbert, B. 62
Moran, Lord 131
Morris, C.J. 16, 57, 64, 66, 76, 85,
    94, 96, 97, 98, 99, 106, 108, 112,
    114, 119, 122, 125, 142, 144, 145
Mrozek, D.J. 151
Mullaly, B.R. 72, 74, 133
Muni, S.D. 110, 124

Nakane, C. 32
Nandy, A. 120, 155
Neild, E. 74
Nicholls, A. 89, 90, 122
Nicholson, J.B.R. 71, 74, 144
Niven, B.M. 100, 108, 113, 134
Norris, C. 26
Northey, W.B. 15, 16, 21, 74, 95, 97,
    98, 99, 105, 106, 108, 113, 114,
    140, 142, 144
Nugent, S. 10

Okely, J. 152
Oldfield, H.A. 102, 141, 151
O'Malley, L.S.S. 32
Omissi, D. 1991. 88, 94, 99, 107,
    108, 122, 123, 141, 146, 148
Oppert, G. 127
Ortner, S.B. 35
Otley, C.B. 58, 59, 60, 83, 84, 86

Padel, F. 8
Pahari, A. 34, 36, 39, 42, 92, 96,
    124, 146
Palit, A.N. 64, 75

Palsokar, R.D. 27, 56
Pant, M.R. 16, 141
Parkin, D.J. 10, 137, 150
Parmanand 109
Parry, B. 98, 101, 116
Pearse, H. 16, 141
Peers, D.M. 57, 105, 112, 124
Pelly, L. 90, 107, 112, 151
Pemble, J. 11, 16, 17, 56, 84, 92, 114, 141, 150
Perkins, R. 25
Petre, F.L. 66, 146
Pickford, S.C. 64
Pignède, B. 38, 39, 40, 43, 47, 53
Pinney, C. 158
Pocock, T. 142
Poynder, F.S. 22
Praval, K.C. 117, 118
Prinsep, H.T. 13, 124
Proudfoot, C.L. 27, 66, 69, 117

Rabinow, P. 10
Rachman, S.J. 131, 132
Ragsdale, T.A. 29, 35, 46, 47, 51, 94, 96
Ramakant 13, 14, 19
Rana, N.R.L. 14
Rana, P.S.J.B. 110
Rathaur, K.R.S. 20, 34, 92
Razzell, P.E. 56, 59
Regmi, M.C. 16
Richards, J. 61, 84
Ridley, H. 65
Roberts, Lord 68, 88, 89, 90, 102, 103, 112, 114, 121
Roland, A. 120
Rorty, R. 12
Rosaldo, R. 105, 120
Rose, L.E. 14, 21, 36, 37, 106, 110
Rundall, F.M. 93
Russell, A. 46
Rutherford, A. 149

Sagant, P. 32, 37, 42, 43, 44, 48, 49, 134
Said, E. 1, 12, 101
Sangren, P.S. 10
Sanwal, B.D. 14, 19
Saxena, K.M.L. 15, 57, 68, 94, 112
Scholte, R. 10
Seddon, D. 32
Seidler, V.J. 88, 123
Sen, J. 13
Shaha, R. 18, 91, 104, 114, 142
Shakespear, L.W. 72, 92, 124
Sharma, G. 27
Sharpe, P. 26
Sheil-Small, D. 9, 19, 21, 22, 80, 85, 113, 147
Shipp, J. 84, 132, 140
Short, N. 86
Shrestha, J. 44, 53
Silverman, M. 158
Singh, H.L. 143, 144
Singh, K. 11, 17
Singh, T.N. 124, 150
Sinha, N.K. 33
Slim, W. 55, 112, 129, 130, 132
Smith, E.D. 8, 22, 26, 71, 111, 133, 134, 135
Smith, T. 15, 145
Spaight, W.J.M. 11
Stevens, G.R. 72, 124
Stiller, L.F. 13, 14, 15, 17, 18, 20, 26, 227, 33, 91, 104, 122
Stoler, A.L. 86
Street, B. 61, 89, 109, 147
Stuchlik, M. 10
Subba, T.B. 26

Tamang, P. 96
Tarlo E. J. 101
Temple, R. 104, 146
Tillich, P. 128
Tuan, Y. 3, 121, 148, 151

Tuker, F. 16, 22, 69, 99, 103, 105, 112, 113, 115, 117, 132, 143, 146
Turner, E.S. 57, 59, 84
Turner, R.L. 126, 135, 136
Twiss, L.O. 64, 76

Vagts, A. 4, 79, 103, 108, 142
Vance, N. 82
Vansittart, E. 15, 46, 92, 93, 94, 95, 96, 97, 100, 103, 107, 108, 109, 114, 122, 124, 142, 143, 144, 145, 151

Wakeham, E. 17, 128, 130
Walker, A.R. 4
Walton, D.N. 127, 131, 148, 150
Walvin, J. 61
Wheeler, V. 2, 3
Whelpton, J. 18
Wilkinson, T. 142
Wilson, Lady 73
Wood, D.R. 75, 83, 113
Woodyatt, N. 65, 67, 74, 85, 100, 106, 123, 147
Worthington, I. 59

Zaehner, R.C. 128

Subject Index

Anglo-Nepal war 6, 14, 15 *passim*, 33, 34, 91, 92, 95, 103, 106, 113, 114, 128, 140, 141, 150

Bengal army 16, 17, 88, 90, 105, 112, 114, 122 (*see also* Indian army)
  mutiny of (*see* Mutiny)
Bengalis 102, 123
Brahman(s) 31, 32, 49, 51, 121, 122, 145 (*see also* NBC's)
  as non-martial 88, 91, 95

British army 1, 2, 22–3, 24, 40, 44, 53, 80, 101, 117, 124, 157 (*see also* Royal army, Indian army)
  and public schools 59 *passim*
British officer(s) 3, 4, 5, 8, 9, 17, 18, 25, 52, 55 *passim*, 67, 79, 80, 97, 114, 147–50 (*see also* Gurkha regiments)
  authors 1, 4, 12, 15, 16, 17, 18, 22, 24, 29, 34, 102, 103, 105, 107, 111, 119, 148, 150, 151, 153, 156–8.
  and careerism 79, 80 *passim*, 116
  as chivalrous gentleman 61–2, 65, 82
  and courage 129–30, 153
  class 4, 150
  culture 74
  as ethnographers 93–4
  as gentleman 63, 65, 82
  –Gurkha soldier bond 3, 25, 69, 88, 92, 107, 112 *passim*, 120, 155
    founding myth of 115
  -Gurkha officer bond 67 *passim*
  as intellectually backward 108
  kin ties among 68, 77, 86
  mess 73
    and women 74–5
  patriotism 62, 153
  private means 58, 84
  and public schools 4, 59 *passim*, 82, 84, 86, 153
  recruitment of 66
  and regiment 67, 76, 78 *passim*, 83, 86, 115, 118, 157 (*see also* Gurkha regiments)
  and shikar 65
  social backgrounds of 57
  and sport 63 *passim*, 82, 84
  and staff college 78–9, 82
British Resident/Residency 13, 14, 19, 20, 34, 103, 106, 108

Chetri(s) 31, 49, 54, 91, 94, 95, 96, 122 (*see also* NBC's)
colonial discourse 2
'Confrontation' 23, 27, 38, 79, 157 (*see also* British army)
courage, western views of 126 *passim*, 148
military views of 128 *passim*

East India Company 13, 17, 19, 21, 26, 34, 54, 113 (*see also* Anglo-Nepal war, Indian army)
'Emergency' 23, 137
ethnographic writing 2

Garhwal/Garhwalis 14, 18, 30, 93
Gorkha (see Nepal)
Gurkha(s)
bravery 126, 131 *passim*, 147, 154, 157
decorations 139, 148
and fate 139, 148
and fear 131–2, 137–8
Brigade 2, 4, 6, 8, 11, 22, 23, 24, 27, 36, 41, 47, 50, 54, 118
Association 77, 86
future of 24
discourse 4
as fictions 10, 12, 156
handbooks 7, 93, 95, 100, 107
images of (*see* representations)
killed 42
literature 4, 7, 9, 10, 12, 24, 62, 87, 100 (see also texts)
as genre 6, 9, 10, 156
role of Foreword in 9
marriages 44
miniaturisation of 148, 155
officers 39, 68 *passim*, 85, 99, 117
pensions 36–42, 51, 54
pensioners 36, 41, 47, 54
as elite 47–8
in towns 50 *passim*, 53

perspectives on courage 136 *passim*
recruitment of 13, 20–1, 23, 29, 33, 35, 36, 42, 93, 154
opposition to 20–1, 38
regiment (s/al) 2, 6, 8, 22
associations 76
Colonel of 9, 71
Colonel-in-chief of 71, 72
cultures 66, 70 *passim*, 78, 83, 153
division of 6, 22, 23, 117 (*see also* 'opt')
eastern 40, 76, 97
as elite corps 66, 82–3
guest nights 73–4
hierarchy of 66, 76
histories 4, 5, 22, 25, 27, 71, 109, 153
identities 75
popularity of 67
publications 76
and Scottish regiments 74
'sons' of the 67–8
western 95, 97, 122
religion 145
remittances 36
representations of 5, 10, 25, 50
chivalry (*see* courtesy)
courtesy of 7, 140 *passim*, 155
as gentlemen 126, 140, 142, 147–9, 156
as honorary Europeans 145–6, 149, 155
humour 7, 144, 155
and Indians, NBC's 144–6
loyalty 7, 25, 88, 107 *passim*, 154, 155
as martial race 87 *passim*, 93, 107, 148, 154 (*see also* martial races, manliness, masculinity)
as pets 3, 121, 148, 155

as public school boys 147,
149, 155
as reflections of British officers 147 *passim*
as simpletons 108, 124
as sportsmen 143–4, 155
stereotypes 100
as yeomen 28, 105, 143
salaries 37, 40, 42
savings 41
service, economics of 36 *passim*
effects on literacy of 45–6
demographic implications of
42–3
impact on women of 44–5
texts 2, 3, 26 (*see also* literature)
Gurungs 29, 33, 35, 39, 40, 43, 91,
92, 94, 95–7, 100, 122, 145

Hawaii incident 110, 118, 121, 124,
156
high caste(s) 11 (*see also* NBC's)
regiment 95

Indian army (pre-Independnce) 1, 6,
15, 19, 20, 21, 22–3, 27, 33, 34,
35, 37, 39, 45, 46, 55 *passim*, 66,
83, 84, 88, 112, 143, 153 (*see also*
Bengal army)
post-Independence 22–3, 50, 69,
77, 117, 120, 146
Gorkhas in 23, 50
officers 67, 114
ICO 69

Khas (*see* Chetri(s))
kipat 30, 31, 40, 43, 48
khukhuri 7, 26, 72, 134, 149, 150,
157
Kumaon(is) 14, 18, 30

lahure 11, 33, 37, 44, 49, 150

Limbus 29, 30, 31, 33, 35, 37, 41,
43, 44, 47, 48, 49, 95–7
line boys 45, 97–9, 100

Magar(s) 29, 31, 33, 36, 41, 46, 91,
92, 94, 95–7, 100, 122, 145
manliness 61, 82, 101, 120
martial race(s) (class/tribe) 11, 25,
35, 87 *passim*, 112, 122, 126 (*see
also* martiality, masculinity)
theory 87 *passim*, 119, 123, 129,
154, 156
persistence of 99 *passim*
Nepalis as 91 *passim*
martiality 88 *passim* (*see also* martial
races, masculinity)
rhetoric of 93, 101, 120, 123, 126
masculinity 25, 88, 101 *passim*, 120,
123, 126 (*see also* martial races,
martiality)
images of 62
cult of 107
mercenaries 19, 127, 142–3, 150,
151
middle hills (see *pahar*)
military writing 7, 8, 88, 94
muscular Christianity 63, 65, 101
Mutiny 27, 34, 57, 70, 87, 88, 90,
98, 103, 109, 112, 133, 146 (*see
also* Bengal army, Indian army)

Nasiri battalion 18, 93
NBC's 95, 146
Nepal (kingdom of) 8, 11, 13, 32
army 13, 16, 18, 20, 27, 34,
70, 114
officers 114
caste composition of 91
durbar 14, 19, 20, 21, 34, 35, 70,
106, 109–10, 113, 150, 154
government (see *durbar*)
resistance to Gurkha recruitment 20–1, 34, 96, 154

and Gurkhas 5, 96, 109–10
independence of 7, 105–6
intellectuals 25, 88, 110
    attitudes to Gurkha recruit-
      ment 110, 124, 142
king of 18, 26, 31
masculine character of 103
    passim, 123
militarist character of 103–5
Newar(s) 51, 95 (*see also* NBC's)

'opt' 85, 117–18, 121 (*see also* division of regiments)
Orientalism/ists 1, 2, 3, 9, 12

pahar 28, 29, 30, 32, 34, 36, 43, 47,
  50, 53, 99, 119, 154
panchayat 47
patriotism 62
  and courage 128

Rai(s) 29, 31, 35, 95–7
Royal army 15, 27, 56 *passim*, 83, 153
  (*see also* British army, Indian army)
  officers 56 *passim*

Sirmoor battalion 18, 20, 34, 71, 93
Sunwar(s) 96

Tamang(s) 29, 31, 47, 49, 95–6
terai 14, 17, 19, 29, 51, 53
Thakuri(s) 31, 49, 54, 91, 94, 96, 122
Tibeto-Burman(s) 30, 31, 33–6, 39,
  42–4, 47–8, 50, 52–4, 76, 95, 154
  languages 11, 29
  leadership 32, 47–9
  motives for enlistment 39–40
Travel writers 3, 6, 8
Treaty of Sagauli 17, 19, 106
Tripartite agreement 23, 111, 151